# HONORABLE CHOICES

IRWIN SADETSKY

Interior Formatting by Indie Formatting Services

## ALSO BY IRWIN SADETSKY

Iraqi Rebound

A Terrorist on Every Block

*For all of the teachers and administrators past and present. You educate students from Pre-K to Graduate School and view it is a calling. May your patience be rewarded with the knowledge that you do make a difference in this very fast moving world.*

*For Mary: because she understands, in a very special way, my intellectual needs and is able to edit, suggest and counsel me. My total love and admiration to her.*

*"Education is not preparation for life; education is life itself."*

JOHN DEWEY

Captain Matt Collins lifted the flap of the tent and saw his Sergeant tied to a chair.

A white robed man had his knife out and was about to gouge out his Sergeant's eye. Matt shot the infidel through the chest with his M9 Beretta.

Matt heard movement behind him and quickly hit the floor as a shot rang out. He turned and fired instinctively scoring a direct hit.

"Captain, I'm hit, I'm hit."

Matt ran to his man. He was bleeding from his gut. "Hang in there."

The young Captain took his K-bar knife out of its sheath and ran to the dead terrorist. He cut a long strip of fabric from the man's robe. Matt tied it around his Sergeant's lower stomach and cinched it up tightly. In one swift move he lifted his Sergeant over his left shoulder and kept his automatic in his right hand.

As he opened the tent flap to get out two men lifted their guns. Matt shot one through his mouth and the other between his eyes. He started toward the check point as he heard friendly fire. The friendly fire merged into an alarm going off. It continued to ring. Matt opened his eyes and thought. *Oh shit! Today I start as the new Principal of the George W. Bush Middle School*

## CHAPTER 1

The smell hit me first. Not rotting oranges, not rotting banana peels, not perfumed floor sanitizer. Got it! It was the lingering smell of kids aged twelve to fourteen in a middle school who were still out on summer break.

I turned the corner to get to the office and a large man wearing a t-shirt that read, "Love me or leave me!" confronted me. "Can I help you?"

"I'm Matt Collins, the new Principal, and you?"

Extending his large right hand to shake mine he said, "Jerry Jackson, your Assistant Principal."

"Nice to meet you. Did you apply for the job I got?"

He pointed to the office, smiled, "Let's go to the office. There's air conditioning running."

We got into the office and Jerry introduced me to Maggie Carter, the School Secretary. Before I could even say hello he took me by the arm and ushered me into the Principal's Office. "Sure I applied, but the Board of Education wanted new blood. The Superintendent wanted me, but you know, politics always win."

I looked into his eyes, "Will we have a problem?"

"No way Boss. If you look good, I'll look good as well."

Since it was August, Jerry & I covered book orders, teacher supplies, staffing, student schedules, Team Leaders, non instructional staff, the cafeteria, the transportation system, new students, Guidance Counselors, and the first day of school.

Most of it was routine since I was an Assistant Principal of a middle school for four years on Long Island, New York. The Long Island Superintendent told me to, "Stick around for another few years and you will get your own school."

I didn't want to wait any longer!

My University, NYU set up a number of job interviews for principal and I accepted this post, even if it was upstate New York. My Committee Chairperson stated that I could take a year off from writing my dissertation for my doctorate and I was very grateful for that. Since I was single, with absolutely no attachments, I decided to farm myself out. I was sure that upstate New York would be just fine.

Risenburg Union Free School District had four elementary schools feeding into one middle school. The incoming sixth grade class population was three hundred eighty five and the middle school population was thirteen hundred ninety. Pretty much what I had as an administrator on Long island.

The school was nine years old. From the outside it looked like a typical cement and brick building. On the inside it was a clone of so many schools that I have known. Nothing special about it, but again, nothing too bad.

Risenburg as a town was smaller than most Long Island towns or hamlets. It had an early nineteen hundreds look with Main Street being the center of town and the cross streets being alphabetical as Aster Street, Begonia, Clover, Dandelion and so on. There was a locally owned major supermarket, a fifty's style diner, Italian restaurant & pizza joint, an honest to goodness luncheonette and three major fast food places. A tailor shop and a general merchandise shop were in the center of town as well. There were other shops on different streets, but I did not have the time to investigate all of them as yet.

The Board of Education was located by the high school as an attached building. I was sure I would take a tour of it after our first administrative meeting with all the principals which was scheduled at the end of the week.

I called Maggie Carter into my office. She was about fifty years old with shining blue eyes and a wide smile. "Sit down Mrs. Carter."

She sat down, straightened her skirt and said, "Please call me Maggie. I'm really okay with it."

"Maggie it is. I'm still going to be called Mr. Collins."

"Well of course," she quickly replied, "I know the principal has to be respected."

"Look Maggie, I really will need all your help to get the school started and functioning well. Being new I'll need your advice and counsel about many things. Where I came from it was said that, 'School Secretaries ran the schools, the administrators bumped into walls.' What do you think?"

Maggie let out a surprisingly loud laugh as she blurted out, "Oh, we are going to get along fine!"

The rest of the day covered my first day newsletter to the teachers and staff as well as a letter to all parents. Within the communications was a "Code of Conduct" for the students in the school. The parents or guardians were requested to sign it along with the students..

During my interview with the Board of Education and the School Superintendent they pointed out that the previous principal did not have good control over the school. I stated that my policy would be based on a zero tolerance policy concerning weapons, drugs and violence being brought into the school. I would be more tolerant on individual cases based upon the student's behavior and the situation. I guess that got me the job.

Late into the afternoon, Jerry, my Assistant Principal came in and asked, "Will it be okay with you if I take the next three days off? I had to revamp my vacation schedule because of your appointment."

I didn't like it. "Sure, I understand."

The rest of the day I spent looking over the contracts of : The Teachers Union, The Custodians Union, The Non-professional Staff Union, The Cafeteria Workers Union, The Transportation Workers Union, and the Administrators Association Contract. Only six contracts to understand and make sure I knew every word and policy.

Maggie buzzed, "How do you like your coffee?"

"Black with nothing in it! Thanks."

Maggie delivered my coffee and waived goodbye. After finishing my coffee, I went back to reading the contracts. When I got to the Teachers Contract and reviewed the School Psychologist section my eyes started to tear up. My former girlfriend of seven months was Adriana Jones who was the School Psychologist in my school. We had a torrid relationship, physically and mentally. The conversations were terrific. We seemed to be on a course toward a permanent relationship except for one thing. She did not want me to go out of town for any position.

I remember the night we broke up. I was invited to dinner by Adriana and I had just returned from Risenburg with a signed contract. Although I knew she would not like it, I thought she would be happy for me.

Forget about it! The dialogue started with, "Hon, I made it. I'm going to be a principal. I just signed a contract!"

"How dare you sign anything without consulting me. You know I'm not going along with you leaving"

Her tone was amazingly nasty and her manner seemed completely out of place. "Look Adriana, I didn't ask you to come upstate with me. I know we can work something out."

"Screw you! Screw you! You're a selfish bastard! Get out! Get out of my house now!"

That was the last conversation I had with her. She refused to answer my phone calls. I wrote to her twice, but never received a reply.

A knock on my door pulled my head out of the contracts and a large man dressed in a grey uniform came in. "I'm Otto Lyons, your Chief Custodian."

I stood up and shook his hand, "It is a pleasure to meet you Mr. Lyons. Your school looks great!"

He smiled, "Please call me Otto. I've been here since its opening and I certainly like to keep it that way."

"Otto, please join me at the small round table."

I felt better talking to staff in a more intimate manner, rather than behind a large desk. My desk was huge!

"So you opened up the school. It must have been exciting."

"I was a custodian then, and had the night shift so I didn't see the ceremony, but I built myself up to become Chief Custodian."

That statement hit me where I was in my career! "I know how tough it is to move up the ladder. Look at me. I was an assistant principal for four years and could not break into a leadership role."

Otto stuck his hand out and shook my hand vigorously, "We'll get along great. I've got a crew who knows what to do and I evaluate them fairly."

"And I will evaluate you fairly as well. I promise."

Otto left smiling and turned his head at the door. "Boss, how about a tour of the building tomorrow?"

"See you at noon tomorrow. I'll bring a bag lunch and we'll eat together."

Looking at my watch I realized it was six p.m. Time to have some dinner and go back to my furnished apartment about two miles outside of town. The town itself had a very nice suburban area with some lovely homes and neighborhoods.

CHAPTER 2

I bought a barbecued chicken, potato salad, and coleslaw to bring back to my apartment. Actually it was an extension of a ranch house that was built for the owners' parents. It was simple, composed of an eat in kitchen with a table and four chairs; a medium sized family room with a thirty two inch television set plus a leather couch and recliner. The bedroom contained a firm queen size mattress, triple dresser, two lamps and a night table. The owner's parents lived there before they passed on. It seemed to me that they were gentle with the apartment. It was clean and well maintained.

There was a side driveway with a canopy that lead to a side door which was the entrance to my apartment. It was completely private and I was thankful for that.

I slept well and the next morning I decided to have breakfast at the local diner. The name described it all, "Main Street Diner." I found parking near the diner and put two quarters in the meter which would take care of sixty minutes.

Upon entering the diner I smelled the wonderful aroma of coffee. It permeated the whole place. A slim waitress came by and waived, "Take any table honey."

I took a booth that looked out over Main Street so I could get a general impression of the town at eight in the morning. Within a minute the waitress came back. " Decaf or regular?"

Her name tag read "Julia". She stood there with the two coffee decanters. "Regular please."

"We have a special today, two eggs, two strips of bacon and toast.

One buck off from the menu."

"I'll take it Julia. Make mine scrambled."

"Thanks Mr. Principal."

"How do you know I'm a principal?"

Julia smiled, showing one tooth missing from her mouth, "Your picture and background were in the local newspaper. My kid is going to your school."

"Thank you Julia. I'll see you at Parent's Night."

I looked around the diner. It made me smile because so many of the newer diners did not have that special fifty's look anymore. This diner had a long counter with chrome stools and red vinyl seats. There was a large glass enclosed pastry rack with gorgeous calorie plus cakes, pies and Danish style pastries. Booths along two sides of the diner had benches of red plaid covering. The red Formica tables were in the center of the diner. It matched all the booths and gave me a feeling of nostalgia. I really liked it.

My food arrived piping hot and I ate steadily while observing the clientele. The patrons were a mixed bag, some business men with suits and ties, uniformed mechanics from the local water company and only two females. One was dressed in a good looking grey suit carrying a leather case and the other sitting with her was dressed in a t-shirt top and jeans.

Julia came back to refill my coffee and noticed me looking at the two women. "Oh that's Nancy Briggs, she's a lawyer and her client is May Gold who is getting a divorce. "

"Thanks Julia."

I suddenly realized that small towns do have their own communication systems through word of mouth and other methods including diner talk. I resolved to be closed mouthed in the diner. Better yet, I should be closed mouthed with shopkeepers and vendors alike. It wasn't Long Island where bedroom communities were indifferent to each other. I ordered a roast beef sandwich to go remembering that I had a brown bag lunch with Otto later in the day.

\* \* \*

Maggie gave me a big smile as I arrived at school. "There is a call from the Business Office, something about an insurance form you did not sign. They asked if you could sign it today so they can get it out. There is a call from a Mrs. Granger, something about getting her son out of physical education. I told her to get a doctor's note, but she insisted you call her back."

"Thanks Maggie, first on my priority list is getting the "Code of Conduct" mailed out today."

"Okay, Mr. Collins. It will be mailed out today." She handed me note paper with Mrs. Granger's phone number as well as the student's file.

"Thanks Maggie. I call that efficient. Looks like you do run the school."

She laughed and blushed slightly. I knew I would be able to count on her at any time. On the other hand I didn't have any feelings about Jerry, my Assistant Principal.

I looked over the file of Norman Granger. After perusing it I came to the conclusion that he was a kid with an above average IQ and good marks throughout his schooling. He was going into eighth grade and his physical education grades were satisfactory. I called Mrs. Granger. "This is Mr. Collins, Principal."

"Oh Mr. Collins, please help my son."

I recognized a voice that was shaky and stressed. "Please tell me what is happening?"

"My son doesn't want to go to school if he has to take phys. ed. He has told me that some of the boys last year picked on him. He was bullied all of last year and never told me or anybody else."

This wasn't my first rodeo when it came to bullying. I looked over my staffing list focusing on Guidance. "Mrs. Granger, this is what we are going to do. On the first day of school, before Norman has to go to physical education he is to report to Ms. Andrews the Guidance Counselor. I will join her and we will discuss this bullying. Please encourage Norman to give us names. Without that we cannot do anything."

"Thank you Mr. Collins. I'll speak to my son."

I wrote a note to Ms. Andrew to see me when she came in. The Guidance Counselors came in one week before school started. It would be good to see her take on bullying. I looked over guidance assignments and realized that the previous principal gave the Pupil Personnel staff permission to do their own scheduling and assignments. That meant that the counselors, psychologist, and social worker worked independently from the schools schedule. I resolved to change this practice, but slowly and carefully.

* * *

I hopped into my car and went to the Business Office to sign insurance papers. On my way out I heard, "Mr. Collins, may I see you?"

I turned around and saw a very tall, completely grey haired gentleman wearing a seersucker suit. He motioned to me to come to him and I complied.

"I'm Eric Bolt, the Assistant Superintendent. I'm sorry I couldn't be in the hiring process because I was in the hospital with congenital heart failure. Welcome aboard."

"Thank you sir. I'm sorry as well. Would you want to schedule some time with me to discuss the middle school?"

"Not necessary. This is my last year. After thirty nine years in education it is truly time to give it up. My wife is thrilled with the idea. If you have any problems try to figure it out yourself."

I boldly thought it was a good move to resolve the Pupil Personnel scheduling problem. "Would you mind if I took complete control of the Pupil Personnel Department in my school?

"No problem for me, but they may give you a hard time."

"Anything in the contract that forbids it?"

"Nope. Let me know how it works out."

He did a one eighty military move and left me with my mouth wide open. I figured that he was a short timer and really did not care about any more personnel problems.

* * *

Otto, the Chief Custodian, knocked on the door. "Time for lunch Boss."

"Okay, I'll meet you in your office in a minute." I grabbed my paper lunch bag and followed him to his office.

"Sit down Boss. How do you like your coffee?"

"No sugar and just a bit of milk." I looked around. It was a small but tidy office with a large board. On it were personnel schedules and work assignments. It reminded me of a factory foreman's office since I worked in a factory many years ago. I took my coffee in a huge mug and drank a bit of it. It was hot and strong.

"Boss, the school is in pretty good shape. My only problem is that some of the tables in the cafeteria are weak and perhaps dangerous and we have no replacements. The kids do a number on them. The previous Principal didn't do anything and when I went to the Business Office Manager he told me to have the Principal write a memo to the Superintendent since it wasn't in the budget. I asked, but nothing happened."

"How many do you actually need?"

"If you can get me four I'll be very happy."

"Okay Otto, I'll get a memo out today since it is a dangerous condition for our students. Would you confirm that if asked?"

"You bet I would!"

We took a tour of the building and I noticed that the custodial workers took pride in cleaning and getting everything ready for the opening of school. The only real problem was the Art Room. "This room is a pig pen."

"Boss, the teacher doesn't really care. She has about fifteen years in the District and her husband is the Editor of our local paper."

"So what. She has to keep up with normal routines."

There have been three principals who have tried and every time it happens there is an article in the newspaper about some problem blaming the principal. It stinks!"

"Thanks for the tip. Perhaps we can figure out another strategy."

The rest of the afternoon was spent on incoming supplies and new book orders. Jerry, the Assistant Principal was still out, and the boxes had to be sorted and matched against the purchase orders. It took Maggie and me the whole afternoon to get it worked out. When Jerry comes back he will be delighted to know that his job would be distribution of said books and supplies.

"Maggie, I'm going to have to have you work on my new curriculum guidelines. I'm glad your shorthand is up to date. I guess Jerry and some of the custodians will have to get the books and supplies out."

Maggie smiled, but said nothing.

## CHAPTER 3

Jerry Jackson came back to work and he seemed different. He was wearing a decent sport shirt and slacks perhaps mimicking my summer dress. He opened my door and looked at me with an impish grin. "I spoke to the Assistant Superintendent this morning and he told me that you were taking over scheduling of Pupil Personnel. I think it's a bad idea."

"Why?"

"They like to run their own show and schedule their Child Study Team and Evaluation Team together. Thank goodness they have their own secretary."

"Have you or any administrator attended their meetings?"

"No. Why is that necessary?"

"Only under the Federal law and New York State law. The teacher or teachers have to attend as well as an administrator. When the IEP is written the parent has to sign off on it. Who sees the team reports?"

"What's an IEP?"

"That's an Individual Educational Plan."

"I don't know. It always goes up to the Assistant Superintendent and then the team lets the teachers know about any modified programs or changes."

"Are the parents involved?"

"I don't know, ask the team. Ms. Andrews usually is the Chairperson."

I fully realized that Jerry did not know anything about special education law and this troubled me. "Jerry, when was the last time you went to any administrator conferences on curriculum and special education.?"

"I was told that the Board of Education thought it was money not spent well."

"Okay Jerry, make sure about the books and supplies today. The custodians will help you since my secretary will have a heavy dictation load today."

Instead of being down Jerry seemed pleased. "That's one job I'm an expert on!"

I reflected about Jerry counting the cafeteria money and the milk money. If he thought that was all there was to being an administrator he was way off base. Sure, perhaps an administrator or clerk, but certainly not an educator! I waved Jerry off without saying anything. I felt absolutely sad.

Maggie buzzed Matt. "There is a service man, wife and child who wish to register and speak to you."

"I'll be right out."

Matt walked into the Main Office and saw a petite blond woman about thirty and a young adolescent, about thirteen, sitting on an office bench. Maggie was helping the soldier fill out registration papers for his daughter.

Maggie looked up, "Mr. Collins, this is Master Sergeant O'Keefe."

Matt shook the soldier's hand, "Thank you for your service!"

'I'm worried about my daughter."

"What's her name?"

"Samantha. She's quite shy and we've been moving around a bit. She's going into seventh grade."

"Finish your paper work and I'll show Samantha and both of you around the school."

Maggie looked up at Matt and Sergeant O'Keefe, then smiled broadly. "My husband was in the army and is a Lieutenant Colonel in the Army Reserves."

Both men nodded.

Sergeant O'Keefe turned to Matt, "Did you serve?"

"Three years, in Iraq and Afghanistan."

"What unit?"

"Company B, 3rd Battalion, 75th Ranger Regiment. I was a Captain when I got out."

Sergeant O'Keefe snapped to attention and saluted Matt. "Thank you for your service, sir. You pulled some real heavy missions in the badlands."

"You know, you go where they send you."

Both men laughed and a special bond seemed to happen immediately .

The paper work was finished and Sergeant O'Keefe introduced Mrs. O'Keefe and Samantha to Matt. "Samantha, this is Principal Collins. He served in the army just like I did. You will be okay here."

Matt looked into the eyes of the frightened girl and grinned. "I'm going to make sure that we team you up with a buddy to show you the ropes. How old are you?"

"I'm thirteen."

"How did you do in your last school?"

"Pretty good, I got all A's except for Math. I got a B minus."

"Well, we will be able to help you get up to at least a B."

She started to laugh and Matt took her hand. "Let me show you the school and classrooms. Oh, we have a wonderful gym and as I understand our Girls Basketball Team won the State Division last year."

They left the office and Maggie went to Google to look up Matt's Ranger Regiment. She read about their exploits and thought, *My God, he went through a lot.* Picking up the phone she called her husband. "Hon, can you look up Matt Collins' service record. He served as an Army Ranger, Company B, 3rd Battalion, 75th Ranger Regiment and was a Captain. He was in Iraq and Afghanistan."

Twenty minutes later Matt returned and waved to Maggie, "I'll be in the diner for lunch."

Matt decided to walk to the Main Street Diner. He used a quick pace and in about ten minutes he arrived. Julia, the waitress, who previously served him, acknowledged him with a smile and wave of the hand. "You know the drill, take any seat you want, Mr. Principal."

Matt settled for a booth in the back of the diner hoping for privacy. He looked at the lunch specials as Julia was pouring his coffee. "I'll have your special, tuna with bacon on rye toast with chips, please."

"Order the egg salad, its much fresher. The tuna was made yesterday, that's why it's the special today."

"Okay. Thanks."

"No problem Mr. Principal."

Matt took Julia's hand, "Please call me Matt when we are in the diner."

She squeezed his hand, "Okay Matt, I'm beginning to like you, that is in a platonic way. Egg salad it is."

Halfway through his meal Matt spotted a large man approaching him. It was Dominic Costello, President of the Board of Education. Matt stood up as a matter of respect. Dominic waved him down and squeezed into the booth. "How are things going?"

"Great, Otto has the school in terrific shape and Jerry is helping out to the best of his ability, but I'm blessed to have Maggie as secretary. She is a blessing!"

"We got your Code of Conduct in this mornings mail. There may be some more kids coming to your office for discipline. They will test the system."

"I'll be tough, but fair. I promise you that."

Dominic maneuvered his way out of the booth and pointed to the west. "I run the real estate office, biggest in town, right down the block on Maple Street. If you want to chat here is my card."

Matt left the card on the table as he finished his meal. He thought, *I wonder who runs the show, the Superintendent or the Board President?*

Julia came by and filled his cup. "That Dominic Costello had no interest in running for the Board until his pushy wife forced him to run. Who wanted the job anyhow?"

"Community service is really important in towns like this."

Julia turned away as she muttered, "Bullshit."

Matt fast paced himself back to the school. Before entering his office he went to Maggie's desk and picked up a pad. He wrote "Guidance meeting with Mr. Collins, Principal, in the conference room at 10:30 a.m."

"Maggie make sure that all three counselors get this note. Make it in a memo form and carbon copy it to me for the record."

"Is there anything wrong?"

"No, just establishing the ground rules."

Maggie nodded, "Do you want me to set up the conference room with coffee, donuts, and pads?"

"No, perhaps another time. The meeting will only last fifteen minutes."

The rest of the day Matt spent researching the new special education laws from the federal and state governments. He wanted to be as sharp as possible when he met with the counselors. Matt handled almost all of the special education teams at his previous middle school. The meetings were long and at times crowded with school personnel.

There were the classroom teacher or teachers, guidance counselor, school psychologist, reading teacher, resource room teacher, speech pathologist, social worker, parent, and sometimes the school physician or local psychiatrist. Matt was the Chairperson and it was usually a vigorous meeting trying to get a proper IEP or Individualized Educational Program for the student. Most of the time it worked.

If a parent objected, there was a route to take including re-evaluation of the student with different testers, meeting with the Board, having a mediation, and having a true judicial review as in arbitration. Matt experienced all of the steps in his years as the head of the Child Study Team.

Again he worked until six p.m. Matt thought, *What jobs can I give Jerry to take some of the work load off me?*

## CHAPTER 4

Matt met with Jerry to check on the progress of supplying the school with new books, workbooks, computer set-ups, and general items as plan books, pencils, pens and chalk. Other items teachers requested before they left last year were added to the mix.

Jerry was happy with his progress. "Tomorrow the job will be finished."

"Okay, tell Otto to continue to help, but be in the conference room at ten thirty to meet with the counselors."

"What's up Boss?"

"I want to set the ground rules as soon as possible."

"Exactly, you want to make sure that they know you have taken charge. Oh, I'm sure John Brown and Shelly Katz will be alright with it, but you better watch out for Beth Andrews. She is the favorite counselor of the Superintendent. He personally hired her."

"I was hired as well and have a job to do to get this school organized into a cohesive unit, not individual fiefdoms."

"Don't you think a velvet glove will get you more cooperation?"

"Oh Jerry, you haven't seen my diplomatic side. It will blow you away."

Matt dismissed Jerry by pointing to the door. "I'll see you at ten thirty."

Jerry left in haste looking like a wounded animal.

Matt sensed that confrontation was not in his DNA.

\* \* \*

Matt entered the conference room at ten twenty. The chairs were well padded with leather coverings and the conference table, shaped as a surfboard, was in grained layered mahogany. It was a very impressive room. The side walls had framed pictures with no particular theme. The back walls had a white blackboard that could double as a screen and a large white clock with a second hand. The opposite wall had a seventy two inch television screen. There were all sorts of covered plugs in the floor where you could set up a computer and send an image to the screen or plug in any audio visual device.

Jerry entered at ten twenty five and sat down to the right of Matt who was seated at the center of the table. At exactly ten thirty the three counselors entered the room. Matt stood up and looked at them one by one, "You may sit opposite Mr. Jackson and me. I'm Matt Collins, your Principal. Mr. Jackson, will you please introduce the counselors to me."

Jerry took his clue well and in a professional manner started the process. "May I introduce in seniority order: Mr. John Brown, eighteen years in the district with ten of them in the old junior high school, he holds a Masters Degree in Guidance."

Matt looked at the senior counselor, he was large boned with a pot belly and almost completely bald. He was wearing a short sleeve shirt ."I see that you will be covering the sixth grade this year. How was that decided?'

"Pleasure to meet you Mr. Collins. We run a rotation every year so I had the eighth grade last year and now I rotated to the sixth. It's easy."

"Thanks Mr. Brown."

Jerry introduced the next counselor. "May I introduce Mrs. Shelly Katz. She holds a Masters in Guidance and a second Masters in Counseling and Therapy. Mrs. Katz has been with us nine years. She opened the school for us and has been involved with The League of Women Voters as well. Mrs. Katz does most of our heavy duty counseling for our special education classes."

Mrs. Katz was wearing a business suit and sensible heels.

"It is indeed a pleasure to know you. When things go wrong in my area, will you have time for me to lie down on your couch for a session?"

Shelly Katz laughed. "Mr. Collins, I'll tell you what I tell the teachers when they come to me. Go home and eat two cookies or a bowl of ice cream. Curl up with a book or watch some dumb television show. The next day you will be fine."

Matt enjoyed her statement. " I see you will be doing seventh grade this year. With that load and special education counseling how do you manage?"

"I have to measure my time, but when I'm in real time trouble Beth helps out in the counseling area. She is quite talented."

"Thanks for the information."

Jerry picked up from Matt's statement. "The counselor with two years experience, but very talented and very organized, may I introduce Beth Andrews."

Beth was wearing a red and white print dress that fit her like the proverbial glove. She had honey colored hair, a smooth girlish complexion wearing very little makeup. She didn't need it. Matt knew she was a knockout. "It is a pleasure meeting you Miss. Andrews. Where did you study?"

"I have a Masters degree in Guidance from Columbia University and a Professional Diploma in Counseling and Psycho-therapy from NYU." Perhaps one day I hope to get my doctorate."

Matt nodded in agreement. "I finished all my course work and have preliminary approval for my doctorate dissertation from NYU. They told me I can have a year off to concentrate on my new position. It looks like we have something in common."

Beth's eyes were shining. "You have accomplished quite a bit for a young man. How old are you?"

This rattled Matt for a moment. He took a deep breath. "I'm thirty two with four years of being an Assistant Principal at a very large middle school in Long Island, New York. It was time for me to move up."

"Why are we here Mr. Collins? You know we have a lot of work to do in a short week."

"I wanted to meet you and inform you that you will be under my complete supervision. The Assistant Superintendent has given me permission for this policy change."

Beth stood up, looked at me squarely. "I guess you will decide if I have tenure or not. You are new yourself. Don't you think the Assistant Superintendent would be a better person to judge me?"

"No, I don't think so. In the every day to day operations of the school the Assistant Superintendent does not see you. I will be able to do so. If you do your job professionally and honorably there should not be a problem."

"May I see you later in the day?"

"Sure, how about three today in my office?

"Done!"

"I would like to thank everyone for coming and wish all of you a great start for the school year. Please feel free to call me at any time. Oh, by the way. I'll be Chairing the Child Study Team this year. Please inform me of any scheduled meetings at least a week ahead of time. Alright, this meeting is over."

They left quickly without looking back. "Thank you Jerry for introducing me to the counselors.'

"Boss, they are in shell shock."

* * *

Maggie met her husband in his office during her lunch break. He had a Stage Seven license from the Securities and Exchange Commission and was a Financial Planner.

The reservist Colonel carried himself straight and erect. "Maggie, your boss, Captain Collins is an honest to goodness hero. He has a Silver Star, a Bronze Star, a Purple Heart, a Meritorious Service Medal and two battle stars for Iraq plus two for Afghanistan. He led a number of black missions that are so classified that when I asked, I was reprimanded by a General in the Pentagon for snooping. He is a warrior first class and I would like to shake his hand and salute him."

Maggie responded quickly, "I knew he carried himself well. This year we are going to have fireworks at the school. Wait and see."

"Why?"

"He sent out to every parent and child a Code of Conduct which really spells out what he expects in terms of their overall behavior."

"Sounds like due process to me."

"It certainly is. He asked every parent or guardian to sign the Code as well as each student."

"Perhaps the behavior of the students will improve. He's a man who will not back down. I know it from his service record. I hope it works out."

Maggie wiped her brow. "I hope it does. I like Matt Collins and I will stand behind him one hundred percent."

"Ask him over for dinner on the weekend. Tell him I really want to meet him."

CHAPTER 5

Matt reviewed his staff's makeup. Most of the teachers, about seventy five percent, had tenure and their evaluations were good to above average. The average amount of total years teaching was eleven. Their ages were in the low thirties and some in their early forties. A few teachers were in their late forties and early fifties. The Lead Teachers, within the subject areas, had very good evaluations from the previous principals.

The remaining twenty five percent did not have tenure and most of them were very new to teaching. Matt surmised that the Board and Superintendent wanted to have a balanced staff and they brought in new faces and new teachers. Matt thought. *I'm going to spend a great deal of time with the non-tenured teachers. I hope Jerry will be able to handle the load I'm going to give him for observations of teachers.*

Maggie buzzed. "Miss. Andrews to see you."

Matt looked at his watch. Exactly three o'clock.

Beth Andrews came through the door and Matt liked what he saw. She had a mid western wholesome look and she carried herself beautifully. Her honey colored hair, blue grey eyes and high cheek bones reminded him of some very sexy movie stars. "Please sit down at the table. I'd rather talk to you without a desk separating us."

She sat down gracefully. "Mr. Collins I wish to apologize to you. I didn't want to put you on the spot about my tenure in front of the other counselors. It just came out."

"Miss. Andrews, I have reviewed most of the staff's evaluations from last year and yours was outstanding. I don't think there will be any problems at all. My goal is the same as yours, helping each student to achieve to the best of his or her abilities. After four years in a middle school I know the storm and stress of these youngsters. Some of them want to test adult roles. We know that at times they are not ready. Their hormones are raging and the outside stimulus through all sorts of media makes our jobs very difficult."

Beth Andrews relaxed in her chair and really took a close look at Matt. He was of above average height, about five feet eleven inches, sandy colored hair, very well dressed and very well groomed. She looked into his hazel eyes. At the meeting they looked brown and as she looked at him now they looked green. He was wearing a long sleeved shirt that helped define the muscles beneath it. A conservative green tie emphasized the color of his eyes. "Oh that's great. We are certainly on the same page. Thank you so much!"

"I don't know if you are going to thank me after our faculty meeting," Going over to his desk he took out the Code of Conduct and gave it to Beth, "It spells it out to the parents as well as the kids."

"I'm encouraged already, the kids need structure as well as the teachers. This will be a good vehicle for all of them. I certainly approve. Perhaps the counselors can play an important role in explaining to some of the offenders the importance of self discipline. I'll read this over tonight and I'll be able to come up with a few ideas to help you."

Matt was pleased by her willingness and cooperation. "That would be great!"

Beth stood up and Matt did the same. He opened the door for her and she brushed by him, not intentionally. He smelled something that reminded him of honeysuckles.

She smiled, "I'll see you tomorrow."

Matt stood there , "Oh, okay, tomorrow."

* * *

Jerry Jackson, Assistant Principal to the George W. Bush Middle School lifted up his fourth glass of beer and told his drinking buddy, "I feel like an errand boy. That young piece of shit of a principal had me running my ass off today."

Bill Jackson, the owner and bartender of "Jackson's Tavern" took his shot glass of vodka and downed it in one gulp. "I'll tell you little brother, don't help too much to make this guy look good. Mom really wants you to become the principal. Why don't you just slow down everything he asks you to do. That will either have him do some of the crappy work himself or fail to keep the school running well. When the Board sees him fail they certainly will fall back on somebody they know and that's you, little brother!"

"Yeah, but the son of a bitch was an assistant in a middle school. He knows the drill."

"What are you afraid of. You have tenure. Big deal if he writes you up. At a hearing it would be his word against your word and the Board knows you better."

Jerry motioned with his beer mug and his brother filled it up again. Jerry really liked his drinks. It didn't matter if it was beer or whisky. He liked to drink.

"Oh shit, I've got to go home to the wife. If she makes one more meatloaf I'm going to kick her ass. What a lousy cook and what a lousy lay."

Jerry staggered out of the tavern and into his truck. He gunned the engine and nearly hit an oncoming car. He gave the car driver the finger, rolled down the window and yelled, "You fucking piece of shit, where did you learn how to drive?" He then gunned the motor and started for home.

The tavern was situated about eight miles out of town, just off Route Twenty in upstate New York. Jerry figured he could drink there without people from the town knowing about it. If they did see him at the tavern he could always say he was visiting his older brother. Pretty good alibi for a drinker.

* * *

Matt finished writing his agenda for the faculty meeting he would have next Tuesday. He made sure to minimize handouts since he was certain the teachers would not read them because their priorities were books, supplies and lesson plans. He realized this and promised himself that the faculty meeting would be less than an hour. The only important item would be the Code of Conduct.

Maggie came into his office and sat down in front of his desk. "Mr.

Collins, I would like to invite you over for Sunday dinner. It's the Labor Day Weekend and I'm sure you're ready to have a good home cooked meal."

"I'll come over on Sunday, but you will have to do one thing for me."

"What's that Mr. Collins?"

"When we are not in front of staff and the public please call me Matt."

"Oh, that would be grand, Matt!"

"Maggie, you have worked so extra hard since I've been here. Thank you for your advice, your work ethic and really being a nice person."

"Matt, I really like you. It seems to me that you actually want to do your best to help the kids. That's what I want to do as well."

She handed Matt a card that contained her address and home number. "Please come about three and we plan to have Sunday dinner about four."

"Sounds good to me. Thanks"

When Maggie left, Matt took on his last project for the day. He did a statistical analysis between the IQ's of the students taking the New York State Common Core Learning Standards for Grades Three through Eight. He started to measure the correlations. The tests were called, "English Language Arts" or ELA and "Mathematics" or Math. His school in Long Island scored eighty percent proficient while most of the state scored seventy percent proficient. He was amazed to find that only ten percent of all students taking the ELA and Math were below proficiency. That meant that ninety percent of the students were proficient. He was stunned.

Matt went into the small file room adjacent to Jerry's office. It had at least twelve large file cabinets all with six drawers. He searched for testing in the previous years and located twenty-twelve and twenty-eleven. Matt brought them back to his office and started his calculations. The tests used then were standardized achievement tests. They were used in thousands of schools throughout the country. The norms for these tests were calculated by geographic regions and the northeastern states had the highest norms in the country. Many educators challenged the high norms, although in most cases the tests were quite accurate.

Matt spent about an hour doing his calculations and found that all the tests scores were well above the normative IQ scores of the students. He did his correlations over and over again and the same results appeared. Only ten percent of the students failed to make average to above average scores.

It was too late in the day to redo his numbers, although he thought, *It smells fishy to me. I think I'll call up my Professor of Advanced Statistics at NYU and speak to. Perhaps I made a mistake.*

It was past seven in the evening and Matt thought it would be a good idea to meet the night custodians. It was the Friday of the Labor Day weekend. He found two men and introduced himself. They were somewhat surprised that the principal would even do that. One man was out on sick leave and they had to cover his areas as well. Matt got the impression that Otto, their boss, did a good job with his men.

Matt left and went to the Italian restaurant named "The Pizza Place." It was divided into two sections. One for takeout pizza and the larger area as a sit down restaurant. He ordered some lasagna. Garlic rolls and a small salad proceeded the main dish. The lasagna came out piping hot. It was delicious and he ate every morsel. As he looked around he thought. *Thank God, no one in the restaurant knows me.*

CHAPTER 6

Matt spent Saturday morning cleaning his apartment. The owners left him a full compliment of cleaning tools including a brand new full powered vacuum cleaner. It took him thirty minutes to read the directions and attach all the proper equipment, hoses and weird looking brushes. He then attacked the apartment with gusto.

In the afternoon Matt drove to town and signed up at the local gym. It had all the equipment he needed including free weights and incline walkers. He was dressed in gym shorts, tee shirt and sneakers. As he was stretching, a familiar voice came from the rear. "Hi Mr. Collins."

He quickly turned around and responded. "Hello." It was Beth Andrews.

Beth was wearing a red tank top and black workout shorts. She looked great and Matt started to sweat a bit. He looked at her intensely. "Please call me Matt off campus."

She mimicked his tone. "Then call me Beth off campus."

"Have you worked out regularly?

"Oh yes. I love to push my body to its limits. No pain no gain. How about you?"

"I really started working out when I was in service. I wasn't a jock in school. In fact I probably was close to being a nerd. Anyway, when you are in the Army the way to keep out of trouble is to be lean and mean. So I really started to improve my body."

"So the Army made a man out of you?"

"I guess so. It worked for me!"

Beth felt herself drawn to Matt. She liked him. He was straight forward, with a no nonsense approach to his job. *He really is interesting*, she thought. "How many push ups can you do?"

"Enough to make me faint!"

Both of them started to laugh as if they shared a very intimate moment together. Beth dropped her towel and Matt picked it up and they touched hands. It seemed to Matt a special moment. "Beth, how about dinner tonight?"

She looked at him. He was handsome, he was bright, he was well groomed, he was muscular and she thought, *Do I dare get involved because I surely am ready for a man.* "Not a date, but two colleagues having dinner. Is the concept okay for you?"

"For now it is, but I can't promise you what will happen during the second time we eat together."

"It will probably be in the Faculty Cafeteria. No harm there!"

They both started laughing again. It was spontaneous and they both liked it. Matt looked at her shapely body. He noticed her muscular thighs and asked her, "Do you do long distance running?"

"I do half marathons. Thirteen miles is my limit. Would you like to do one with me? It is exhausting!"

"I'm used to short runs, perhaps five miles or less, but I'm willing to try if you help me pace myself. Would you?"

Beth felt that special feeling in her lower body and in her mind. She had not had that for a number of years. She was involved with her boyfriend for two years and then an awful breakup. "Matt, I would love to help you pace yourself."

"Okay, why don't we meet away from town. Do you know that barbecue place on Route Twenty, it's called Henry's House. It has a red roof and a large modern entrance painted in silver."

"I know it. How about seven thirty?"

Matt nodded. I'll see you then colleague."

* * *

Matt was dressed in a designer muted gold shirt with dark khaki pants. He had loafers on and decided to wear socks. He arrived at seven fifteen and waited by the benches in front of the restaurant. A small red sedan drove up and a hand waved to him. It was Beth. She parked the car and quickly walked up to him.

Beth took his arm and they entered. They were seated quickly in a booth near the rear of the restaurant. As Matt slid in, Beth slid in beside him. Her thigh rested against his and she smiled. "I'm starving. Let's order."

She was wearing a flowered dress with a scoop neckline. He smelled her fragrance, it was spicy and sweet at the same time. Her skirt was short and as he looked down her hemline came up over her knees. Beth was delicious to him. Matt felt an urge and tried to calm down. Thankfully the waiter arrived.

During their meal they focused on the early years of their lives. Beth came from Western Pennsylvania, a suburb called South Fayette. It had a superb school district and was fifteen minutes to Pittsburgh. Her parents were retired and lived in Florida. "I was lucky enough to go to Smith College. It's a private, independent women's liberal arts college located in Northampton, Massachusetts."

Matt was impressed. "Isn't Smith the largest member of the Seven Sisters?"

"It is. When I was there we had about twenty six hundred women. It was marvelous. I studied social studies and education. When I got my degree the Smith Placement Center gave me a number of schools who needed Social Studies teachers. I ended up teaching in the Yonkers Middle School for five years while I got my Masters at Columbia and my Professional Diploma at NYU. I was able to get to Columbia since Morningside Heights was twenty five minutes away. NYU was a struggle, but it's a great school. They are really flexible with your plans. Of course they are really expensive as well. I doubled up on courses during the summer. That was great! Then the opening came up in Risenburg and I decided to get away from New York City and the hustle and bustle. I'm really enjoying the change of pace. Where did you grow up?"

"I grew up in Levittown, Long Island, New York. I'm what they call an 'Islander.' Levittown is a true example of a suburb. It started out as a potato farm until old man Levitt bought all the land and started building small, affordable homes for returning service men after World War Two. It has about fifty thousand people living there today. Many people did not move. As their families became bigger they built dormers and extensions to their homes. The trees that were planted are beautiful and most of the people take great pride in their community. I would describe it as a middle class community. The school district placed me in the honors program and I made high school in three years, so I was sixteen when I graduated."

"You told me at the gym that you were sought of a nerd in school. What did you mean?"

"I was Captain of our Quiz Bowl Team. We entered 'Jeopardy' style competitions sponsored by local universities. I was lucky enough to compete for two years and visited Stony Brook University, Hofstra University and Long Island University. It really was fun. We never won any championships, but it was still fun. I went to Long Island University because it was close to my home in Levittown. The professors and teachers there were marvelous. We both seemed to like social studies. What a coincidence!"

"When did you join the Army?"

My folks weren't rich so I got a ROTC Scholarship for school. During the summers I went for officer training. I signed a contract for a four year enlistment. Sure enough, I became a Second Lieutenant at the age of twenty. Four years in service, three years teaching and four years as an Assistant Principal and here I am! Thirty two years old and lucky enough to get my first true leadership job."

"You mean to say you weren't a leader in the Army?"

Matt sort of whispered as he held his jaw tightly. "That was a different world and it was a different type of leadership. I'd prefer to forget about it and focus on the present."

Beth noticed a painful look on Matt's face as he dismissed talking about his service. She realized that he had issues with his service. He reminded her of her father. Beth's father was in the Vietnam war and chose not to discuss it with anybody. Her mother could not make him talk about his war experiences as well. It just wasn't discussed.

Beth conjured up horrible scenes and moved closer to Matt instinctively, perhaps as a nurturing person who wanted to comfort him.

Just then the waiter came and offered them a delightful array of desserts. "Matt, will you share a dessert with me?"

"Sure, you pick it out."

The chocolate mousse came to the table with two spoons. Matt and Beth made quick work of it. Beth insisted they split the check and

Matt acquiesced. It was a delicious meal, but the exciting part was the sharing of their lives.

Matt escorted Beth to the parking lot. It wasn't well lit. He was ready to say goodbye when Beth kissed him on the lips. Not a long kiss, but a meaningful kiss. "I had a great time Matt. Thank you. Next time it will be a date."

She drove off and left Matt stunned in the parking lot. He really liked her a lot, but thought, *I better be careful at school. Keep it professional and keep away in school.*

Matt slept very well that night. There were no nightmares and no night sweats. His last thought was of Beth kissing him.

CHAPTER 7

On Sunday morning Matt called the local florist. They closed at noon so he drove to the florist shop on the corner of Main Street and Clover right after breakfast. He wanted to bring a nice bouquet of fresh flowers to Maggie. The young woman who was behind the counter took one look at him and blurted out, "Mr. Collins, how nice of you to visit the shop. Let me introduce you to my mother. Mom, come to the front please!"

A very nice looking middle aged woman came out from another room and shook Matt's hand. She had seen his picture on the front page of the local newspaper. "Welcome to the store Mr. Collins. My daughter Cynthia will be working for you. She is a first year teacher. The Superintendent hired her right before you came".

"What is your last name Cynthia?"

"Blackburn, I'm going to be part of the Science and Math Team in Sixth Grade."

"Well Miss Blackburn, I'll see you at eight thirty Tuesday morning. It is a pleasure meeting you."

Cynthia ran to the back of the store as Mrs. Blackburn rang up the sale. "That's fifteen dollars less ten percent for school personnel, that will be thirteen fifty plus tax."

"Mrs. Blackburn, with all due respect, I cannot accept the discount. It really is against my principles. I do hope you understand."

She smiled. "No problem, Mr. Collins. I do understand."

After paying, Matt drove back to his house to put the flowers in water before going over to Maggie's house at three. He was anticipating an enjoyable and relaxing time at her house.

* * *

The house sat on top of a huge lawn. It was an old fashioned Victorian with its distinctive turrets and front porch. It was quite impressive. The entrance to the house had characteristic bricks in unique patterns and there was a large double door for the entry. Matt rang the bell and a distinguished looking gentleman opened it. "Matt, I'm Jason Carter, Maggie's husband. Welcome to our home. Let's go into the family room."

"I really like the Victorian style Mr. Carter. How old is this house?"

"Please call me Jason. It was built in nineteen-sixty and we bought it in nineteen-ninety. We really love it. Our two sons had plenty of their friends over here. That front lawn saw plenty of action."

Maggie came in carrying a tray of munchies and some cold punch. "I'm afraid to tell you Matt, but Jason and I don't drink."

"I hardly drink at all. If I do it usually some wine or a wine spritzer. My hard drinking days were in the service."

Jason took a sip of punch and wiped his mouth. "Oh yes. I was in Nam and I do remember something called drinking."

Both men laughed in a knowing way. "Jason, what do you do?"

"I'm a financial consultant and have my own practice in town. I've helped a number of teachers and administrators with their financial plans and retirement plans. It's never to early so start."

"Perhaps I'll look you up eventually. I just have to get things going first."

Maggie looked at both Jason and Matt. "Matt, I asked Jason to look up your military record because of what you said to that soldier when he was registering his daughter. You were so kind to him."

"We are a band of brothers and brothers help each other."

Jason sipped his drink. "I was flabbergasted by what you did in service. Why didn't you stay in? They would have fast tracked you up to Bird Colonel in no time."

"Jason, I put my time in, served my country, and took care of my men. Sometimes you have to do things on a mission you don't like, but if it serves the greater good you do it. As for the awards and medals, you know, I was there at the right time and the right place."

Maggie looked at Matt with tears in her eyes. "I'm so proud to have you as my boss. I guess we can't tell anybody about your service career."

"Right on Maggie. Why don't we just leave it alone. I know how to fight a battle if it comes to it. I don't think there will be too much combat at the middle school."

They all laughed and finished their punch. Maggie got up from her chair and motioned to the dining room. "Let's eat."

The dinner was wonderful. Roast beef, au jus gravy, garlic mashed potatoes, snap beans and plenty of homemade rolls. Maggie's home baked apple pie topped off the meal in a marvelous fashion.

Jason wiped his mouth with a cloth napkin and motioned Maggie to sit down. "Matt, I want you to know that you have a friendly and confidential ear right in this house. I like you! Maggie has said that you are really for the kids. If you are feeling down, wish to bounce an idea off me, or need something, anything, let me know or let Maggie know. We are here for you!"

This was a wonderful gesture by super people. "Thanks. I just may have to take you up on that, but not right now. I'm really very organized and motivated to give the kids at the school the best and safest environment. It may take some doing, but my mission is to have a cohesive staff pulling together."

Matt thanked the Carters for their hospitality. He was very pleased with the reception they gave him and with support they offered him.

As he entered his car his cell phone rang. "Matt, it's Beth. How about coming over to my place tomorrow for a Labor Day brunch? About eleven."

"Will there be any staff there?"

"No, just Jennifer and myself."

"Who is Jennifer?"

"My cat . Well yes or no?"

"Of course yes. Where do you live?'

Beth gave Matt the necessary information and Matt drove home in a cheerful mood. He liked Beth and it was apparent she felt the same way. A thought came to him as he listened to some mellow love song on the way home. *I hope this works out.*

* * *

Beth lived on the other side of town where the new condominium developments were built. She was on the third floor of a five floor building. Each floor had four condo units. The elevator smelled of disinfectant and Matt got out of the elevator just in time to sneeze. He cleared his eyes and walked over to her door. The bell sounded weak, but in ten seconds Beth opened it. She looked at him and hugged him. "Come on in and I'll give you the tour."

Matt handed Beth a box of candy. He had purchased it at the convenience store that was open every day of the year. "If you eat only one you don't have to count the calories."

"Thanks Matt." She placed the candy on the kitchen counter and pointed to the refrigerator. "Look, I have all the appliances including a dish washer. Isn't civilization great, however it is just a work kitchen." She took his arm and directed him to a dinette with a table and four chairs. A chandelier hung over the table. She turned on the lights. "This is my desk, my table, my work station and probably the best thing in the condo. I'm sub-renting this from a salesman who has been transferred to the west coast. He wants to have a rental income and I'm obliging him."

Just then a black and white spotted cat ran under Matt's legs. The cat started rubbing against his leg and Matt obliged the cat by picking her up and holding her. "Well, it looks like I made a conquest. Jennifer is in love."

Beth grinned and motioned the cat to leave Matt. The cat instantly obeyed. "You don't make a conquest that soon. There has to be dating, courting, understanding, a partnership, and togetherness before any conquest is made. Don't you agree?"

Matt thought for a moment. "Sure."

"Nothing more to say about that?"

"Well sometimes when two people click it just happens and togetherness is sort of natural. Don't you agree?"

"Let's continue the tour. This is the family room. It has a thirty two inch television that works plus cable.The rest of the furniture is okay."

He observed a large leather couch, a nice coffee table and two bean bag chairs. "Don't try to sit in the bean bag chair. I'd have to call the firefighters to help you out of it."

"It all looks very comfortable. Do you like sports?"

Beth continued holding his arm against her body. "I love baseball and football. I'm not too keen on professional basketball."

"Basketball is exciting in the fourth quarter, not before. The game is too long."

Beth steered him into the bedroom. "This is where I dream and have all sorts of fantasies. Do you fantasize?"

Matt's face turned red. " Yes, I do."

"I'm sorry I embarrassed you." She came close to Matt and put both of her hands on Matt's cheeks and kissed him with closed lips. She continued kissing him and opened his mouth with her tongue. Beth pressed her full body into Matt and held him tightly. She whispered in his ear, "I'm not a tease, but I'm not going all the way with you today. I have to feel safe with you. I'm really not sure. I'm very attracted to you."

Matt released her. "Look Beth, I'm really attracted to you and I'm not going to push myself on to you, but that kiss really rocked me."

"If truth be told I had no control over that. I just had to taste you. You excite me and I'm trying to control myself. If I let go of my control we would be in bed right now. I don't want to be a one day or a one night stand."

Matt decided to change the subject. "Let's eat. I'm hungry!"

There was a moderate sized balcony that was adjacent to the work kitchen. Beth had a small grill and a work table on it. "I have some minute steaks on the grill. How do you like your eggs?"

"Scrambled well."

"Matt, please help me place our food on the dinette table." Beth seemed to be very organized. She removed a fresh fruit salad from the refrigerator and then from a breadbox she handed Matt a basket of fresh rolls, bagels and bread. Matt took the items and placed them on the table. Butter, cream cheese and jam followed.

As Beth was stirring the eggs Matt took it upon himself to take the minute steaks off the grill. He placed it on the table as Beth came out with the eggs. The timing was impeccable. "We certainly make a good team in the kitchen."

Beth smiled broadly, "Thanks for the support."

They ate and chatted about the opening of school. Matt felt very comfortable in this situation. About an hour after eating they had cleaned up. Matt headed for the family room. He sat down on the far left side.

Beth came in a moment later and sat down right next to him. Again her thigh was up against his. She was happy.

Matt looked at her, "You are a very warm and kind hearted person. Taking a man in and feeding him so well!"

She giggled, "I only choose men who I can control. Matt, may I control you?"

He didn't know what to say but muttered, "Okay."

Beth put her arms around him, hugged him and then kissed him. She trailed her hand to his stomach and stopped. "I want to do this. Okay?"

Matt nodded as he felt her hand unzip him and fondle him. He wanted to respond, but Beth pushed him back. "No, this is my treat and I want to control you. You said it was okay."

Matt leaned back and let Beth take over. She was skilled with her hands, she was skilled with her mouth, she was skilled with her tongue and she was a lovely giving person.

When Matt left her condo he felt wonderful. He found a mature, bright, loving, sensitive woman who was quite independent. He had wished to consummate their relationship, but she insisted that she just wanted him to lay back and enjoy everything. It was a relationship he didn't know how to handle, but he enjoyed it. Oh yes he did enjoy it. Big time!

CHAPTER 8

The first day of school for the teachers was the Tuesday after Labor Day. Students would return on Wednesday. Matt wanted to make sure that the teachers were given as much time as possible to set up and have their Team meetings. He resolved to keep his meeting to no more than one hour.

Previously he had made arrangements with Otto to set up two large coffee urns and with Maggie's help, to get plenty of donuts and fruit for the meeting. When Jerry and Matt came into the cafeteria at eight in the morning they saw a spotless room. The chairs and tables were glistening. Otto and his crew had done a masterful job.

Jerry and Matt distributed only one handout, "The Code of Conduct." Previously Maggie had placed in each teacher's mailbox a newsletter describing the activities and special meetings for the week.

Matt utilized a modified PERT system. It meant Program, Evaluation, Review, Technique. The technique stated specific tasks, staff to perform the tasks, time needed, measured outcomes, and of course, responsibility. Perhaps it would be the first time many of the teachers would see a management style format. He had used it successfully in his previous school and the staff looked forward to the newsletters. Matt picked up the technique in the military, but of course the outcomes were at times quite dangerous.

By the time the staff got their coffee and donuts it was eight forty five. There was a podium set up for him to speak. He stepped to the side of it, "Good morning. I'm Matt Collins, your new Principal. I came out of Long Island, New York with four years experience as an

Assistant Principal of a large middle school. This is my first school where I have been given the privilege to lead. If you do well this school year the students will do well and I may have a job at the end of the year."

Laughter rose from of the audience. "Okay. This meeting will last no longer than one hour, I promise. Who has the most seniority in the school system?"

A grey haired, well-dressed small woman stood up. "Mr. Collins I believe I am that person. I have thirty five years in this District."

"What is your name?"

"Hope Patton. I teach math for the sixth grade."

"Thank you Miss Patton. I'm going to task you with this. The moment the clock behind me on the wall gets to nine forty five please strand up and tell me it is time to end. I promise to do so!"

The staff started to whistle and applaud. It seemed they appreciated the gesture. The rest of the time was devoted to new laws in special education, team responsibilities, the New York State Calendar for Testing, and the Code of Conduct.

Matt had given the staff a short five minute break before discussing the Code of Conduct. "Okay, ladies and gentlemen. The Code of Conduct has been sent home this week to every home of our students. It is to be signed by a responsible adult who is in charge of the student and also signed by the student. I want the homeroom teachers to keep a log in terms of collecting the Code. On Friday morning please send the completed log to my office. Any questions?"

Shelly Katz, Guidance Counselor stood up, "Do you want the counselors to help out. Sometimes the story is that the dog ate the code." The staff laughed loudly.

"Thank you Mrs. Katz. I'm going to leave that up to the homeroom teachers. I have faith in their judgment. If they think something is funny, I mean not right, and wish to send a kid to Guidance, then of course. I'm leaving it up to the teacher's judgment."

Again there was applause from the teachers. "Look folks, I was told by the Superintendent and the Board that discipline was lacking in this school. I believe in the eleventh commandment." Every head turned toward Matt and not a sound could be heard since this was something new, "The eleventh commandment says be specific!"

Hope Patton jumped up from her chair, "Mr. Collins it is nine forty five."

Matt yelled to his staff, "Have a great year. I'm behind you one hundred percent."

Instead of walking out the teachers stood up and applauded. Then they went to their classrooms to set up for Team meetings.

Jerry wiped his brow. "Whew, that was a whirlwind meeting. I've worked with a few principals and they never got applause."

"That's because the meeting took an hour and the donuts were fresh. Nevertheless I want you to check with the Lead Teachers to make sure all their books and supplies are in. If there is a problem try to help them as a top priority."

"Okay. Will do." Jerry thought, *This is what my brother advised me to do. Slow down, perhaps a few books might be missing. The Team Leaders will complain to Matt.*

* * *

The Board of Education Building was attached to the high school. There was only one way in or out. The Board building was quarantined from the high school. Perhaps it was a good idea. There was no sense having the top brass walking the hallways of the high school or students roaming the Board building.

Matt arrived ten minutes early for the administrators' meeting with the Superintendent, Assistant Superintendent, Business Manager, and School Attorney.

He met the principal of the high school and the four elementary school principals as well. They were experienced and very knowledgeable.

Right before the top brass walked in, John Ward, the High School Principal sarcastically asked Matt, "How do you figure test scores? The middle school sends me, supposedly, ninety percent proficient students and my English and Math teachers complain that a great deal of the kids still don't know their basics."

Matt shrugged his shoulders. "Hey, I'm the new kid on the block. I'll let you know after the first semester is over."

John Ward nodded. "Matt, please do. Let's have lunch next week. How about a week from this Friday. I have some concerns to talk about."

"Sounds good to me."

The rest of the afternoon was spent going over the practices and procedures of the District, the latest New York State Curriculum Guidelines, and the budget picture for the school year. The meeting ended at three. Matt decided to go back to his school to check with his secretary and Jerry.

* * *

The moment he got into his office he sensed a problem. Maggie was deep in a conversation with Jerry and Otto. "What's happening?"

Maggie was the first to speak. "Jerry said that Otto delivered the new eighth grade math books and Otto said he did not handle those books at all. The Lead Teacher wants the books for tomorrow's classes."

Jerry put his hands on his hips in a obstinate manner. "I'm sure Otto had that responsibility. Damn sure!"

Otto interjected. "Mr. Collins, I never touched math books for grade eight."

Matt realized that this was a no win situation. "Jerry and Otto, please go into the supply closets and check on the new books together. Let me know if there may have been a short from the publisher. Did the eight grade math workbooks arrive for the slow learners?"

Jerry was quick with his answer. "Yes sir."

Matt buzzed the Math Team Leader's room. "Mr. Lyons, tell your teachers to prepare first day lessons for a review of basics. Drill and skill sets might be appropriate including basic algebraic formulas. I don't know if the publisher shorted us or if it is an administrative error."

"Thanks for the suggestions Mr. Collins. We will be prepared with or without books."

At five in the afternoon Otto came into the office and told Maggie that he found the books in the cafeteria's supply closet. He personally would distribute the books to the eighth grade math teachers' rooms.

Maggie buzzed Matt. "The books were found. Funny, that has never happened before."

Matt quickly responded. "Maybe there is a bad elf running around the building."

Maggie scoffed. "Bad elf my ankle."

Matt asked the reading teacher to see him before she left. She appeared ten minutes later.

Juanita Jones had dark hair, dark eyes and a dark complexion. When she verbalized, "Do you have a problem Mr. Collins?" It sounded as if an elocution teacher spoke. It was crystal clear and perfectly articulated.

"I want to compliment you on keeping all the New York State testing scores as high as they are."

Juanita Jones replied. "I never expected them to be so good. I still cannot figure it out. Some of my remedial readers were in the top ninety percent."

"Thank you Miss. Jones. Keep up the good work this year."

Matt called Professor Francois Lebo who was his teacher of advanced statistics at NYU. After the pleasantries Matt got down to business. "It seems I have a group of very above average students in this upstate middle class community, or something is wrong. Tests from the last three years have shown that the students were ninety percent proficient in math and language arts. I have reviewed the standardized tests of years twenty eleven and twenty twelve. I included all the students in grades six through eight and correlated them against the mean IQ of the District's student testing program.. There is a huge distortion in the analysis. I also did the same with the current New York State tests. The same distortion took place."

"Did you recheck your numbers and formulas?"

"Yes. I did it three times. On an empirical basis the high school principal has told me that he has had to place a number of ninth grade students in remedial math and reading. This included part of the ninety percent who were marked proficient. My middle school reading teacher cannot determine how some of her remedial students became so proficient as well. What do you think?"

"I think you have a problem and it sounds like the students have gotten the answer keys or the teachers have changed the answers or the independent scorers screwed up."

Matt remained silent for a moment. "I think it has to be collusion in the school. The answer keys are extremely hard to get and the independent scorers really have no interest in any students."

"If there is collusion then a serious conspiracy has taken place. Be careful, very careful with who you talk to because these test scores have probably made the Superintendent a happy man and the Board of Education ecstatic. Tread lightly and see if you can get some prima facie evidence from staff members. I'm not a psychologist, but guilt is always a good way to get people to talk. Keep me abreast."

"Thanks Professor"

"The bill will be in the mail."

Maggie, opened the door and wished Matt good night. Matt's head was in some files and he muttered, "Good night."

He thought, *I have to become a detective in a school I don't really know as yet with a staff I just met and it seems to me I am on my own. I don't think I can trust my assistant to do anything.*

There was a knock on the door. It was past six in the evening. "Come on in."

Beth stood in the doorway. She worked from early this morning to the early evening and she looked ravishing. "How was your day Matt?"

"Considering it is the day before the kids come in I would have to say that it was the best mediocre day I have had!"

"Come on, you had applause today. You are a rock star!"

"Beth, you are the rock star in my eyes."

"I'm going home and plan a dinner for this Friday night. I want to show you that I can chew gum and cook at the same time."

"I'll bring a bottle of red and a bottle of white wine to make sure."

"Good night Matt, I'd kiss you, but we are working."

CHAPTER 9

Matt arrived at the George W. Bush Middle School at six thirty in the morning. He was wearing a navy blue suit. A white on white shirt accented the navy and white striped tie. His shiny Bostonian shoes pinched a little and he reminded himself to get a new pair. The teachers were due in at seven and the first buses would start to come in close to seven thirty.

Maggie came in and introduced Matt to the ten-month salaried clerk who worked with her. "May I introduce Charlotte Greenburg who has worked with me for six years."

Matt saw a large woman of fifty who was wearing a proper business suit with a bit too much makeup. "Pleasure to meet you Miss Greenburg."

"Oh, just call me Charlotte, everybody else does. I usually make the coffee for the office. I collect five dollars a month from Jerry, Maggie and now you."

Matt withdrew five dollars from his wallet and gave it to Charlotte. "I like my coffee strong!"

"I like mine medium and I make the coffee."

They both laughed at the same time and Matt knew that Charlotte would fit in with his office style.

She turned around and went to her desk which was closer to Jerry's office. Thinking of Jerry reminded Matt that he had not seen him around at all. He quickly went to his desk and called Jerry's home.

Jerry picked up, "Hello."

"Jerry, this is Matt. It's the first day of school. Where are you?"

"Sorry Matt. I have an intestinal virus and can't make it in. Maybe I'll be better in a few days."

"Feel better Jerry. Come in when you can. Please call the office each day you aren't able to make it in."

"Okay Boss."

Jerry sat in his kitchen sipping his first cup of coffee of the day. He thought, *What a bad day Matt will have without me. Screw him!*

Matt considered this serious situation. He would have to do double duty without his assistant. Lousy luck.

"Maggie, Jerry is out with an intestinal virus and will not be in for a few days. I'll have to cover his areas as well as mine. I'll be in the cafeteria and on the playground so the kids can see an administrator. Perhaps threat motivation will help."

"That's funny. Since I have known Jerry he's never missed a first day of school."

"Funny or not, it will be a struggle without help."

Matt went outside to the bus platform to make sure the bus duty teachers were there. He was relieved to see all three of them were on station. This would have been Jerry's job. The first buses started to come in and Matt observed the youngsters getting off.

His four years at a middle school gave him great experience with the age range. The physical and psychological development of the students were dramatic. There is no consistent or normative quality of these students apart from, expect the unexpected.

The girls start to develop more quickly than the boys with menses starting at the average age of twelve. He remembers the School Nurse at his previous school explaining to the staff that at times the younger girls would have cramps. Further, sanitary tasks that go with early menstruation proved a problem. Facing body changes as well caused anxiety among the twelve to fourteen year old group. Many times a female counselor or nurse can be and would be a vital resource in a school.

The self concept of the boys, at times, will cause anger and bewilderment with their own peer groups. Since the girls develop faster many boys feel insecure with their sexuality. Peer groups are very important to the boys and at times a male teacher might become a role model to boys. The awareness of the opposite sex is acute with a great deal of fantasizing done by the boys.

Uncertainty reigns as students ages twelve to fourteen try to test adult roles. The guidance counselors are always looking out for ideation of suicide threats and severe bullying. It is a difficult age, very difficult to deal with whether you are a parent or an educator.

Only one bus came in late. Since it was standard procedure to have an extended homeroom period for the first week Matt was relieved. Matt had to ferry some frightened sixth graders as well as some new students to their classes. He didn't have Jerry around to take youngsters to their classes. Matt considered the bad luck having Jerry out, and a grain of doubt sneaked into his mind.

Before he knew it the second period bell rang and Matt headed for the first floor main corridor. He wanted to be a presence for the students to see. The third period bell sounded and he was on the second floor showing his presence again. Principals are no longer Gods to the students in a school. They are thought of more as wardens. Warden or God, Matt wanted the kids to know that he was all over the school and not in his office.

When Matt came back to his office he found two girls seated apart on the office bench. Maggie pointed to his office and they both went in. She read the note. "These two girls were arguing in my class and I could not quiet them down. I'm sending them to the Assistant Principal for punishment. Signed, Faith Higgins, Art Teacher. Room 208."

Matt read the note as well. "Maggie, is this standard procedure in the school?"

"It depends. There are some teachers who would rather send arguing kids to the Guidance Office. If there is a physical confrontation, then they go to the Assistant Principal."

"And Mrs. Higgins?"

"Never to guidance, always to the office."

"What grade are those girls in?"

"Eighth"

Matt stepped out of his office and called the girls in. "Sit down and listen to me very quietly. Normally you would be seeing Mr. Jackson, but he is ill so I'm doing double duty. Do you understand?"

They both nodded and one of them started to cry. "I've never been to a principal's office in my life. What are my parents going to do to me."

"What's your name?"

"Jennifer Williams."

He looked at the other girl. "And what is your name?"

"Carmen Sanchez."

Matt took a coin out of his pocket and asked Carmen. "Heads or tails?'

"Tails."

Matt flipped the coin. "Heads it is. Okay Miss Williams you have one minute to tell your story."

"Carmen told me that she was going to flirt with Robert Kaye. I told her to lay off because he's just into sports and bikes. He's just a kid."

"Carmen, your story?"

"I told her not to tell me what to do. Then we started yelling at each other."

"Did Mrs. Higgins try to calm you down?"

Carmen shook her head. "No she just wrote a note and told us to go to the office."

"Jennifer, is this true?"

"Yes sir."

"I assume you read the Code of Conduct rules for the school. You both were wrong. Carmen, for telling Jennifer and Jennifer for telling Carmen. If I see you in this office again I will contact your parents for a special meeting. Do you understand? Both of you sit on the bench under detention for this period only. Then go back to your schedule."

They left quietly, almost as little lambs. Matt wrote a note to Mrs. Higgins asking her to see him before she went home. He might as well start the education process with her now. Otto already warned him about her sloppiness and her husband being the owner of the only newspaper in town., but Matt had a duty to perform.

Period three had no major outbursts. The Cafeteria Manager, Julia Di'Salvo introduced herself and asked that he step into the cafeteria during period four. "Sometimes the two teachers on duty talk together and don't watch the kids. Then all hell breaks loose."

"Does Mr. Jackson ever come into the cafeteria to check on the duty teachers?'

Julia Di'Salvo laughed. "Mr. Jackson comes into the cafeteria to take a portion of pie or French fries. I don't know if he knows teachers are on duty."

"I'll be in during period four."

* * *

The cafeteria was large. It was noisy and it was typical of what he experienced in his prior school. As he approached the tables the students quieted down. Matt sat down at a table with some sixth grade boys. "What are the choices today?"

One young boy had enough courage to answer. "We have fries, burgers and chocolate milk. I'm eating the red jello for dessert."

Another boy raised his voice since he was sitting on the opposite side. "I'm having a grilled cheese sandwich with coleslaw and an apple for dessert."

"Thank you guys. I'll see you later."

After Matt left one of the boys remarked. "He doesn't sound like a principal."

The kids laughed, but there was respect in their eyes.

Matt looked at the two teachers on duty. When he had come in they were talking together. As soon as they saw him they moved away and started walking up and down the cafeteria. Obviously they knew what the procedure was for cafeteria duty. Matt resolved to get a device that worked well in school cafeterias. It was a very large stop light that had a red light, yellow light and green light. There were noise settings that were programmed into the device. If the light remained green there was no problem. If the light turned yellow there would be a bell that would warn the kids that it was getting too loud. If the light turned red there would be a siren sounded and it would signal the kids to quiet down. Most of the time it worked well.

* * *

Matt returned to his office and Maggie turned her head towards the office bench. "Mr. and Mrs. Costello would like to see you. Something about their daughter's math teacher."

Matt remembered Dominic Costello as the President of the Board of Education. He considered, "Ask them to come in, Maggie."

Mr. Costello sat down and introduced his wife Marie. She immediately got down to cases, "My daughter Nora is in eighth grade. She called me about her third period math class. She hates the teacher and claims he keeps looking at her breasts."

"Mrs. Costello, this is a guidance problem for the teacher, your daughter and you to work out."

"Oh no. We're not into that psychology crap. I want her changed right now!"

"Mr. Costello, do you feel the same way?"

"Of course I do."

"Well I am not going to change her until I get a recommendation from her counselor. Look at it this way. If I changed her without following the proper procedures other parents would want to do the same thing and we would have anarchy."

Marie Costello's face became red and she stood up tall. "You better remember your decision when it comes to your job. Don't you know about my husband's position?"

"Of course I do. I respect the public service that your husband renders. My concern is that he use it in a judicious manner."

Dominic Costello stood up, "Can you get us in to see her counselor today?"

"I certainly can. Hold on for a moment."

He dialed Beth Andrews extension. "Miss Andrews, this is Mr. Collins. Will you do me a great favor and see Mr. and Mrs. Costello right now to work out a problem that their daughter Nora is having with her math teacher. Good, fifteen minutes."

Mr. Costello took his wife's arm. "Thank you Mr. Collins."

When they left Matt called in Maggie. "Maggie, please bring in your pad."

Matt dictated a memo to himself describing the visit from Mr. and Mrs. Costello. "When you get that typed out please give it to me for my signature. Start a file called "Personal', Mr. Collins."

"Perhaps the file should be called 'Private" and kept locked in your office file?"

"That's a better idea. Let's do it your way."

* * *

It was half way through the fifth period and Matt decided to go outside to the field. The seventh graders would be outside having recreation. He needed some fresh air after the confrontation with Marie and Dominic Costello.

It was a typical field. There was a long grassed area where football or soccer could be played. Diametrically opposite at each corner of the field, there were large baseball backstops made of metal mesh. Matt observed groups of seventh graders playing some ball, girls chatting, and some boys running races. A pretty typical scene. There were two teachers on duty and they were walking around covering the large field.

Matt turned his back to the playground to walk back to the school when he heard screams. There was a large crowd of kids about forty yards away. Matt sprinted toward the crowd and pushed his way through. A boy was on the ground. Matt listened to his breathing and there seemed to be none.

A teacher came over and Matt directed her. "Call nine-one-one right now." She took out her cell phone and complied.

Matt started CPR. He knew exactly what to do. His military training kicked right in. He was in a zone and knew that he had to save this boy. Visions of him trying to save one of his men severely hurt on a mission came to his mind as he kept on doing CPR. He kept on thinking, *Don't die. Don't die. Don't die.*

The EMT tapped Matt on the shoulder. "We have him now."

The ambulance was on the field since there was an emergency entrance for vehicles on the street side. The two uniformed men placed an oxygen mask on the boy and listened to his heart.

"You saved this kids life buddy. Nice job!"

Everybody heard what the EMT said and the kids started applauding while teachers began to clap.

Matt wiped his brow. His blue pants were grass stained and he was sweating profusely. Matt asked one of the teachers, "How long did the ambulance take to get here?"

The teacher, nearly in tears, responded, "Twenty five minutes. Oh, Mr. Collins, you really saved his life!"

"What's his name?"

The other duty teacher replied. "Joseph Green, sir."

"May I borrow your phone?"

He called Maggie at his office. "Please call the parents of Joseph Green and tell them to go to the hospital. Their son is there."

The duty teacher, Helen Muir took back her phone. "Mr. Collins, I saw what happened. Joseph just fell down. No one pushed him or hurt him. He just sort of fainted."

"Please fill out a statement describing what you saw. It's important for the record. Give it to the school secretary, please."

"Sir, I will do anything you ask me to do. I have never seen anybody so intense trying to save a life. As far as I am concerned you are number one for me!"

Matt got back to the office and tried to get the grass stains off his knees. He couldn't get it clean. Maggie looked at the pants. "Matt, give me your home keys. I'll get you a pair of pants from your closet and bring it back to school."

Matt agreed and within thirty minutes Maggie brought back a pair of grey slacks that would look well with his blue jacket. "The word is all over town that you saved Joseph's life."

Matt went into his office bathroom and changed. He called the Assistant Superintendent's Office to alert him about the accident. Eric Bolt's secretary stated that he was not in his office, but she would give him the message.

Matt went out to the bus platform and made sure that the teachers were on duty. The kids filed out and one of the boys he spoke to in the cafeteria yelled, "Hi Mr. Collins. Have a great day!" The other kid waived.

Matt returned to his office after all the buses left. Waiting for him was Faith Higgins, Art Teacher.

"Please come into my office Mrs. Higgins."

A woman about forty years old marched into the office. She sat down in the chair opposite Matt's desk. "Well, I'm here,"

Matt went to the small table. "Mrs. Higgins, please sit down by this table. Its more conducive to taking to colleagues."

"Do you consider me a colleague? I work for you."

"No, you work for the District as I do. We are in different roles, but all focused on the same goal, educating children."

"That's the point. How can I educate them when their behavior is so poor."

"When I was in the service I learned a great deal about discipline since I was an officer. The first was that you had to earn the respect of your people. It's the same way in schools. May I suggest you develop a few strategies and tactics before sending children to the office. If you cannot control them, then I will have to give you a poor evaluation in terms of control of class."

"Are you threatening me Mr. Collins?"

"Far from it. In fact I will help you with a tactic that will help you keep your class happy and looking forward to coming to your room."

"I have been teaching for fifteen years and I know what to do."

"Perhaps you have been teaching for fifteen years and have been doing something wrong, in terms of discipline, for fifteen years."

"Well, I'm not going to take this abuse from you."

Matt went to his desk and buzzed for Maggie. "Please come in with your pad."

Maggie came in with her dictation pad. "Yes sir."

"Mrs. Carter will you please record, using short hand, my conversation with Mrs. Higgins." Matt turned to Mrs. Higgins, "You may call in a union representative to witness this conversation or you may give us approval to continue."

"Okay. Go ahead."

"Mrs. Higgins, in order to improve your discipline techniques I am requesting that you try a few tactics with the overall mission that the children will respect you as an Art Teacher."

"I'm listening."

"Try to find out from your students what interests them. Spend a lesson, even two lessons to see what they like for example: dirt bikes, baseball, make-up, fashion, TV shows, movies, trips, travel, dancing, weight lifting and I could give you a dozen more. Have a student write these interests down on your board. Try to get a consensus from your class what the three best interests might be. The kids love to vote on things. Then design your lessons around their interest levels."

"What if I'm not interested in any of their topics?"

"You told me you have fifteen years of experience. I'm sure you know much more than a thirteen year old! Improvise your lessons if necessary. The goal is to have the students enjoy art and test their creativity."

'"What about the children who interrupt?"

"May I suggest this tactic. Take them outside your door and speak to them. Ask them for their cooperation. Don't demand it, just ask. Another tactic is to contact their Guidance Counselor for a meeting. Perhaps you can get some insight about the disruptive students. Another tactic is to have a conference with their parents. They all have signed the Code of Conduct. That is due process before major disciplinary action. Sending a student to the office is a major strategy to think over since I would have to suspend the student. You would have to write up a bill of particulars for the record. Are you willing to try some of my suggestions?"

"Yes of course I will try them."

"Fine. I'll have Mrs. Carter give you a copy of this conversation."

When Mrs. Higgins left Maggie stood up and put her hand on the knob of the door. She then turned around. "Do you know who you are dealing with?"

"Yes. A teacher who needs help in classroom discipline. Nothing to do with her husband or the newspaper. Otto warned me."

"Well Matt, you had a hell of a first day!"

Matt smiled.. He thought, *End of day one!*

Matt's phone was ringing when he entered his apartment. "Hello."

"Hello Mr. Collins, I'm Sharon Silver, reporter for the Risenburg Tribune. I'd like to interview you about the incident on the playground that happened today."

Matt immediately had his defenses up. "I'm sorry Miss Silver, but you will have to go through channels with the central office. I have no idea how the youngster is doing."

"Oh, Joseph Green is doing better. They are running tests on him. I've already interviewed his parents. They will be coming to your office tomorrow to thank you"

"I'm glad to hear that he is doing better, but I'm afraid I cannot comply."

Matt hung up. He was happy to hear that Joseph was doing better, but he was concerned about law suits against the teachers, himself and the District due to accidents on the playing field. He had to be deposed four times in his previous position and was in court once. It was not a pleasant experience. He learned that in two out of the four cases the District insurance lawyers settled out of court. They won the court case and the other case was still open.

Matt belonged to SAANYS, School Administrators Association of

New York State. One of the benefits was legal assistance with no cap set. When he became an administrator he took out a million dollar personal liability insurance policy to be on the safe side. Many of his fellow administrators did the same thing.

Matt was starved. It was almost nine in the evening. He decided to go to the Main Street Diner to have a late dinner.

* * *

There was a different waitress on duty tonight. She was professional, but not chatty. This was perfect for Matt tonight. He ordered liver, bacon and onions with decaf coffee. While waiting he devoured the rolls and butter before the food came. Matt ate with gusto. He enjoyed basic American food.

Matt waived to the waitress and she walked over to the table. "May I have the check?"

"See Harry. He's the owner."

Matt approached a very large man who had a white apron on. "Are you Harry?"

"Yes I am and you're Matt Collins, the Middle School Principal. Julia, the day waitress told me about you. You are an okay guy!"

"Thanks. May I have my check?"

"It's paid for."

"By who?"

"By me."

"Why?"

"Because Julia calls me up and tells me how you saved that kid's life. Because my son who is the EMT told me you saved the kid's life, because Joseph is my God Son and the Greens are best friends with my wife and myself, because just get out of here before I cry! I'm so happy Joseph made it!"

This time Matt decided not to argue about any gratuities to him. He felt happy that Joseph made it and how the situation affected so many lives.

* * *

Upon entering his apartment Matt saw his message light blinking from the base of his master phone unit. It was a call from CNN. They wanted to interview him about the incident. There was a call from the School Attorney for information. There was a call from a reporter from the Times-Union in Albany and another call from a reporter from the Post-Standard in Syracuse. Matt thought, *This is getting out of hand.*

He decided to get some sleep before making any decisions about publicity. His first morning call would be to the School Attorney. Hopefully he should be getting the duty teacher's write up and summary of the incident tomorrow morning. It was time for him to sleep. That didn't work.

After tossing and turning until midnight he decided to do some deep meditation. He learned the technique in the army especially after coming back from some very tough and brutal missions. It usually worked. If that did not work a sleeping pill would put him to sleep, but with a terrible headache in the morning.

## CHAPTER 10

Matt pulled into the front parking lot. There was a sign painted on the curb that read, "Principal's Parking."

As he got out of his car a truck pulled up beside him. It was Jerry. "I heard about the kid yesterday. I should have been out there instead of you. I'm feeling better."

"Great Jerry. I really could have used you yesterday!"

Both men entered the school and Maggie ran to get Matt a cup of coffee. "Here Boss, you are going to need this today. Keep sharp and alert because it's going to be chaos around here, and I'm not talking about the kids."

Jerry got his cup of coffee and looked at Matt. "What's the plan Skipper?"

"The kids come first. Jerry please make sure to get the incident report from Helen Muir, she saw the whole thing. The kid just fell down. No one pushed him or anything like that, he just fell down on his own."

Maggie moved between Matt and Jerry. "Who has the highest priority for adult visits for you today?"

"Anyone from Central Office. Try to keep the press out. I'm sure I'll get a visit from Mr. and Mrs. Green."

Matt heard the buses coming in and he saw Jerry scurrying out to take charge. That was the good news. He looked again and saw the Superintendent, his Assistant and a woman with a camera around her neck. He thought, *Oh shit, here it comes!*

Dr. Frederick Hull was generous in his praise of Matt. Eric Bolt, the Assistant was flowery in his praise. Dr. Hull introduced Jan Thomas. "Jan is our District photographer. We plan to give these shots to the newspapers upon request. Is this okay with you?"

"Yes sir, that will be okay. I did hang up on a reporter from the local paper."

"We'll take care of that Matt. Don't worry about it."

The photos were mainly group shots of the officials shaking Matt's hand and having their arms around his shoulders. It was over in ten minutes.

Jerry came into his office with the report from Mrs. Muir, yesterday's duty teacher. It was one paragraph long and ended when Matt started CPR. It was concise and well written with her signature on the bottom. Matt added a written note to the School Attorney as well, indicating he was willing to write a more formal report if necessary. "Maggie, please fax these to the School Attorney and call his secretary to make sure he sees it. Give me about fifteen minutes of uninterrupted time."

Matt had to decompress. He did not want to have pictures taken with his superiors. It seemed as if they were trying to pump up or inflate the District's valor. All he did was help a kid. He felt that Jerry coming back so quickly meant that his sickness was a phony. Matt called Beth in the Guidance Office. "I need your help. I'm feeling used by the District. They just left with their photographer. All they wanted was their faces with mine."

"Matt, that's the price of being a middle manager. You are in charge of your school, but you have bosses. Just like me. Grow up and welcome to the real world!"

"Thank you for the advice."

"That will be five cents please."

They both laughed together and Matt felt better about the situation.

Matt answered his buzzer. "Mr. and Mrs. Green to see you."

The Greens' came in and Matt ushered them to his small table. Mrs. Green was a small woman, perhaps in her late thirties and Mr. Green was just a few years older. "We want to thank you personally for saving Joseph's life." Mr. Green's voice was emotional and Matt thought the man might start to cry.

Mrs. Green spoke up. "I'm a Registered Nurse Mr. Collins. Joseph had prolonged apnea. It means a person has stopped breathing. Since you kept his heart beating the doctors called it a respiratory arrest. They told us this condition is a life threatening event that requires immediate medical attention and first aid. Well, you provided the first aid that started his heart. Now the doctors are running tests. It could be bronchiolitis, meningitis, a seizure or stroke, or maybe a heart or lung condition. We've called in a specialist who is coming in from Syracuse."

Mr. Green stood up and shook Matt's hand. "I own the supermarket in town and my first name is Vincent. If you want to speak to me tell my workers I want to speak to Vincent, that's the only way you will get through."

Matt thought for moment. "Joseph will need tutoring if he is to stay out for a long time. I can arrange that."

Mrs. Green quickly responded,, "No, I think he will be back to school on Monday."

They left the office and Matt looked up at the clock. It was already approaching the fifth period of the day. He wanted to go to the cafeteria to check on noise levels, but Maggie buzzed. "Mrs. Stuart, President of the PTA is here to see you."

Mrs. Maureen Stuart was dressed right out of the cover of Vogue. She was in her mid thirties with very blonde hair, a shapely figure, and perfume that you could smell ten feet away. "Oh Mr. Collins, I am so proud to meet you. The whole town is talking about you. I'm sure the Executive Board of our PTA will be excited to meet you next Tuesday evening. We meet the second Tuesday of every month for ten months in the conference room. Either the Principal or Assistant Principal usually attends. Will you attend our first meeting?"

"Of course I will be there. Do you expect me to present anything to you?"

"Only if there is a need."

Matt looked into her eyes. She could not hold his intense look. "I may have a proposal for the PTA regarding doing something special for the kids."

She got up and shook his hand. "I'll see you at seven thirty next Tuesday in the conference room."

Matt quickly went on line to see how much the Noise Traffic Light would cost. The best one would cost nine hundred and seventy dollars shipped to the school. It would be the actual size of a real traffic light. The students would have instructions about using their "inside voices" for green and their "whisper voices" for yellow or "no talking" for red. He thought, *That would be a good project for the PTA.*

Matt never got to the cafeteria. Maggie gave him the typed copy of his conversation with Mrs. Higgins the Art teacher. "I'll put a copy in her mailbox."

"No Maggie, please give me her copy. I think I'll take a walk up to the Art room.

\* \* \*

Matt fast timed it up the stairs and opened the rear door of the Art room. He quietly sat down. The students were talking about their interests and hobbies and a girl was writing the information on the black board.

"Welcome Mr. Collins," Mrs. Higgins pronounced in a loud voice, "and what is your hobby or interest?"

"I love boating. Especially sailing." Matt came to the front of the class and not a sound was made by the class. They were in awe of him. "I used to own a boat on Long Island and when I had time I would sail all over the coast line. It was fun. I'm so pleased that Mrs. Higgins gave you time to discuss interests and hobbies. What will you do with all this information?"

"I'm glad you asked me that." The crafty teacher replied. "We will start a pictorial scrapbook that will contain pictures and captions focusing on interests or hobbies. It will be up to each student to decide."

There was a happy buzz in the class as Matt dropped off the report on her desk. He winked at Mrs. Higgins and she smiled broadly to him.

The rest of the day seemed anticlimactic. He decided to have dinner at one of the fast food restaurants on Main Street. Fried chicken, mashed potatoes and gravy sounded good to him.

CHAPTER 11

Matt awoke feeling energized. He thought of Beth and their date tonight. He reminded himself to buy red wine as well as white. It seemed to him that Beth had him guessing. She seemed wise beyond her years. He really liked her. A lot!

Fridays in most schools are happy days. The kids, as well as the teachers, are looking forward to a weekend off from school. The weather was still beautiful. Only a few trees were beginning to show autumn colors. Soon the trees would look magnificent in their dazzling fall splendor.

On his desk was his next week's newsletter that he wrote yesterday. The teachers were going to get a dose of structure even if they didn't like it. The most important message in the newsletter was a meeting of Team Leaders with Matt and Jerry set for Tuesday. Teacher Assistants would cover their classes. Matt designed it for two periods. Eighty four minutes should be enough time to settle any problems.

Matt wanted to establish goals for the year and meet the Team Leaders as early as possible. He was looking forward to the meeting next Tuesday.

In his experience, Matt realized that the three grade level Team Leaders had more to do with the day to day operations of the school then he did. They coordinated the ongoing operations of a grade. Scheduling of tests, assemblies, field trips as they related to the instructional program and cross grade level activities were their responsibilities.

Maggie buzzed. "Mr. Collins. The Library-Media Teacher, Miss Peck is here to see you. There is a real problem in the Media Center.

Dolores Peck walked in. She was a knockout auburn hair, dark blue eyes, a figure out of Playboy magazine and tall. She was wearing spike heels making her

Matt's equal in height. Matt waived her to the small table and as she sat down she crossed her legs up to her mid thigh. There was nothing to miss since her light sweater accented a very shapely bust.

"How can I help you Miss Peck?"

"Mr. Collins, one of my computers is missing. I have a Monday morning routine to check all equipment. I had thirty computers and now I only count twenty nine."

Her voice matched her beauty and I had to focus on the problem. "Has this ever happened before?"

"No sir. This is my fourth year in the school. I got tenure last year."

"Go back to your center and give me the following information. Make, type, model number and serial number of the missing computer. May I have that as soon as possible. Please do it quickly."

She got up, turned around and left. There was nothing wrong with her rear appearance at all. He thought, *If I wasn't involved with Beth I might take a crack at Dolores Peck!*

Matt dialed Otto's extension. No answer. He buzzed Maggie, "Using only the hallways, not the classrooms, page Otto to come to the office."

A minute later Matt heard, "Mr. Lyons to the office. Mr. Lyons to the office."

Otto appeared in less than five minutes. "What can I do for you Boss?"

"One of our computers in the Media Center is missing. Did you have any substitutes working on Friday night?"

"Yes, we had a new man recommended by one of the Board members. This was his first night."

"May I have his name and address."

Otto left and returned promptly with the information. "Maggie, please come in and close the door behind you."

"Problem?"

"A missing computer from the Media Center. Do you know the

Chief of Police?"

"Sure, Chief Miller. He's been with us for ten years."

'How can I get him to move quickly on this without seeming to be pushy?"

"Let me call my husband and see what he can do."

Matt started to work on an observation schedule for Jerry and himself when his phone rang. "Mr. Collins, I'm Chief Miller. How can I help you?"

"I have a computer missing from our Media Center and there was a new custodial substitute working the night shift Friday night. One of the Board of Education members recommended him . I'll have all the information about the missing computer and I'll have the substitute's name and address for you if one of your officers could sort of find out if he may be our man."

"This will take a bit of diplomacy. I'll handle it with Otto Lyons, your Chief Custodian. I'll be over in an hour."

Matt called Otto's extension. "Otto, Chief Lyons will be coming over. Ask Miss Peck for all of the computer information right now and give it to the Chief. He said he wants to handle it personally. Make sure to give him the name of the Board member who recommended your substitute."

"You've got it Boss."

Matt learned enough about school politics when he worked on Long Island. Although Board members in New York State did not get paid, they wielded a great deal of power when it came to hiring, major contracts for the District, selecting vendors and other indirect personnel. He didn't want to point a finger at a Board member if the recommendation turned out to be a bad decision. No one wanted to recommend a thief!

Matt was able to get to the sixth period which was the eighth grade cafeteria period. The cafeteria was a zoo. The noise level was atrocious and there were students running from table to table. He saw one student walking on top of a table. Matt turned his eyes to the duty teachers and found them chatting away in the far opposite corner. A male teacher spotted Matt. He blew his whistle three times and ran up and down the lanes blowing the whistle and shouting, "Shut up! Shut up!"

Matt stepped into the center of the cafeteria, raised his right hand

and put the pointer finger of his left hand on his lips. He turned around twice and all the noise and activity stopped. "Young ladies and gentlemen of the eighth grade. I am supposed to give approval for your end of year trip to Washington D.C. for three days. If you continue to act out as you were doing here there will be no trip at all. If I have to come into this cafeteria to reprimand you again there will be no after school clubs for the first semester." Matt summoned up his military voice and ended with, "And I mean business. Go ahead and test me."

The cafeteria was church quiet as the students ate their lunch. Matt approached the two duty teachers and in a whisper told them, "Please see me at the end of the day."

Maggie came into the cafeteria and motioned to Matt. As they were walking to the office she whispered ion his ear, "Mr. Bird, the Business Manager is angry and here to see you. Something about the health and safety of the students. Matt, he is really pissed!"

When Maggie used his first name he knew she was into protective mode He came through the side office door and asked the Business Manger to come in.

"Mr. Bird. a pleasure to meet you."

"Don't give me that polite business. Your memo to the Superintendent got his balls in an uproar and he placed all the crap on me to find out what is happening."

"What is the issue?"

"An emergency request for four cafeteria tables. You said you would not be held responsible if they collapse on the students."

"That's exactly what I said."

"Who the hell do you think you are Mister?"

"I'm the Principal of this school and under New York State Judicial decrees I am under loco parentis, which means I act as their parent. That means that if they are in danger I have to take care of that danger and Mister, it's up to you to respond. Get the hell out of my office and order those tables today!"

John Bird, the Risenburg Union Free School District's Business Manager, sat on his chair and looked at Matt. "Boy, you have a lot of guts. When you said the word 'Mister" in that tone, I knew you served. Where did you serve?"

"Three years, in Iraq and Afghanistan."

"What unit?"

"Company B, 3rd Battalion, 75th Ranger Regiment. I was a Captain when I got out. Where did you serve?"

"Two years, Iraq and Afghanistan"

"What unit?"

"The 10th Mountain Division out of Fort Drum, New York. 4th Brigade. I was a First Lieutenant when I got out."

Matt walked over to him and shook his hand. "You were warriors. We used to get news that some of your boys did some major damage in Indian Country."

"Yeah, we knew of your gang and some of the black ops. We heard about it, and we thought you guys were off the wall crazy."

"You want some Joe, I mean coffee."

"No, no thanks. I have to go back to my office and order four cafeteria tables. It seems some crazy guy needs it."

John Bird stood up and he and Matt hugged. "Good luck brother," John whispered.

Matt met with the two cafeteria duty teachers and asked them to roam around and be more aware of the students behavior. He did not write them up or discipline them.

CHAPTER 12

Beth bought a Prime rib chef-style cut roast beef. She asked the butcher to de-bone it and have it tied. She knew it was one of the more expensive cuts, but well worth it. She thought, *I want to show Matt that I am multi-dimensional. I can cook, counsel, and make love in a masterful manner.* She had gone to different stores with the intent of making this meal perfect. The beautiful matching napkins and tablecloth were bought at the large General Store as well as a set of nice wine glasses. The fresh vegetables from the roadside farm stand and, of course the beautiful roast from the specialty butcher in the market.

She had previously put fresh sheets and pillow cases on her bed and sprayed a light linen scent on the pillows. Beth wanted to consummate their relationship tonight. She felt excited and was eager for this relationship to be meaningful.

\* \* \*

Matt selected a light foam green long sleeved shirt, black sport jacket, grey pants and black loafers. His clothes fit him well. He looked tailored and well-dressed in a casual manner.

Steve, Matt's older brother by three years would always tease Matt about his clothing. His brother was an immaculate dresser who intuitively knew what to wear. Currently Steve was the CEO of a large company based in "Silicon Valley" in northern California. He offered Matt many superlative positions in his corporation, especially in Human Resources, because it would fit in with his experience and background. Matt refused to take the bait, but knew his older brother was always watching out for him.

Matt was anxious about tonight. He really liked Beth. He liked how animated she was, how full of life she was, and how loving she was. Her intellect was outstanding and he felt alive when they were together. There seemed to be endless topics they could discuss in depth.

Matt picked up the package of wine and started to leave when his home phone rang. He looked at the phone's screen and it was from Chief Miller. "Hello Chief."

"Good news Mr. Collins. Your computer will be back to your school on Monday. It currently is at the Station House."

"Great! May I ask how you got it?"

"Off the record now."

"Okay, off the record."

"I called the Board member who recommended the substitute custodian and told him the story of the missing computer. He said he would go over the man's house and check it out. Well, lo and behold he found the lost computer and delivered it to my office about an hour ago."

"Great. Did you mention my name?"

"No, I took all the credit. Let's not ruffle any Board members decisions about their recommending lousy substitute employees."

"Thanks Chief."

"Mr. Collins, you handled yourself very well. If you need anything let me know."

"Thank you sir."

* * *

Jerry Jackson sat home brooding. His wife of twelve years looked at him and shook her head. "Now what's wrong?"

"I can't catch a break. This new principal is now a hero and the town, as well as the Board loves him. How am I going to ever become a principal?"

"Jerry, we have no children and have saved up a bit of money. Why don't you start looking around in other districts."

"Nobody really knows me."

"Why don't you join Principal's State Association. You told me Mr. Collins highly recommends that organization. You could go to meetings and meet other administrators. Get the lay of the land."

"Get me another beer. I'll think about it."

* * *

Friday evening, Matt was greeted with a light kiss on the lips by Beth. She looked radiant. Her dress was blue and it accented her blue-grey eyes. Stepping back, Matt noticed her honey colored hair was let down. It looked great. Normally she had it set in a more professional manner as a bun or upsweep. She looked stunning!

"Here are white wine and red wine. I don't know what we will use tonight."

"Red meat tonight means red wine. I'll put the white in the refrigerator. Maybe we can drink it later when we relax. Matt, please open the wine and sit down."

"It will be my pleasure."

Matt saw the wine corkscrew device on the dinner table and proceeded to open the wine. The table was set beautifully! He thought, *I keep on seeing more and more of the best from her. I hope I can live up to her standards.*

"Matt, please pour the wine."

Beth lifted up her glass. "This is for us. Let's have a great school year and I hope our relationship will blossom."

Matt was surprised by her toast. "May our relationship continue to blossom!"

Beth smiled and drank the whole glass of wine as he sipped a bit of it.

The salad was crisp, cold, delicious, delightful and tasted like the Greek salad he had when he was in Greece on a tour. He consumed at least three huge slices of roast beef. The vegetables and potatoes were out of this world. If Beth wanted to prove to him that she could cook she got the gold star tonight.

"Matt, don't expect dinners like this all the time. It would ruin my budget. I just wanted tonight to be special."

"You're a wonderful cook. I know that tonight is special."

Beth brought out an old fashioned apple pie. It was still warm and she had put vanilla ice cream on top. They both ate with gusto. Coffee ended the meal.

Matt noticed that the wine bottle was nearly empty. "Do you want more wine?"

"No. I'm going to clean up. Why don't you go and watch TV until I'm finished cleaning up."

Matt helped to clear the table and then went in to watch TV. Luckily there was a baseball game on and he became interested in it. He looked at his watch and it was almost nine. Exactly at that time Beth came in from the kitchen. She smiled, took his hand, and escorted him to her bedroom. Matt followed, excited with anticipation.

Their lovemaking was sweet, with each person trying to satisfy the other. Matt felt at home with her. They both fell asleep locked in each others arms.

Before Beth fell asleep she knew that he was the one. She smiled and gently drifted off to sleep.

Sometime during the night they made love for a second time. It was natural. It was satisfying. It was loving. It felt so right to both of them. Matt heard Beth whisper in his ear, "I love you."

Matt waited just a bit and whispered, "I love you more."

They stayed locked together until the morning.

The morning coffee smelled wonderful to Matt. He went over to the chair where his clothing was draped and put on his shorts. Going into the bathroom he washed up and put Beth's toothpaste on his fingers to brush his teeth. He then walked into the kitchen and saw Beth in a pink robe making breakfast.

She looked at Matt. His body was beautiful well muscled, lean and slender. Beth noticed a scar that ran from his right shoulder down to the inside of his right arm. Instinctively she knew it was from the war. "Sit down, I'll get you some juice."

Beth served Matt a small glass of juice, but before she left he pulled her on his lap and kissed her. She laughed, kissed him back and quickly returned to serve toast, bacon and eggs.

They ate quietly with Matt going to the toaster a second time. "Hon, do you want toast?"

Beth liked that he called her "Hon." It was a sign that it really had become a relationship. "No, thank you sweetheart."

At the kitchen table they discussed how their relationship would impact their positions. They agreed that it would have to be a professional relationship with absolutely no loving interaction at school If any of the staff would find out it would upset the delicate balance of the school. Kids would not tell the truth to Beth and faculty members would have to watch their complaints against administration. On the other side, Matt would have to make sure that he would not favor Beth in any manner.

They agreed to meet that evening at a restaurant some twenty five miles outside of town on Route Twenty. Matt dressed, looked at Beth smiling and left.

\* \* \*

"The Black Swan" restaurant was one of those old fashioned establishments that catered to a economically higher class. The menu was strictly ala cart.

"Matt, Can you afford this place?"

"Tonight you can have anything you want. Tomorrow we eat beans."

Beth laughed so hard that the bread she was eating nearly slipped out of her mouth. "You are silly and I love you."

Matt reached out and took her hand. "I love you."

They both had the lobster special and attacked it with zest. Later they had espresso to finish the meal. Matt called for the check and the waiter responded by saying, "The bill and tip have been paid for by Mr. and Mrs. Green. They are regulars here and they spotted you coming in. If you're looking for them they already left. You know that he owns that supermarket in town. He's very generous."

Matt looked at Beth, "I guess something like this happens all the time in movies, but not in reality. We're twenty five miles out of town."

"The only people who can afford a place like this would be people like the Greens where money is no object."

"I'll speak to them and thank them. I'll ask them to keep quiet about our date."

They both drove their separate cars back to Beth's apartment.

While driving back Matt felt elated. He really loved spending time with Beth. She reminded him of fresh air in the early spring and sunshine at the height of the day. Combined, they presented him with a warm gentle person who had a positive view of life. He loved that about Beth.

* * *

Matt brought enough clothing and toiletries. He started to strip down.

Beth looked at him and smiled. "Why are you undressing?"

"Because I'm ready?"

Beth ran to him and jumped on him as she wrapped her legs around his waist. She whispered, "So am I!"

## CHAPTER 13

Sunday was a first experience for Matt and Beth. After breakfast they started to make love and it continued past their lunch. Finally about one in the afternoon Beth got up from Matt's embrace. "I'm hungry."

"So am I."

They raided the refrigerator and had cold roast beef sandwiches and beer. The loving couple continued to look at each other. Beth finally proclaimed, "I've never had a day like this in my life."

"Neither have I. Shall we stop?"

Beth came to his side of the kitchen table and sat on his lap. She gave him a deep open mouthed kiss and then replied, "No, I just started."

Matt felt reenergized and he gladly followed her lead. They ended up on the area rug in the family room.

Beth looked down at him, "I love you so much and I'll do anything for you." She moved in over him and slowly let herself become engaged.

Matt issued a happy groan as they became one again. "Oh my God, you are insatiable and I love it!"

Matt left in the early evening. He recognized that Beth was the only woman he would ever want or need. The weekend was extraordinary.

\* \* \*

Matt arrived, as usual, at six thirty in the morning and saw Jerry's parked truck. He entered the school and Jerry offered Matt a cup of coffee he had just brewed. Matt accepted it. "Hey Jerry , what made you an early bird today?"

"I just feel I let you down and I've got to show you my 'A' game."

"If you read my newsletter you know that I need the lists of kids who have not brought in the signed Code of Conduct. Will you be my point man and call the parents or guardians and find out what happened?"

"You've got it. I'll have a report by the end of the day."

"Don't forget that we are having a meeting with the Team Leaders at period two and three tomorrow. The agenda was published in the newsletter."

"Be careful. They may throw a few curves at you that you can't handle."

"I'll have you Jerry, to run interference."

Both men laughed. Jerry nodded. 'Boss, its not football, its hardball."

They both turned to their respective offices. Matt waived to Maggie as she came into the office.

Matt received another call from Sharon Silver, the reporter for the local newspaper. This time he was courteous. 'The District gave you a nice statement and many pictures. Don't you think you've covered it enough?"

"Mr. Collins, I want to do an in depth story about you. Your resume and early information was read when it was released by the District when you signed your contract. I want to interview and get your opinion about education, discipline in schools, our District and how we run our schools."

"Thank you for all your interest in me, but the answer is no." Matt hung up.

He called Maggie into his office and handed her information about the large stoplight that he wanted for the cafeteria. "Maggie, please prepare an information sheet for the Executive Board of the PTA. I'm meeting with them tomorrow night and I'm going to ask them to purchase this for the school."

Maggie looked at the sheet. "This is great. For the first time in a long time I can see something concrete suggested from a principal to help kids. I'll make it real pretty."

She returned to her office determined to create a professional brochure for the PTA.

Maggie buzzed, "There is a student to see you. I recommend you see him now."

Thirteen year old Joseph Green came in. "Mr. Collins, I want to thank you for helping me. I don't remember much, but everyone says you saved my life. Thank you."

"Joseph, I would have helped any kid who was in trouble. I just spotted you."

"I guess you have good eyesight!"

"I sure do."

"Joseph are you on any special medicine?'

"No sir, but I have to go back to the hospital on Wednesday for some more tests."

"Okay. If you need anything special, like a note to quit gym classes, ask the doctors to give it to you."

"I like gym."

"Only if the doctors say okay."

"Sure thing Mr. Collins. Thanks again."

Matt dialed the School Nurse. "Mrs. O'Dwyer, I just finished speaking to Joseph Green. He is going to the hospital for tests on Wednesday. Make sure to keep an eye out on his progress.'

"Sure thing Mr. Collins. I'd like to see you to schedule classes for sixth grade girls."

"What's the topic."

"Menses."

"Permission granted, but do the scheduling with the Sixth Grade Team Leader. That's his job. He has responsibilities."

"Yes sir. This will be a first. I'll do that right now!" She immediately hung up.

Maggie, buzzed, "Superintendent Hull on the line."

Matt responded in a military manner. "Yes sir."

"Matt, I want you to give a half hour presentation on your new Code of Conduct to our Chamber of Commerce. That's this Friday at noon. We meet at Henry's House, the barbecue restaurant on Route Twenty. Do you know it?"

"Yes sir. How many will be there?"

"About twenty."

"I'll bring handouts."

"I know you will do a great job for the District"

"Thank you Dr. Hull."

\* \* \*

On Tuesday morning Matt and Jerry sat in the conference room as they discussed the agenda for the Team Leader meeting to be held the second and third periods. Items included were text book and work book needs, equipment and supply needs, field trip plans, support for new and non-tenured teachers, Teacher Assistant roles, Code of Conduct review, and the New York State Testing program.

Jerry reviewed the agenda. "That's a lot to cover in eighty four minutes."

"If I keep control and don't let other items interfere, we will be alright. I want you to be aware of this and if any of the leaders start going off on a tangent please bring them back to the agenda item. Do it diplomatically, but do it!"

"Yes sir. Diplomatically!"

All three Team Leaders came in at the same time. Matt waved them to their seats and gave them the agenda. "Ladies and gentlemen, please review the agenda . If there is anything else you wish to discuss please tell me now."

Tim Franklin, Team Leader of the eighth grade looked at the agenda. "Please add room cleanliness. I'm getting some flack from the teachers about your new administrative rule."

Matt looked at Tim Franklin. He was tall, about six one, with a ruddy complexion and very dark eyes. Tim was wearing a beige cardigan over an ordinary shirt and brown tie. "I'll put that down as the first item. Mr. Franklin why don't you introduce yourself to me."

He seemed startled. "Okay. I teach social studies and language arts and have been working in the District for thirteen years. Took my undergraduate degree at Oswego and got my Masters from Albany."

Matt looked at Julia Lovell. She was heavy set and short. Julia was wearing a pants suit outfit of dark green She wore hardly any make up at all. "I'm Julia Lovell, Sixth Grade Team Leader. I've been in this school for eight years and before that I worked in the Syracuse schools for four years. I moved here because my husband was transferred to the area. I teach math and science and have been Team Leader for five years. Got my degrees from Syracuse University."

Sam England did not wait for Matt. "I'm Sam England and I'm the Seventh Grade Team Leader. I teach language arts and social studies. Ten years in the District with both degrees from New Paltz, SUNY."

"Thank you Mr. England."

Sam England seemed aggressive in his tone. He was about five nine with curly blond hair, and light eyes. He was wearing a blue suit that was out of fashion some five years ago.

Assistant Principal Jerry Jackson knocked on the table. "I want to discuss the first few items because it is my responsibility."

The first few items were handled well since there were no complaints. That is until the topic of field trips.

Tim Franklin looked at Matt. "There is a rumor among the eighth grade kids that they may not get to Washington D.C. because of their behavior. Can you clarify that for us, Mr. Collins?"

"I told the eighth grade the other day in the cafeteria that if their behavior did not change I would cancel their trip."

"Don't you think it would have been better to discuss this with me?"

"Most certainly, but there were two kids walking on top of tables, other kids running around and throwing items at each other and two duty teachers who were talking in a corner and not paying attention to their duty."

"Oh, I didn't know."

"That's why I want to discuss the code of Conduct with you."

They finished discussing the standard field trips that the classes have been doing for years. Matt nodded his support and did not change anything..

"I would like to discuss support for new and non-tenured teachers. Have any of you asked this group to watch you teach? Especially if you were starting a new topic or giving a master lesson on a subject. It would be alright with me if you assign Teacher Assistants to cover classes for this reason. Please talk to your experienced teachers as well"

Julia Lovell clapped her hands together. "What a wonderful idea. I'm going to try it."

Both men nodded, but remained silent. Jerry looked at them

sternly. "Don't you think that's a good idea?"

Sam England responded. "I don't get paid enough to be a model for new teachers. That's not for me!"

Matt smiled, "As I understand it you get a stipend of twenty five hundred dollars a year for your duties. You are being paid for your leadership. Any fool can count field trip money."

"I'll think about it."

Sam England looked at Tim and then at Matt. "Okay, I'll try to speak to my senior teachers about some good master lessons to demonstrate."

"The next item on the agenda is Teaching Assistants. Starting this year the New York State education law permits all assistants to provide direct instructional services to students under the general supervision of a licensed or certified teacher. That means that regular teachers provide direction and guidance to teaching assistants concerning the educational program. Make sure your teachers know about this. That means, at times, you may call grade level meetings and keep assistants in the classroom to teach specific lessons that you have designed. Any questions?"

There were none. The Team Leaders seemed quiet as they wrote some notes on their pads.

Jerry looked at Matt. "How about a five minute break for coffee and donuts?"

After the break all three Team Leaders were very happy about the structure of the Code. They felt that having the parents sign the document as well as the kids gave it a very high priority.

Matt was pleased. "School has been in session six days so we will see how this plays out. Thank you for you positive response. We will evaluate it after the first marking period in ten weeks."

Jerry picked up on the conversation. "The last item on the agenda is testing."

Matt was quick on the draw with his response. "The high level of performance by the student's over the last few years is wonderful. Do you think that this will continue?"

All the teachers nodded in the affirmative. Julia Lovell put her hand up and Matt recognized her.

"I think the incoming sixth grade will do very well this year. We make sure to keep our special ed. kids out of the count as well as our

ESL, English as a Second Language out of the count. This raises the score."

The fourth period bell sounded and the teachers picked up their pads and left the meeting. Matt thanked them as they left.

"You covered quite a bit Boss."

"Not a bad beginning, Not bad at all."

## CHAPTER 14

Immediately after the meeting, Jerry and Matt discussed the teachers' reactions. It seemed Matt wanted Jerry's feedback on the meeting. He also asked how to make the meetings better. Jerry thought, *In another time I think I would love to work for this guy. He really is a team player and respects my position and brain. No, I've got to take him down as hard as I can.*

Jerry Jackson left school at three and went speeding down the road.

\* \* \*

He entered Jackson's Tavern. Jerry's brother Bill quickly drew a sixteen ounce cold mug of beer for his brother. "Here you go little brother. You look like shit."

"I feel like shit. This Matt Collins is a stand up guy. No bullshit, no hidden agenda just a professional who wants to help kids. I feel like an asshole trying to take him down."

"Well what do you want to do?"

"I don't know. My wife wants me to look outside the District for a principal's job. Maybe she's right."

"What do you think?"

Jerry swiftly finished his beer. "Let me have a double vodka. I need something to get me going."

"I'll let you have the double, but that's it. You've been drinking much too much lately."

"Screw you. I can control my liquor!"

Jerry drove home after consuming two more beers. He felt confused. The situation with Matt was puzzling.

* * *

Matt worked late into Tuesday evening. Beth, Jerry, Maggie and Otto all knocked on his door to say goodbye. He understood the dynamic of saying goodbye to the boss. Yet the "good byes" were more than business. They were sincere. The gesture itself was honest and he felt good about it.

He looked at the list of students who did not return the signed Code of Conduct. Jerry had left early and had made no calls. Maggie had correlated the list and put the home phone number and a second contact number next to each student. The sixth grade had only seven students. Grade seven had twelve and grade eight nineteen. That meant thirty eight phone calls. He vowed to do all of them by tomorrow night. He picked up the phone and called the first parent.

Matt made twenty calls. He found, in most cases, that the parents never got the document for one reason or another. Some just forgot and promised to send it in. Some parents signed the Code and gave it to their children, although it never got to the teachers.

He made a list for Maggie in order to send out a second copy of the Code. Matt made out a list for teachers to check with the students who did not return the Code. Matt stretched and looked at his watch not bad twenty calls in less than two hours. He decided to go to the Main Street Diner for dinner. He thought about liver, onions and bacon. That motivated him to move quickly and lock up his office. He had an Executive Board PTA meeting that evening.

After dinner Matt entered the conference room at exactly seven thirty in the evening. He looked around and Maureen Stuart, President of the PTA, took his arm. "Ladies, may I present Mr. Matt Collins our new principal."

"It is a pleasure to meet the parent leaders of the school."

The smiles from the five women in the room were instantaneous He knew that in this setting diplomacy and sensitivity would be the best strategy. There were mutual greetings from all. Mrs. Stuart introduced her Board and gave out the evening's agenda.

Matt sat through the reading of last month's meeting, Secretary's report, Treasurers report and Presidents report. They did some very nice community projects including a brand new telephone chain for parents of the school in case of an emergency.

Then it came to Matt's report. He gave them a statistical report in terms of grade enrollment, gender, teacher enrollment and the status of the school. He mentioned that four new cafeteria tables are coming soon and that the Code of Conduct is working so far. Then Matt looked at each of the Board members. "I have a concern and it's the noise level and discipline in the cafeteria. Even if I put another teacher on duty the kids noise level will not go down. Here is what I propose. I would like the PTA to buy a special Noise Traffic Light. It is the size of a regular traffic light and it will be installed by my custodial staff. We will instruct our students about using their 'inside voices' for green their 'whisper voices' for yellow and 'no talking" for red. It has worked very well in many school districts."

Matt gave out the information to the Board members and they studiously read it. Matt was waiting for questions and there were none. "The cost, as you can see is nine hundred and seventy five dollars complete."

Mrs. Stuart looked at Matt. "Mr. Collins will you please wait outside. I want to discuss this with the Board and I don't want you to think negatively about any of us if we say no. Will you do this, please?"

"Of course."

It took only five minutes and Matt was called back in.

"The school will get its Noise Traffic Light."

Matt smiled. "I wish to thank you so much. I know it is a major part of your reserve funds. Have your Treasurer work with Maggie for the details. When it is installed you will see how it works."

The meeting ended fifteen minutes later and, for the first time, Matt felt tired.

* * *

Beth called her parents after dinner. She wanted to talk to her mother about Matt and their situation. After the few pleasantries about health and welfare were over, Beth got to the point. "Mom, I met a man who

I really love. He is kind, he is fair, he's not sexist, he listens and doesn't try to solve my problem's and he's also gorgeous."

Beth's mother was extremely supportive of her daughter when she had a very nasty breakup a few years ago. "Beth, I'm happy for you, although it is too soon to really love a person. Perhaps you mean you really like a person do you?"

"No Mom, I love him. Not only that, I like him."

"Why?"

"His values. He is fair and completely honest with everybody around him."

"What does he do for a living?"

"He's a principal."

"Is it your school?"

"Yes."

"You are in big trouble young lady."

"Oh Mom, we can work it out."

"It works out if one of you leaves the school. Perhaps you can get a transfer."

"No, maybe next year I can shift to the high school, but not this year."

"How involved are you?"

"Mom, I'll do anything for him. I mean anything!"

"Have you?"

"Oh yes, and oh yes, and oh my God!"

"I'm thrilled that your relationship is that deep. Perhaps you better start thinking about the type of future both of you will have "

"I will Mom. Right now we're making sure nobody in school will know about it."

"Sweetie, it will come out sooner or later. I think you are better off cooling the relationship down until you decide what to do."

"Thanks Mom, that's good advice. Kiss Daddy for me. I love you."

"Good bye Beth. Love you too."

After the phone call Beth began to think deeply. *If we announce our relationship it may hurt Matt's ability to work with the Guidance Department. If he gives me an easy assignment the others will think its favoritism. If he gives me hard assignments the others will think he's making sure that I will show every body up. Oh yes, the administration may not like it and it would hurt his career in Risenburg.*

She fell asleep concerned. Should she tell Matt about the phone call with her mother and all of her other worries.

Matt called Beth and woke her up. She looked at the time and it was close to eleven in the evening. In a whispered voice, "Hello "

Matt interrupted her, "Beth, I just got the PTA to buy the Noise Traffic Light!"

"I'm glad, but we really have to talk about our situation."

"Why?"

"Because going together in this small town will affect our careers."

"Look, the three day Columbus Day weekend will be here in a week or so. Why don't we get out of town and discuss our options.'

"Okay, but until that time I really want us to keep a low profile. Agreed?"

"I'm disappointed, but I agree."

Matt did not sleep well that night.

CHAPTER 15

As scheduled, Matt met with the Guidance Department on Wednesday at noon. He decided to meet in the conference room. The counselors filed in and sat on one side of the conference table. Matt sat on the other side. "Thank you for coming at this time. I'll be brief. There is only one agenda item for me and then I'll open it up for you. Have you had any difficulties performing your duties so far?"

Shelly Katz, the Seventh Grade Counselor started to laugh. "We thought we were coming to your office for a spanking."

Matt laughed loudly and continued to laugh. The counselors joined in.

John Brown, the Senior Counselor stopped laughing. "Mr. Collins this is the first time in my career a principal has shown genuine concern for counselors. Thank you. I'm in need of an office chair. Mine is falling apart."

Matt wrote on his pad. "So noted."

Beth Andrews looked at him kindly. "Our substitute secretary isn't on the ball. We would rather have someone else."

Shelly Katz pointed at Matt. "How do you feel about being a hero? The kids are in awe of you. I've seen them quiet down when you pass. The eighth grade girls are gushing over you."

Matt turned red. He was embarrassed. "Gushing? I don't know about that."

"Mr. Collins, you have the opportunity to turn this school into a model school. Your Code of Conduct is specific and almost all the kids will comply. The parents are for it as well. The teachers like it and when you can get teachers to like something that's amazing!"

"Thank you. I will consider keying in on that dynamic. I mean I'll check it out."

Again, they all laughed.

Mrs. Katz raised her hand. "One more thing. We have to teach modules about career education. Some of the lessons are straight forward. See the movie, answer the questions. Would it be alright if the Teacher Assistants do that instead of us?"

"I'll meet you half way. Ten minutes before the period ends I would expect the counselor to come back to answer questions."

All the counselors were positive. They left quickly. The meeting took twenty five minutes and it was a good one.

Matt stayed late again. He wanted to complete his Code of Conduct telephone survey. This time twelve of the eighteen parents stated they never got the Code. Six parents signed it, but it never got to the teacher. He wrote a note to Maggie to send out new Codes and wrote notes to teachers to question the students.

It was past nine when he finished. He went over to the "Pizza Place" and had two slices and a drink.

Matt slept very well that night.

Thursday was uneventful other than running a disastrous fire drill. It seemed that the teachers and students thought it was a big joke. There was playful pushing and the teachers did not take charge in terms of quiet behavior. After the bell, signaling the students to return to their classrooms, Matt got on the school public address system. "Attention, attention, this is Mr. Collins. The fire drill that just happened was a disaster. You are to remain silent and follow your teacher's orders. In five minutes we will do it all over again and this time it better be perfect!"

Maggie looked at Matt with great respect. "Do you think it wise to do this over again?"

"Maggie, we will do this over and over again until it is perfect. I am responsible under New York State Law to have fire drills that are safe and orderly."

Matt called Jerry out of his office. "Jerry, take the back of the school and the left side. I'm going to take the front of the school and the right side. Pull out any kid who doesn't obey and let me know of any teacher who screws up!"

Maggie looked at Matt and realized how superlative a soldier he must have been. He had command, knowledge and courage to lead. She thought, *How lucky we are to have him be our leader.*

The fire drill bell rang and there was no problem at all. Later, in the Faculty Room, teachers discussed Matt's style of leadership. Almost all of them liked his approach. In fact some of them were in awe of him.

\* \* \*

On Friday the Superintendent met with all of the administrators for a meeting. Most of the time was spent on administrative matters as lost book orders, lack of supplies that did not make it to the schools and poor teacher substitutes.

The meeting ended at noon. John Ward, Principal of the High School spoke to Matt in the hallway. "How about that lunch we were supposed to have? My treat."

Matt agreed and they ended up in the rear booth of the local pizzeria. They agreed to share a pie with meatballs and sausage.

Wiping his mouth with a huge paper napkin John Ward swallowed. "Matt, have you found out anything about testing results so far?"

"Well, the ESL and special ed. kids don't take the test. I know that parents can opt out their kids if they are special ed., although they have to take the tests if they are in school. ESL is different. They have to take the New York State ESL English Test."

"That's a small group of kids. Anything else?"

"Not yet. Give me time."

They finished their lunch and returned to their schools in one hour.

\* \* \*

In almost all schools, Friday is a get away day. The teachers leave right behind the students. The school becomes very quiet and Matt liked this time to go through the classes and see the condition of the school. It was not snooping, it was part of his job. He realized that although many staff members were neat, the opposite was true as well. Matt took notes as he checked the condition of the classrooms

Matt heard his name being called and turned around to see Beth standing near her office. "I thought you would be going home why are you here?"

Beth moved to Matt and stood very close to him. "I know we have to cool it, but I need you so much. Let's go to Syracuse and get a motel for the weekend."

Matt stepped back. "Beth, we agreed to cool it and I'm going to. I'll make plans for Columbus Day. I promise."

Tears in her eyes, "Okay." She turned quickly and left.

Matt sighed and thought. *This is really going to be a big problem for both of us.*

He left the building with a feeling of sadness and no plans for the weekend.

## CHAPTER 16

Dear Staff,

The last few weekly newsletters I have written asked you to do the following by the end of the week:

1. Remove any papers from the floor. Not the real little stuff.
2. Have all chalk boards washed. Students may do that.
3. All computers and audio visual equipment locked up.
4. Plan books be one week ahead and locked in your desk.
5. Specialists equipment stored and locked plus desks cleaned.

"Better keep yourself clean and bright; you are the window through which you must see the world." (George Bernard Shaw)

Matt Collins, Principal

Matt had Maggie distribute this letter to the total staff. He hoped this would motivate many of the staff members to keep their work stations and rooms clean. He knew he wasn't a neat nut, but the school had to do better in terms of cleanliness.

Jerry came into Matt's office holding the letter, "Boss, are you nuts? This letter will have a bad reaction from the staff. You should have bounced it off me."

"Why do you think this will have a bad reaction?"

"This is mainly a mature staff. They don't want to be treated like children"

"Jerry, I walked around the school late Friday afternoon. It was fifty-fifty. Some rooms neat and clean and others a pig sty. We are supposed to set examples for our students. This includes how we groom ourselves as well as the condition of our rooms."

"Okay. I'm sure you will hear from our Union leaders."

"So be it!"

As Jerry left Maggie buzzed. "Beth Andrews on line two."

"Hello"

"Matt, are you batty? The teachers are talking about your letter. Most of them feel you have insulted their professionalism. Watch out for a grievance."

"Thanks for the input. I've got to go. Good bye."

At lunch time Maggie buzzed. "Jennifer Stanton, President of the Teacher's Union would like to meet with you during her seventh period."

"Tell her that would be fine with me and please be prepared to audio the conversation."

Matt looked up Jennifer Stanton's file. She was a thirteen year teacher of Social Studies and English. Her evaluations were superior and included a few letters of commendation from previous principals. This was her second year as President of the Union.

A few minutes after the seventh period bell rang Jennifer Stanton came into his office with Sam England, the Seventh Grade Team Leader. Matt motioned them to his small table. "What can I do for you?"

Jennifer Stanton was about six feet tall, ruddy complexion, well groomed brunette wearing a plaid business suit. "Mr. Collins I'm afraid I have to serve you with an official grievance."

"What is the content?"

"We, as professionals, are not custodians and do not think that we have to do what you suggested."

"Is any part of my letter part of you contract/"

"No sir."

"Then as the Principal of this school I think I have the right to direct and instruct you to do the deeds I asked you to do."

Sam English replied, "Most of the teachers do what you suggested. There are only a few who mess up. Please rescind the order and go after the individual teachers who are messing up!"

"Thanks for the suggestion. I took a tour of the school Friday late afternoon and noted the rooms that were okay and the rooms and areas that were messy. It was fifty-fifty. That's why I wrote the letter."

Mrs. Stanton shock her head. "Why do we have to lock our plan books in our desks."

"Because when teachers get sick the substitutes have to use their plans."

"Mr. Collins, the teachers respect you," he sounded very sincere, "and I ask you to withdraw the rules and ask the Team Leaders to try to enforce cleanliness."

"I wish I could, Sam. The problem is that you are a teacher with a specific curriculum responsibility, not really an administrative one. I thank you for your concern."

The Union President stood up and shook Matt's hand. "Okay. Let the process begin."

"Meanwhile advise the teachers that my rules stay in place."

Both responded simultaneously, "Yes sir."

* * *

Matt left the school immediately after the eighth period and went home. He turned on some light classical music and brewed himself a strong cup of coffee. Second guess thinking started up: *Should I have taken Sam's advice was I too strong are my standards too high what will the Superintendent think. Hell. I've been in combat, this is chicken shit! Let's rock and roll!*

CHAPTER 17

On Wednesday Matt notified the Building Grievance Committee in writing and sent memos to the Assistant Superintendent and Superintendent of Schools in terms of his decision at the building level.

The Teachers' Contract called for the following sequential steps for grievances:

Note: all days are working days and not weekend or official holidays.

1. Conference with the building Principal three days for determination

2. Meeting with the District Grievance Committee of Teachers five days for determination.

3. If approved by the District Grievance Committee conference with the Superintendent or his designer ten days for determination

4. Conference with the Board of Education twenty five days for determination

5. Meeting with an arbitrator for a binding decision ten days

Matt figured that the process could take up to fifty working days to settle. He took out the school calendar and scanned it. Then he counted the actual working days. The decision could be made by the end of the second week of January. At the moment it was two days before Columbus Day in October. Hopefully, by that time, the teachers would shape up in terms of their rooms.

Matt buzzed Maggie to come to the office.

"Yes Mr. Collins."

"Maggie, this is personal, please put on your friend hat."

"Okay Matt, what's up?"

"I don't know the Syracuse area and I need a suggestion from you for a bed and breakfast place for a long weekend."

Maggie smiled, "For two?"

"Of course."

"There's a wonderful B&B near Union New York that has charm, great views, free bikes to ride including a tandem bike. Better yet, you are half an hour to Syracuse and there are wonderful restaurants all over. The color of the autumn trees will make it a wonderful experience. I'll give you the information as soon as possible."

Within the hour Matt made reservations for the long weekend. He was looking forward to spending uninterrupted time with Beth. He called Beth and gave her the information.

"Oh Matt, I'm delighted with the plans."

"Don't forget to bring at least one girly dress for a Saturday night date."

"I love you Matt!"

"I'll pick you up at four thirty. Love you too."

* * *

Friday was a disaster. There were twelve classroom teachers who called in sick as well as the Art Teacher, one Physical Education Teacher, Speech Teacher, Computer Teacher. Sixteen teachers in all. Added to this was the absence of three Teaching Assistants. That gave them a four day weekend instead of a regular Columbus Day three day weekend. Matt was pissed.

Jerry came into the office, "Mr. Collins, we don't have enough classroom substitutes. We have to cover eight classes. Any suggestions?"

"Maggie, bring your pad and give the following information to every teacher as soon as they arrive. Jerry, you assign the classes personally. Have the remaining two Teaching Assistants cover the classes for the day. Put the Library Media Teacher to cover a class and the three Guidance Counselors to cover classes. Let's see, that's six. Okay Jerry, you and I will cover the toughest classes, the eighth grade. Plus, to make it easier, all first period classes are cancelled.

Instead of Art, Music and Physical Education make that class a recreational period in the auditorium. The kids can dance on the stage with music, or listen to music, or talk to each other. The Music Teacher and the Phys Ed Teacher will have to cover the auditorium. Okay, let's do it now!"

The day was a difficult day. Some teachers did not provide plans. The substitutes had to do the best they could. During the supervision of the students in the auditorium the Music Teacher felt faint and reported to the nurse for two periods. The Physical Education Teacher had to handle three classes on his own, He sent four students to the office for rough housing. Maggie had them sit outside the office on chairs.

When Jerry had a free period he was able to go to the office and confront the four students. They were shaking in their boots when he got through with them.

During Matt's free period he took extra duty in the cafeteria. Luckily it was pizza day and the kids were happy. He managed to sit down and eat pizza with some of the students. They liked the idea.

Maggie handled the front office with calmness and expertise. She kept a list of teacher requests, complaints and what she later said was "garbage."

Jerry and Matt took extra duty at the bus ramp for dismissal. There were no late buses and by three thirty the school was empty.

Matt looked at Jerry and Maggie and wiped his brow. "Thank you for all your work and help. This school could have been a zoo, but we made it into an interesting day. Go home now. I'll cover for you. Thanks again!"

Otto, the Chief Custodian walked into the office. "Boss, some kid busted a few pipes in the south quadrant bathroom. There was some minor flooding. I called our District Maintenance, but they were let out early. What should I do?"

"Call a plumber and have him bill the District on my authority. I don't want a broken bathroom on Tuesday when the kids come back."

"Great idea, I'll do it now!"

Matt called the Business Office and received quick approval for the plumber. He checked the time four fifteen. Time to go his luggage was already in his car.

\* \* \*

Beth was on time and they quickly took care of her luggage. They drove out of town heading towards Union, New York. Matt figured their ETA would be about five thirty.

"What music do you want? The car has blue tooth and I've got Pandora."

"I like folk ballads, rhythm and blues ballads and a lot of love songs by the great singers the last twenty years. No heavy metal, no funk or new wave for me at all."

Matt nodded. "I like the standards, traditional pop and vocal pop. Sometimes I enjoy light classical music as well. I keep away from heavy stuff whether it's rock and roll or classical."

The drive took a little over an hour. As they pulled up to Johnson Manor a young man about sixteen came down a short flight of front stairs. "May I take your luggage? What name is the reservation under?"

"Collins!"

They met Mrs. Williams the owner-operator and her son Richard. Within fifteen minutes they were ushered into their very large room with a king size bed. The décor was something out of "Architectural Digest." The theme was the nineteen twenties and there were many antiques in the room. It was tasteful and very well done.

"Perhaps you can join us and two other couples for complimentary wine and cheese in the sitting room at six thirty. There is a directory of many of our fine restaurants no more than twenty minutes away. Tell them that you are staying at the Johnson Manor and you will get a table."

When Mrs. Williams left, Beth came to Matt and kissed him. "Thank you in advance for this special weekend. I love the room and the area. Where did you learn about this place?"

"I asked Maggie about B&B's in the Syracuse area and she recommended this place. She and her husband have been here a few times and love the area. Let's wash up, call a restaurant for dinner and go downstairs to enjoy wine and cheese."

\* \* \*

The sitting room was something out of Queen Victoria's era. The rich velvet chairs and brocade couches were highlighted by antique lamps. There was a beautiful green and gold Chinese rug that brought everything together.

The two couples were a bit older than Matt and Beth. One couple, the Silvers, ran a small publishing company specializing in non-fiction. The other couple, the Birds, were on their honeymoon. They both had lost their spouses a few years earlier and met each other on a senior dating service. He was a stock broker who worked for a prestigious Wall Street firm. Mrs. Bird was a free lance artist. The talk was casual and they all enjoyed the crackers, cheese and wine served by Mrs. Williams. Matt and Beth excused themselves since they had a seven thirty reservation at a steak house near the manor.

* * *

The wine was superior, salad crisp, vegetables tasty and the steak was outstanding.

Matt and Beth discussed their situation. She stated her mother was concerned about their having an in-school romance. It could hurt both their careers.

Matt felt frustrated. He thought. *I really want this to work out. What a choice for me. Career versus relationship!*

"Beth, this is a situation that truly is a work in progress. Let's keep our heads up and see what develops."

"Okay Matt, but I know you could suffer a real setback in your career if our relationship angers the Board or Central Administration."

They both agreed to keep it as cool as possible. The couple knew it was risky.

Dessert was a brownie drowned with dark chocolate syrup and vanilla ice cream on top. They loved it!

* * *

Beth showered first and Matt followed. They lay on their king size bed and stared at the crystal chandelier. Matt reached over and pulled Beth onto him. "I love you and I lust for you!"

There was a mutual rush by both of them to consummate their love. It was hot and burned through both of them quickly.

After the initial encounter their lovemaking was slow and probing. Beth wanted to know everything about Matt's body. When she viewed the five inch scar on his back she traced it with her fingers. "Matt, tell me how you got this scar?"

"Oh that was in the war. I'm okay."

She kissed him gently. "No sweetheart, how did you get this scar?"

Matt slipped out of her embrace. "I don't want to talk about it. Two years in Iraq and Afghanistan and I got out alive. A few scars, but some of my men never made it home." He began to shiver. "Beth, it's not good to bring up those memories. Its not good for me!"

Beth took him in her arms and rocked him. "My poor baby my poor love oh I am so sorry so sorry."

Matt fell asleep quickly. Beth looked at him and realized that underneath that polished, mature, and confident person lay a wounded soldier. Psychologically injured by the war. She understood post traumatic stress disorder as a professional counselor. This was the first time she experienced it first hand. Matt's shivering and stress in his voice troubled her deeply. She resolved to help him some way.

Saturday morning was a surprise. After having a superb breakfast of eggs, bacon and waffles Beth and Matt decided to go kayaking. Fortunately the temperature was sixty five and the boat rental was ten minutes away. Within twenty five minutes they were paddling in sequence down a beautiful river under a gradually warming river.

Half way through their trip they rowed to a small area lined with trees. They docked the kayak on the shore. Matt stretched, sat down on an abandoned log and took a mouthful of water. "Beth, come on over and have some water."

Beth finished the whole bottle, wiped her mouth and kissed Matt on the lips. "Oh what a great day. It reminds me when I was a kid. My parents loved to go camping and it made me feel so good to be out of doors. We would look up at the sky at night and try to find all the constellations. I can still smell the marshmallows over the fire. It was grand."

"I didn't have any out door experiences like that although I played a lot of baseball. I wasn't too good, but my parents would try to make every game. I loved that they were there."

Matt and Beth talked about childhood experiences and their feelings. Each felt a new depth to their relationship as they shared many stories of their youth.

* * *

They returned to their room to shower and change. A bit later Mrs. William's son Richard knocked on the door. "The Silvers and Birds have decided to rent a pontoon boat for the afternoon. There is a large lake about forty five minutes from here. They plan to leave about one. The Birds have a large van that seats six. They asked if you want to share with them?"

Matt looked at Beth who nodded in the affirmative. "Okay Richard, tell the Birds and Silvers we will see them downstairs at one."

Luckily the B&B had an open refrigerator for guests. Beth went downstairs and made salami sandwiches for both of them. They topped it off with coffee made in the room with a small automatic coffee maker. Dessert was marvelous New York State apples. Mrs. William's sign stated the apples were picked from a nearby apple orchard.

The rest of the day was sheer fun. All the couples were in vacation mode and the funny jokes shared had all in hysterics. Fortuitously, the pontoon boat was easy to handle and the boat rental provided fishing gear, bait, and buckets. It was enjoyable to fish and at times catch some bass. Near the end of their rental they hit into a major school of bass and caught many. They agreed to bring the fish back to the B&B. Perhaps Mrs. Williams knew of a restaurant who would cook their catch.

Mrs. Williams did something better than recommending a restaurant. She suggested she make a fish fry dinner, if the group would help. All the parties heartily agreed. Mrs. Williams' assigned tasks to everyone. The men went about filleting the fish. The women set the table and made the salad. All the couples cut up and peeled fresh fall squash, carrots and onions. Richard peeled and cut the potatoes.

Mrs. Williams wiped her brow. "Why don't all of you come back in about two hours for dinner. I think this is marvelous!"

Beth went to her side and hugged her. "Thank you for doing this!"

* * *

When Matt and Beth entered the room Beth pointed to the upholstered chair. Matt sat down. "What do you need Beth?"

"I need nothing except you to watch." She thought. *Matt needs to know I love him and support him and will do anything for him. I will help him with his PTSD.*

Beth very slowly disrobed. "Look at me Matt. Really look at me. I want you to know me!"

When she was finished undressing she came close to him and kissed him. She smiled, "Take off your shirt."

He complied.

"Take off your pants."

He complied.

"Take off your shorts."

He complied.

"Now I am going to kiss every part of your body and you remain still and enjoy my love making!"

He complied and smiled.

At a certain point Matt groaned, "Oh my God!"

They showered together and just managed to get downstairs in two hours.

The fish fry was a great success. Mrs. Williams' cooking was home style but with plenty of spices and butter. Lots of butter! They finished the meal with an ice cream cake that Richard got from the local store. No one counted calories that evening.

* * *

Matt and Beth slept in on Sunday since the plan for the day was brunch up to eleven thirty. They dressed in sweats since the temperature dropped to the low fifty's. After brunch they borrowed the tandem bike and started to explore the beautiful countryside. After two hours they came to a small village where they purchased water bottles and candy bars. They parked the bike and explored the village. Most of the shops were closed. Matt spied a closed store that had as its sign, "The Celtic Shoppe." There were small boutique shops catering to women as well as a candle store and candy shop. As they turned a corner they saw people leaving a beautiful white church. That prompted a question by Beth. "Matt, what is your religion?"

"I'm Catholic, although I haven't gone to church in years. With a name like Collins you might think its English, but my mother researched it. The clan Cullane or O'Coileain also had names as Cullen and Cullinan. Ask the Irish and they will have a story for you. My mother's maiden name is O'hara and her father came from County Sligo in northwestern Ireland. Your boyfriend is Irish! What's your religion?"

"I'm Episcopalian. I went to Sunday School and went through all the rituals in order to please my parents. I think of myself as more spiritual than having a religion."

The rest of the day was spent in returning to the B&B and having a wonderful Italian dinner at a local Mom and Pop restaurant.

* * *

Matt and Beth left immediately after breakfast. The heavy traffic was heading into Syracuse as Matt drove seventy miles an hour on a near empty road the opposite way. Beth sat close to him and on occasion they held hands.

She placed her hand on his thigh. "Matt, I had the best time of my life this weekend. I really mean it! I feel so comfortable with you."

Matt smiled and squeezed her hand. "I had a great time. We really are beginning to know each other and the more I know about you the deeper my feelings are for you."

"I'm proud of our relationship and I think that the school staff should know about it. We are adults."

"No more shadows. There's a staff meeting this coming Wednesday. Would you mind if I announced it at that time? Of course Maggie and Jerry first.

"I trust you. I won't tell anybody until then."

CHAPTER 18

The return to school after a three day weekend is rough on the students as well as on the staff. It's getting back to the mission, the routine, the flow, and picking up from last week. Matt felt it in himself as well.

"Maggie, please pull the attendance records of the staff who were out last Friday. Please go back four years. Is this possible?"

"I'll have to call the Personal Department, but it can be done."

"That is your number one priority this morning."

Matt realized that he would be in deep water with the staff if he was to admonish any staff member for one Friday absence. He wasn't looking for that. The Principal is charged with overall responsibility of the school. When there were not enough substitutes to cover the classes it was up to him to have the classes covered. He was probing for a pattern.

In his last experience as an assistant principal he was charged with checking on teacher absences. When he found a few who had either a Friday flu or a Monday malady he checked with the principal. A letter was sent to the staff members who exhibited a three year pattern. It was an informational letter requesting a medical note if this were to happen again. Since it was not in the contract the teachers complied. A by-product of this was the approval of the rest of the staff who did come in to work before a holiday.

"Here is the list of staff members who fit the category. Quite frankly, I'm surprised." Maggie quipped.

Matt smiled at her sarcasm, "Now come on Maggie who else but the School Secretary would know!"

Out of the sixteen staff members who were out there were seven who were out consistently on a Monday or Friday before or after a holiday. This covered a four year pattern. Matt decided to take to task all of the seven. He was particular in his wording especially as he requested a doctor's note for absences. "Maggie, please have each staff member who gets this letter sign a receipt that they received it."

"Mr. Collins, its going to hit the fan again!"

"Maggie, that's my job. Not to do anything after that last terrible Friday would be giving in to slackers. I'm not that type of administrator!"

"I guess I haven't seen courage in a long time. Thanks Boss!"

It hit the fan before school ended. The Art Teacher, Mrs. Faith Higgins came into his office by pushing past Maggie and opening Matt's door. "Look here Mr. Collins, you just can't demand a doctors note just like this. This is immoral this is unprofessional this is what they would say is chicken shit! Who the hell are you you young squirt, telling us who have lived in Risenburg for years. I won't stand for it. I've already filed a grievance and I'm going to tell my husband to make sure you are ridden out of town."

She turned on her heels and left without giving Matt a chance to answer her.

"Maggie, please write this memo to Mrs. Higgins. 'You are directed and instructed to make an appointment with me, Principal of the George W. Bush Middle School through Mrs. Carter, School Secretary. I will not tolerate your aggressive actions pushing Mrs. Carter and barging into my office.' Send copies of this to her file and the Superintendent and Assistant Superintendent."

After the students left the school, Jennifer Stanton, President of the Teachers Union came in with a sheet of paper in her hand accompanied by Sam England. "Mr. Collins, regretfully I have to serve you with another grievance. The issue is requesting doctor notes for Friday or Monday absences before or after holidays."

Matt smiled, "Regretfully I had to do this for only seven members of your Union. This does not cover all of you since I found a four year pattern with those individuals. I certainly do not need doctor notes from the rest of the staff."

Sam England walked over to the office door and made sure it was closed. "Off the record Mr. Collins the teachers who heard about it were overjoyed about you taking into task the offenders. What a lousy Friday we had, trying to cover classes. The problem is that asking for the doctors note is really pushy. Couldn't it be just an information letter noting their pattern. Perhaps that will keep them from doing it again."

"Mr. England, you are very practical and I admire that trait. However I have experienced this type of situation before and only playing hardball will produce good results. No, I will not do what you suggest."

Mrs. Stanton stood up. "We will take this to the District Grievance Committee of Teachers and you will hear from us. Thank you."

Matt followed up with sending his information to the Superintendent of Schools about the second grievance. He sent a complete data package with the attendance information of all of the seven staff members involved.

Beth called him. "You are certainly causing the troops to talk about you."

"Bad or good?"

"The offenders bad! The non offenders very good, in fact spectacular! Matt, they are keen over the way you are running the school. Most of the teachers really admire you as their leader. In fact some of the teachers have told me they love you"

"And you?"

"Come over to my apartment tonight and I'll show you how much love there is!"

"Hon, I'm tired and I need my strength for tomorrow's faculty meeting. Enjoy the rest of the day. Love you!"

Maggie buzzed. "Mr. Theodore Higgins, Owner and Editor of The Risenburg News on line two. Watch out, he records everything."

"How may I help you Mr. Higgins?"

"Mr. Collins, what type of nonsense are you doing insisting on doctors notes for absences?"

"I'm sorry Mr. Higgins, due to our District policies you would have to deal with the Superintendent and the School Attorney on grievances, policies and specific information. How else may I help you?"

"Screw you Collins, I'm going to tear your asshole out!"

Matt answered in a military manner, "Are you threatening me Mr. Higgins? If so I'm going to call the Chief of Police and file a complaint against you."

Matt heard a grumble. "Are you threatening me, Mr. Higgins?"

"No. I'm not." Higgins hung up.

Matt called Jason Carter, Maggie's husband. "Jason, this is Matt Collins. You stated that if I needed any help you were willing to help."

"Yes. Of course."

"May I see you today?"

"Sure, come on down to the office. My client load is light today."

\* \* \*

Jason Carter's office was on the corner of Main Street and Elm. There was a welcoming room with a smart looking desk and chair for a secretary or associate as well as a wall full of flyers about retirement, long term health insurance, annuities, and other financial instruments. The second room decorated with soft furniture, dark wood tables and chairs as well as three computers, white blackboard, and a large coffee urn with a coffee set up. It was warm and comfortable.

"Nice working conditions you have here Jason." They shook hands and Matt continued, "I've got a problem with Theodore Higgins, owner of the newspaper. He threatened to quote, tear my asshole out, if his wife had to produce a doctors note. It seems she has been absent either on a Monday or Friday before or after a holiday, for the last four years. In fact, there are seven staff members who also are in the same position. The teachers filed a grievance, but most of them are very pleased that I caught all of the offenders."

"I will hold all of this as confidential, trust me on that. What did you say?"

"I told him there are District policies and he can talk to the Superintendent or the School Attorney. Then he threatened me, so I asked him if he was threatening me because I would call the Chief of Police if he was. He thought better of it and stated he was not."

"Well, don't expect any brilliant articles about you or your school from now on. On the other hand he knows that you will not back down and that's good. I suggest that if the Superintendent tells you to pull the letters ask him to put it in writing to you. I think that Dr. Hull, your boss is gutless. Just keep on doing what you are doing. You have a great talent in leadership and we really need it here."

"I want to do the job, but I'm afraid that I'll be out of here because I'm doing the job too well!"

They both laughed. Jason poured coffee for the two of them and they discussed lighter topics. Matt expressed how pleased he was with the B&B suggestion.

CHAPTER 19

Matt arrived early and went through his agenda for the faculty meeting. His main concern was keeping it short and to the point. During his Army service he remembered a Master Sergeant telling his men about the Eleventh Commandment. "Be specific!" Matt loved that phrase and was going to use it at the meeting. He had a concern about after school clubs and activities. Jerry told him that the supervision of the students was poor and the previous principal had threatened to cancel all of the activities if the teachers, who were the activity leaders, didn't come down hard on the kids.

Yesterday Matt received the New York State Testing Schedule. It covered tests from the middle of April into early June. Although it was October, he would have to meet with the Team Leaders to work out an effective schedule. He was aware of the suspicions held by the High School Principal. The test scores were just too high.

The last item was teacher observations. The contract called for two observations for tenured staff and four observations for non-tenured staff. He wanted to cover specific criteria that he would be looking for as he observed. The Assistant Principal would carry half the load and Matt decided to call in the Department Chairpersons from the high school to do at least one observation. He would have to work out a schedule with the High School Principal, John Ward.

After the sixth period bell Matt called Beth. "Please come to the office now. I want to tell Maggie and Jerry about us."

A few minutes later Matt, Beth, Jerry and Maggie were sitting around the small table in Matt's office. Matt took Beth's hand and held it firmly. Jerry and Maggie both looked at the couple strangely. Maggie blurted out, "You two are dating. Is that what you wanted to say?"

Beth's eyes glowed as she squeezed Matt's hand. "No, more than dating. We are a couple!"

Jerry blurted out. "Congratulations Boss!"

"We wanted to let you know before we told the staff at the meeting today. I'll tell the staff at the end of the meeting."

Maggie stood up and hugged Beth. "You are getting a fine man."

"I know Maggie, I'm so lucky that I found him!"

"Boss, thank you so much for telling us before the staff. I feel validated as a real colleague of yours."

Maggie and Jerry left the office. Beth closed the door and requested. "Please, may I have at least one kiss."

Matt took her in his arms and delivered his answer to her.

* * *

Maggie set up two large coffee urns, donuts, fruit and granola bars for the meeting. Matt and Jerry arrived five minutes early and the staff poured in. They were chatty and seemed at ease.

Matt noticed that Beth took the last seat in the last row near the rear door. Obviously she was going to make a fast get away when Matt announced that they were a couple.

The items of the agenda flowed well. His statement of The Eleventh Commandment, "Be specific!" went over very well. There were a few questions and they were valuable.

"I have one more item that's not on your agenda. It is personal, yet I wanted the staff to hear about it first. "

There was complete silence in the room. Coffee cups and food were set aside and all of the audience looked directly at Matt. "Beth Andrews and I have been dating and we are a couple." To Matt's amazement there was applause. "I will not observe her formally nor evaluate her. I will leave that to the Chairman of the Guidance Department and Central Office. Further, I will not try to give her easy tasks nor hard tasks. Let life go on as normal as possible. Any questions?"

Shelly Katz, Guidance Counselor stood up. "You have my

permission Mr. Collins to come to me for therapy if you screw up. I love Beth and you better not hurt her!"

This brought down the house. Laughter and joyful noise permeated the room. Matt yelled, "The meeting is over. You are dismissed!"

* * *

Beth had her head on Matt's shoulder as they watched the six thirty news. Her apartment was bigger than Matt's and all important she had a queen size bed compared to Matt's full size bed. The extra six inches seemed valuable to Matt. Beth indicated that she had no problem sleeping with Matt at his apartment. Giggling and kissing Matt's cheek, "I'll sleep with you even if you have a cot. I have my ways."

Dinner was roast chicken, potato salad and coleslaw brought in from the local supermarket. A scoop of ice cream finished the meal.

"Matt, don't bother with the dishes. Come to bed now."

The passion of her voice and her body language stirred Matt. He complied and the moment caught both of them in the height of passion.

Matt woke up and looked at the clock on the night table. It was two in the morning. The couple had made love passionately for nearly three hours before falling asleep.

* * *

On Thursday, during period three, someone pulled the fire alarm. The school emptied out and the students and teachers did a nice job thinking it was a drill. Matt looked at his alarm system control panel and noticed the alarm was pulled right next to the Seventh Grade Science Room.

As the students went back to their classes Matt stood at the side of the door of the Science Room looking at each student entering the class. He gazed into each student's eyes as they passed him. All of a sudden a girl started crying and ran down the hallway. Matt caught up with her and took her hand. "Let's go to your Guidance Counselor. I'm sure Mrs. Katz isn't going to punish you. What's your name?"

"Patricia Mullen."

Matt noticed that Patricia had a large wart on her nose and on the side of her right cheek. Her clothing, although clean, seemed slightly worn. "I'm not going to punish you Patricia if you tell Mrs. Katz the truth and Mrs. Katz knows when kids are lying."

They entered the Guidance suite and Matt took Patricia to Mrs. Katz. "Mrs. Katz this is Patricia and she knows how to pull a fire alarm. She promised me to tell the truth to you and I promised her that if she did I would not punish her. Is that right Patricia?"

"Yes sir."

Matt notified the Science Teacher that Patricia was in Guidance.

* * *

Upon his return to his office Maggie informed him that the Superintendent requested him to call. "Dr. Hull, this is Mr. Collins.'

"Mr. Collins, what's this about doctor notes."

"I gave you my spread sheets on the seven teachers in question. This is only for them since they seem to be the worst offenders."

"I would have just written them an information memo and verbally told them not to do it again."

"Sure, and do you think Mrs. Higgins would listen. Sometimes you have to play hardball."

"You are the new boy on campus and seem to be causing waves."

"Look Dr. Hull, if you don't like my decision, write me a memo indicating you go along with the teachers grievance. That would end it."

"No, I'll bump it up to the Board of Education."

"Why don't you wait until the District Committee of Teachers meet. You may be surprised."

"How so?"

"Most of the teachers in my school were very pleased with the decision. In fact the Union President used the word 'regretfully' as she filed the grievance. Let's wait and see."

"Alright, I'll wait and see."

Maggie buzzed. "Mrs. Katz to see you, if you have a moment."

"Sure. Maggie please ask the cafeteria to save me a tuna fish sandwich. I think I'm going to be locked in for awhile."

Mrs. Katz and Matt sat at his small table. "This kid is in bad shape. She's turning in on herself and has admitted to me that she is thinking of suicide. Pulling the alarm was a reaction against some mean girls bullying her about her face and a call for help!"

"What's her background?"

"Single mother working two jobs to make ends meet and a pair of twin boys in third grade. Patricia comes home from school and has to take care of the twins, do her homework, make dinner and pray that there is enough money in the house to pay the for food clothing and shelter."

"Are they on welfare?"

"No, the mother makes too much. It's a situation of the "Working Poor." They make too much for welfare, too much for Medicaid, and they just make it every day. If the mother gets sick and can't work it is a true tragedy. They live from paycheck to paycheck."

"I'll see what I can do. More information later."

* * *

Munching on his tuna sandwich Matt called the School Nurse. Mrs. Anita O'Dwyer had been in the school for five years and knew many of the families. "What do you know about Patricia Mullin and her family? She's in seventh grade."

"The name doesn't ring a bell. What can I do for you?"

"The kid has ugly warts on her nose and cheek. Do you know of any dermatologists or plastic surgeons who do pro bono work?"

"Obviously you want to help. I'll make a few calls and get back to you."

The rest of Thursday went smoothly. Matt finished his newsletter for the following week and gave it to Maggie for publication. He informed Central Administration that he would be leaving early, at the eighth period in order to do some personal business.

Matt smiled as he drove out of the town and towards Syracuse. He was on a mission.

CHAPTER 20

Maggie buzzed Matt. "Jennifer Stanton to see you."

"How can I help you Mrs. Stanton?"

"I just wanted to let you know in person that the District Teachers Grievance Committee has refused to take the grievance from Mrs. Higgins and the other teachers in terms of doctor notes. It was felt that you were justified in your actions. I'll give you a memo later on today."

"Thanks so much, Mrs. Stanton." He thought. *That was easy!*

Matt notified the Superintendent of Schools. "I didn't expect that decision, but I am pleased. We still have one more grievance to go through."

"I'm sure you and the Board of Education will back me. Why don't we leave it to the arbitrator."

"Perhaps. We will see."

That ended the phone call and Matt was perturbed. Dr. Hull seemed to protect himself and didn't like to back up his administrators. No wonder the school had so many principals in such a short time.

The rest of Friday seemed slow-moving. Near the end of the school day Beth called. "Where are we going tonight? I want to dress appropriately."

"You are always appropriate."

"I hope not. There are times I don't want to be."

"I'm puzzled, when?"

"When I'm in bed with you."

Although Matt was alone he flushed. "God Beth, you turn me on just by talking."

" I hope so. I love you so much!"

"Okay, we are going to eat at an elegant French restaurant called Rousseau. Its about a one hour drive towards Albany. They have an elegant menu and a pianist. I'll pick you up at six thirty. We have a seven thirty reservation."

* * *

Matt dressed in a tailored black suit that his brother Steve bought for him as a gift when Matt became a principal. It was the first time he wore it. Steve made sure to buy a handsome white on white shirt and a silk tie with a two tone silver pattern. It must have cost Steve over a thousand dollars, but money was no object for his older brother.

Matt knocked on Beth's door and as she opened it he saw the most beautiful woman in the world. She must have gone to the salon because the modified upsweep accented her lovely face. Beth was wearing an off-the-shoulder black dress that accented her marvelous figure. "Mademoiselle, your coach awaits. You look ravishing!"

Beth did a small curtsy. "Thank you Monsieur, you look debonair tonight. I love your suit and tie!"

It took less than fifty five minutes to get to Rousseau. The restaurant had a beautiful fieldstone frontage and manicured greenery surrounding it. Matt thought. *This is the right place for tonight!*

They were seated by a tuxedoed maitre d' who made sure to hold a chair for Beth.

She looked around and was dazzled by the elegance of the crystal chandeliers and the beautiful oil paintings throughout the restaurant. "Matt, this is a very expensive place. Can you afford it?"

"I certainly can. I broke open my piggy bank for this special date."

Matt ordered striped bass and Beth ordered a petit steak.

"Would you like wine?"

Beth shook her head in the negative. "Not tonight, I want to savor the food, the music, the ambiance, although I will share a dessert with you later."

They enjoyed the fresh green garden salad and French bread A house dressing, made at table side by the waiter was extraordinary.

The slow pace and quiet atmosphere was relaxing to the couple. The entrees were served and were marvelous. Matt knew about striped bass because he came from Long Island. It was great. Beth stated it was the best steak she ever ate. They both were pleased.

The waiter came to take the dessert order. Matt requested that dessert be delayed.

He took out a small box and gave it to Beth. "This gift will tell you about how I feel about you."

Beth opened it and found an eighteen inch silver chain holding a beautiful silver locket some three inches wide. It had two tiny hands, gently clasping a crowned heart. Around the outside of the locket were six carved crosses. "Oh Matt, it is beautiful and I love it. What does it mean?"

"This is the Claddagh symbol. In the seventeenth century an Irish fisherman lived in Claddagh, an ancient fishing village, outside Galway. He was captured by pirates and sold to the Moors. Robert Joyce's heart was broken because he would never see his beloved Margaret again. This was the woman he dearly loved.

He worked for diligently and became a skilled silversmith himself. After many years he was released and returned home. Before he returned he made a ring for his true love. The design consisted of two small hands clasping a crowned heart. It was the symbol of his never-ending love for Margaret.

When Robert returned to Claddagh he found Margaret still waiting for him. They lived to a ripe old age."

Beth placed it around her neck. It looked beautiful against her black dress. "Thank you for the gift and the special story. I understand" Beth began to cry. "Excuse me, I'll be back soon."

Matt did not know how this gift would affect Beth. It was obvious that it was very meaningful. He was concerned that it was perhaps a bit too early to give her a romantic gift.

Beth returned to the table. "I'll treasure this gift. You have made it very special for me and I love you for it!"

"I was concerned that giving you any gift so soon in our relationship would spoil it."

"No, sweetheart. The opposite is true. It made it mature and real."

They shared a chocolate mousse for dessert and left. Both did not say too much on the way home.

Beth asked Matt not to stay over. "I really need some alone time. How about we go to the Main street diner for pancakes on Sunday?"

"Are you up to exposing us to the whole town?"

"Sounds okay to me. I'll meet you on Sunday at ten."

* * *

On Sunday, Matt was waiting in front of the Main Street Diner at ten in the morning. Beth drove up a few minutes later and they were ushered to a booth quickly. The waitress was efficient and placed the order swiftly.

Matt looked around and saw many people he did not know. Beth looked as well. "Matt, I can't see any one I know."

"Same here."

Their orders came and Matt downed his pancakes with great enthusiasm. Beth had ordered a western omelet and she too enjoyed it. The coffee was just right. Their breakfast talk consisted of sharing stories of disastrous blind dates and foolishness.

Matt put a nice tip on the table and approached the cash register in the front of the diner. There was Julia, the first waitress who had served him at the Main Street Diner. "Good morning Mr. Principal, oh I forgot, Mr. Collins. How are you?"

"Julia, I'm a happy man. May I introduce Beth Andrews, she's the Eighth Grade Guidance Counselor at our school."

Beth shook Julia's hand. "Nice to meet you. Do you have any children in the middle school?"

"One boy in sixth grade. He's a true red head. You can't miss him."

"I'll look for him."

Matt paid his check and as he was leaving Julia leaned over and whispered to him. "She is a beauty. Better keep her."

He whispered back. "Oh, I certainly will."

The drive was wonderful. Most of the trees were giving up their leaves and the crisp smell of autumn permeated the air.

Since they had driven in separate cars Matt left his car at the diner. Beth wanted to show Matt the suburbs of the town. "There are some lovely homes just a few miles outside of town. Some of the kids go to private schools and of course there is the Parochial School at the east end of Main Street."

"Do you know about the Parochial School and their kids?"

"Sure, I had to place a few of them over the years. I found most of them equal in Language Arts, Reading, Science, and Social Studies. They were almost all a year below in Math."

"How come?"

"Testing. They use a completely different set of tests. One difference is the state doesn't require the non-public schools to give State tests. Public schools must give the tests."

"On Long Island, I was told that all the schools took the Common Core tests." "Better check on that. I doubt it. Hey let's change the subject!"

Matt and Beth enjoyed their togetherness as they drove through wooded areas and farm land. They spotted a Green Market and decided to investigate.

The market was developed by farmers in a cooperative manner. They sold fresh vegetables and invited vendors to come and sell their goods. There were bakery products, delicious muffins, rolls, bread and pastries. All sorts of art work were displayed. Gadgets and gizmos were being sold as well. Some tables had antiques and collectables. Walking through, Matt and Beth spotted a silversmith who designed her own jewelry.

Matt saw a unique pair of earrings that would go with Beth's new pendant. "Beth, look at this. Won't this go with your pendant?"

Beth kissed him on the cheek. "I'll buy it."

Matt interjected, "No, I'll buy it."

"No, although we are a couple, I have enough money to buy things on my own. Matt, I'm a big girl and I do big girl things!"

Matt smiled and thought. *She certainly has a mind of her own. I really like that.*

They carried bags of fresh fruit and vegetables back to the car. Then they returned to the Green Market to have a late lunch. Beth and Matt munched on turkey and bacon sandwiches and shared a huge pastry for dessert. The coffee, served from the back of a van was delicious. They had two styrofoam cups to wash down all their food.

"Matt, I don't think I'm going to have dinner tonight. The morning breakfast and this lunch were enough for me."

"Okay but I may cheat later in the evening. Let's go back."

It was a glorious Sunday and meaningful because they were free of hiding their relationship from anyone. They were a couple, a very strong, united couple.

CHAPTER 21

Matt and Jerry started observing teachers this week in earnest. Each observation had to be a minimum of one period, which was forty two minutes. Immediately after that the administrators would go back to their office and write up the observation. Within two days a conference would take place between the teacher and the administrator. Items as: teaching of content; key and pivotal questions; medial summary; student participation; student discipline; rapport between teacher and student and the condition of the room were taken into account. Suggestions, if necessary were given to the teacher. It was a long process where the conference could take up to forty five minutes.

The suggestions for some of the teachers were written up in a special format called "Teacher Improvement Plan." It possibly involved taking courses at the University, observing teachers in other schools with the same subject matter being taught, watching demonstration videos of Master Teacher's teaching, as well as help in discipline of students using guidance techniques and a myriad of other modalities.

The weeks continued into the second week of November. There weren't too many hurdles. The focus was still on observations and conferences.

Finally the Noise Traffic Light came to the school. Otto installed it where all students eating in the cafeteria could see it. Matt and Otto both worked on the controls and it was time to give it its first test.

Since many of the teachers had to take cafeteria duty they seemed interested in the instructions. A one page sheet of instructions was written to the total staff. The Home Room Teachers were requested to go through the instructions with the students. On Wednesday Matt gave Otto the okay to uncover the light and start it up.

The kids were in awe of the light. They stayed very quiet and the light remained on green. Matt went into the middle of the cafeteria and raised his hand. "Okay kids, the PTA has bought this special light for you and me. Let's hear you yell and scream for twenty seconds."

The light went into red immediately. All of a sudden the kids voices died down .It seemed to be a success. Matt decided to show it to the PTA Board.

On Friday the PTA Board came in and they were thrilled with the results. Actually the teachers were thrilled as well. Finally the kids had some form of norm to measure their voice level. It was a success. Matt thought. *Sometimes little things can really make a difference.*

\* \* \*

Harold Daniels, a fourteen year old student of the George W. Bush Middle School locked his bedroom door. He opened up his closet and behind a box of summer clothes he pulled out his gun. It was a Bushmaster M4 Type Carbine. Harold took one of his four magazines and rammed it home into the gun. It was a semi-automatic and held thirty rounds. A few day ago he broke into the house gun safe and stole it. It was his father's gun.

He was angry at Miss. Andrews, his counselor, for recommending that his mother get psychotherapy for him. He was angry at Mr. Jackson, the Assistant Principal for disciplining him in front of the other students. He was angry at Mr. Franklin, the Eighth Grade Team Leader for pulling him out of class. He was angry at the eighth grade girls and boys laughing at him because he stuttered. He was angry at his father for abandoning his mother and himself last year. He was angry at his mother for dating any man who had on a pair of pants. He was angry because his mother slept with some men who she dated. He was angry because he was to see a psychologist after school today. He was in a rage!

\* \* \*

The morning started well. Matt and Jerry were on target with their observation schedule and there was talk about Thanksgiving plans for next week. Jerry was going fishing with his brother and Beth was flying to Florida to be with her parents. Matt would visit his parents on Long Island. He heard from his brother Steve that he was flying in from Silicon Valley in California. Matt was looking forward to the holiday.

Maggie reported that her clerk was sick and there was no substitute available. She stated there was no problem with her handling the office alone.

Harold had purposely come to school late. He carried his weapon in a large blue canvas bag. Upon entering his school he walked directly to the office. Maggie saw him first. Harold took out his semi-automatic and fired one shot at Maggie. It missed her. She screamed and hid under her desk. Harold shot once more at the desk and then started to Jerry's office.

Matt was in his office finishing up observation reports when he heard a familiar sound. Two gun shots. He was tuned in and immediately went into a combat mode. Matt opened his door and saw a teenaged boy coming out of Jerry's office.

Harold saw Matt and aimed his gun at him. Simultaneously Matt rushed Harold and as the gun went off Matt was already in his roll on the floor, just like the United States Army Rangers taught him in combat school. If you are very close to your enemy he cannot use his rifle.

Matt sprang upwards and gave Harold a karate chop on the back of his neck. Harold went down, unconscious. Matt took the gun and threw it in the corner of the office.

"Maggie, call nine one one and hurry!"

Five minutes later the first patrol car rolled up to the school. The officer saw the situation and handcuffed the unconscious boy. "What happened?"

Maggie's voice was shaken. "This kid came into the office and fired a couple of shots at me. I hid under my desk. Then he went into Mr. Jackson's office looking for him.

Mr. Collins came out of his office and the boy fired at Mr. Collins. Mr. Collins disarmed him. That's all I know."

"Mr. Collins what happened?"

"I heard two shots from the outer office came out and saw the boy coming out of Mr. Jackson's office. I ran as fast as I could to close the distance and rolled as he shot. Then I disarmed him with a karate chop on the neck."

As the news spread rapidly the office was filling up quickly. There was the Police Chief, the Lead Detective on the case, two patrolman, Maggie, Jerry and the boy. Jerry Jackson identified the boy as Harold Daniels, an eighth grade student. Maggie gave the detective the mother's work number.

Mrs. Daniels was called and told to meet the Chief of Police at the Station House. Harold came to as the police officers took him out of the building. He was still in handcuffs. The detective took the gun and blue handbag containing extra magazines to the station house.

After they left the building Maggie collapsed. Jerry and Matt rushed to her side. Matt called the School Nurse who quickly took Maggie into the Nurse's Office.

Jerry put his hands on his face and whispered. "He was after me. I disciplined him yesterday."

"He's a very sick boy. He's angry, frightened, and mentally ill. Jerry, take the rest of the day off."

Matt stayed in the outer office and called the Superintendent. He outlined the scenario in short sentences. The Superintendent seemed concerned. "I'll call the Chief of Police and get the details. Thank you Matt. Good job."

Matt called a teacher assistant to cover the office. He went to the Nurse's Office to see how Maggie was doing. Upon entering the office he spotted Jason Carter, Maggie's husband. "How is she doing?"

"She's alright. Her first combat."

"Maggie, I want you to go home and only come back to school when you feel comfortable."

Maggie rose from the cot and walked over to Matt. She hugged him tightly. "Thank you for saving my life. I will always be in your debt."

"Go home Maggie. Take a shot of whisky, lie down and hug Jason, in that order."

Maggie laughed and cried at the same time.

Jason Carter walked over to Matt. There were tears in his eyes. "Matt, thank you from the bottom of my heart. You saved my girl."

Matt nodded and left the room. He was filled with emotion as well.

The teacher assistant wrote two notes to Matt when he was gone. She placed them on his desk. "Sharon Silver, reporter called." And again, "Sharon Silver, reporter called."

Beth called him, "What happened?"

"I'll tell you later. Don't go home. Stick around your office and I'll call you when things quiet down."

Later in the day, about four thirty Beth entered Matt's office. She ran to him and held him. "I already know. Oh my God, you could have been killed."

"How did you find out?"

"Jason Carter called me. He told me to take care of you and told me the story. The man was concerned about your past history and your condition today. We talked a bit about Post Traumatic Stress Disorder and he told me that you were in the middle of a lot of action when you were in service. This incident might trigger some problems."

Matt looked at her in amazement. "I'd like to be with you for a few nights at your place if its okay with you?"

She rushed to him, put her arms around him and hugged him. "As long as you want to stay my darling."

CHAPTER 22

On the Tuesday of Thanksgiving week Matt and Maggie were asked by the School Attorney, Richard DeLuca to come to his office for a deposition. The attorney representing fourteen year old Harold Daniels was at the meeting.

Nancy Briggs, Attorney at Law was a woman in her late thirties who down played her looks. She had striking dark eyes and a cream complexion. Her black business suit acknowledged that she was a professional. "Good morning Mr. Collins," her handshake was firm and hard, "it's a pleasure to meet a hero."

Matt pulled his hand away. "I was in the right place at the right time. Thank God no one was injured or killed."

Maggie shook her hand. "Good morning Nancy. I haven't seen you in church lately?"

Matt thought. *Small towns seem to have a way of bringing out all the dirt or gossip.*

Richard DeLuca motioned all of the parties to sit. "We are going to tape this deposition. It's really not a joint deposition since I will go first and Ms. Briggs will go second. If you have any questions just blurt them out. If you want to go off the record just say so. Any questions?"

The statements that Matt gave and that Maggie gave were similar to the police reports. Richard DeLuca finished his questions. "Ms. Briggs, they are all yours."

"Let it be known that I stipulate that the statements that Mr. Collins and Mrs. Carter just gave are acceptable to me, up to a point.

Just one question to Mr. Collins, were you trying to kill Harold Daniels?"

"No I was not," Matt looked squarely into her eyes, "I was trying to disarm him."

"Isn't it true that you were an Army Ranger?"

"Yes."

"Isn't true that you were trained that in any combat situation you were trained to kill the adversary."

"Yes."

"Again, I ask you this question were you trying to kill my client?"

"This wasn't a combat situation since I had no rifle, I had no pistol, I had no helmet, I had no bullet proof vest, I had nothing except the motivation to stop some kid from killing."

"Weren't you trained in hand to hand combat?"

Matt stood up. "Let's go off the record. Shut the recorder, please."

Richard DeLuca cleared his throat. "Ms. Briggs, If you continue to go down this dirty alley I'll have to bring up Harold's mother's activities with every single man in this town. Then we will talk about his state of mind. Then we will talk about her being a poor parent"

"Stop!" Nancy Briggs shouted.

"Well?"

Matt interjected, "I was trained in hand to hand combat to fight soldiers, not boys!"

Nancy Briggs smiled. "Okay Mr. Collins. Answer the question that way on the record and we are finished."

The recorder was turned on. "I was trained in hand to hand combat to fight soldiers, not boys!"

"Thank you Mr. Collins. This deposition is finished."

* * *

That evening Matt and Beth had dinner at the Carter's house. Maggie made a delicious meatloaf, garlic mashed potatoes and sweet carrots. Her dessert was apple pie, home baked. "Thank you for an all-American meal." Beth wiped her mouth. "It was wonderful!"

Jason Carter helped Maggie clean up. In less than thirty minutes they all were sitting around the family room. "Matt, I was told that you were accused of trying to kill that boy. Is this correct?"

"No. Not really. I think Ms. Briggs watches too many lawyer movies. She was trying to get the subject on me, not her client. It really didn't work."

"Don't kid yourself. Nancy Briggs is one sharp cookie. She's going to ask the judge to treat Harold as a juvenile, not an adult. Your statement stated that you weren't trying to kill an adult that he was a boy."

"Jason, I don't want the kid tried as an adult. I think he's emotionally unstable and needs help. Plenty of help. I'll go to court and fight for him if asked."

Beth cried out. "Matt, he tried to kill you. He should be put away!"

"No, I don't think so, he's a mixed up kid with a lot of problems and"

Maggie cut Matt off. "I heard from Julia, at the diner that Nancy Briggs wants to get this case to go to Syracuse. She thinks a big city judge will try him as a juvenile and even before that have him psychologically tested."

Jason Carter laughed. "Maggie, is this straight."

"Julia can hear conversations from fifty yards. She is usually ninety percent correct. This was a meeting between Nancy Briggs and Mrs. Daniels. They don't want anything to do with this town."

Matt stood up and went over to Beth. "I have one more day with my sweetheart before we both go our separate ways. I'm going to Long Island and Beth is going to Florida. I'm going to miss her for four long days!"

Beth kissed Matt on his cheek.

Matt took hold of Maggie's both hands. "Thank you so much for the meal and the conversation. It's nice to know that you and Jason are true friends."

* * *

Matt and Beth went to Beth's apartment. They showered together and dried each other off and ended up in the bedroom. "You have a beautiful figure."

"Hon, I'm okay, but things will start to droop. I guarantee that."

"You work out all the time. That will stop it."

Beth closed the door to her bedroom and ran to Matt. She jumped on him and entwined her legs around his waist. Kissing him on his ears, his forehead, each eye, each cheek and finally his neck she murmured. "I'm going to eat you up tonight!"

She nearly did!

* * *

The last day before Thanksgiving was quite different from the previous holiday. Almost all the teachers remained in school and there was no problem with substitutes.

The students were in a very happy mood and most of the teachers made sure it would be a light day. There were no new concepts taught or anything major happening. The teachers were asked to clean up their rooms to give the custodial staff a chance to have a lighter day before the holiday. Most of the teachers complied.

Matt had his bag packed and in his car. He was going to go to Long Island to see his parents and his older brother Steve. There was a great deal to tell after some three months of school.

## CHAPTER 23

As he drove to Long Island from upstate New York Matt reflected about his family. His parents were both college graduates who excelled in school. It was never stated that "if he went to college" it was always stated "when he went to college." The dye was cast very early in his life that education was one of the highest priorities. Matt's brother Steve had the same recollections about education

Dad had a Masters Degree in Electrical Engineering and Mom had a Bachelors Degree in Hotel Management. They met because of their degrees. The story told to him by both parents was that at a convention his father became infatuated with the cutest Assistant Manager of the hotel he was staying at. Bingo! Within six months they were married and living on Long Island. His mother left her career and became a housewife who raised two boys.

Matt's father worked for a major aircraft corporation, Grumman, that supplied almost all the planes to the U.S. Navy. When the Navy had a contract his father made good money, but when there was no contract the family was on a tight budget

Matt's brother Steve, inherited the scholarly genes from his parents and was class Valedictorian in his high school. Matt followed, graduating at sixteen. He was placed on the fast track early on in his schooling. Looking back he wished that he did not have to be accelerated that quickly.

The family was well rounded and there were severe penalties if he or his brother lied. Telling the truth and having good values were built into them very early in life. Supporting the family as the highest priority was instilled into both boys.

Matt chuckled out loud remembering one incident that concerned Steve and his parents. Matt was in the center of it as well. It seemed that Steve, who rarely dated, was asked out to the high school prom by a very precocious and mature young lady.

Matt was fifteen and Steve was eighteen. All he could think about was how beautiful the girl was and his brother was a really lucky guy. When Steve came down the stairs from his bedroom he was handsomely dressed in a pale blue tuxedo. He smiled and stated to all that he was really excited. The family car was washed and cleaned by Matt just a few hours before. It was Friday evening and everything was set for his brother to have a really good time at the high school prom.

At eleven in the evening Mom received a phone call from Steve. It seemed that he would be delayed and he would be back at midnight. Steve told his parents not to wait up for him. The family went to bed at eleven that evening.

Matt heard the noise from downstairs and looked at his bedside clock. It was four in the morning. He opened his bedroom door and saw Steve tip toeing into his room. Matt went back to sleep and thought nothing of it.

The family tried to have breakfast together on weekends. On Saturday morning at eight thirty every one asked Steve about the prom. Steve described the hall, the food, the decorations and the great band. "Mom and Dad, I had a wonderful time!"

Mom chuckled, "What time did you get in?"

Steve quickly replied, "A little before twelve."

Matt knew it was a lie and he never heard Steve lie at all. He looked at his brother and lowered his eyes. This was a really tough call. Never lie and always support your family were the basic values of his family. Matt remained silent. He was caught on the horns of a dilemma.

Later in the day Steve went into Matt's room. "Matt, I just had trouble explaining to Mom & Dad that I was in a motel with my date. I'm not a virgin anymore. Thanks for not saying anything. I owe you."

Matt has kept the secret to this day. He would never betray his brother nor would he want to hurt his family who had such high standards. He grew up from that incident. Things aren't always black or white. Sometimes grey is the correct choice.

Crossing the Throgs Neck Bridge from the Bronx to Queens he saw the water. The bridge straddled the East River and Long Island Sound. He remembered the fun days at Jones Beach on the south shore of Long Island. His family camped out in the Catskill Mountains. There were plenty of swimming holes and lakes to swim in as well.

There was a feeling of joyful anticipation as he headed home on the Long Island Expressway. He hadn't seen his brother in close to a year. It was time to catch up with the whole family.

* * *

Beth's plane came in at seven in the evening. As she was crossing the threshold where security ended and families could reunite she spotted her dad. Beth speeded up and hugged her father. "Oh Dad, I'm so happy to see you. Where's Mom?"

"She's a bit under the weather today. I'll tell you more after we get your luggage."

"Anything bad?"

"Not bad, but treatable."

Beth's father usually was a man with many words. He was a life long career politician in New York State. If his party was out of office he would always have some job heading some bi-partisan committee that the State needed. It worked that way in New York State. Beth thought. *For my Dad to say, "not bad, but treatable" means only one thing. My mom is really sick!*

The drive took less than an hour. The guard at the gate waived as they drove through a beautiful senior community in the heart of Florida. Her parents saved and sometimes struggled a bit, yet they achieved their dream. They lived in a beautiful estate home in one of the best areas of Florida, close enough to two airports and close enough to fine dining when they wished to indulge. They were often out listening to classical music, going to road shows, and enjoying well known entertainers. It was an idyllic life.

When Beth opened the door of the house and saw her mom she started to whimper because her mother had lost a great deal of weight and her hair was completely grey. "Oh Mom, I love you so much. Tell me about it. Please!"

* * *

Matt approached the heavily treed lined street that was his home for many years. His parents chose to stay in Levitttown. They built a huge dormer that spanned the total roof line and built two large rooms. That was for his brother and himself. They had plenty of room plus large closets. The many shelves kept things organized. It was a joy living there.

Matt spotted his brother's rental. It was one of the best German models available. He grinned as he parked behind his brother's car in his made-in-the-USA middle sized sedan. Matt thought. *My brother is in a different league. Financially and perhaps socially.*

The reality came through as soon as his mother opened the door. There was a statuesque blond woman behind her. Mom kissed Matt. "Matt, may I introduce Linda Kersey, your brother's fiancé."

Linda came over to Matt and hugged him. She was at least five foot ten in her heals and stunning. Her figure was well proportioned, with large breasts and perfect hips. Matt mumbled in her ear, "Nice to meet you. Congratulations."

They were ushered into the living room. "Where are Dad and Steve?"

"They went to the deli to buy some cold cuts. They'll be back soon."

Linda sat next to Matt on the couch. "Matt, I know Steve did not tell you about us and that you're surprised. The fact of the matter is that this has happened so fast for me as well. I'm your brother's Chief Financial Officer. We work together day and night. I'm a CPA and handle all of the corporation's finances. Well, about six months ago we started to date. Then we started to really get involved. Steve never mentioned marriage and I have had a previous disastrous marriage so I wasn't particularly looking for that. I love your brother and I was happy with the way things were until a week ago. Steve declared he loved me and gave me this ring."

"It's beautiful. My brother has class. Not only in jewelry but in the woman he is to marry."

Linda's eyes started to tear up and she hugged Matt. "Oh Matt,

Steve told me what a great guy you are. I'm so happy that I'll be part of the family."

At that moment Steve and their dad walked in. "Dad, Happy Thanksgiving!"

Matt's father hugged him tightly. "I'm so happy to see you Son. Did you get the news?"

"Oh yes." He looked at his brother and chokingly said, "Congratulations, you sly old fox!"

Both brothers embraced. "Little brother, she's terrific, just wonderful!"

Mom came out of the kitchen. "Okay, lunch is ready. Cold cuts, rye bread, potato salad, coleslaw, pickles, relish and mustard. Come and get it.!"

Sitting around the kitchen table the five of them discussed wedding plans. Steve took the initiative. "We want to get married in Palo Alto. The company is there and Linda's parents live nearby in San Carlos, about eleven miles away. They have modest means so Linda and I will pay for the wedding. We will also pay for your airfares and any extras. Plan to stay with me at my house."

"Not necessary Son."

"Very necessary Dad. I'm well off."

"I can afford it Son."

"Okay, since we're family I'll let you in on a secret. Linda. What am I worth, personally?"

"Steve has liquid assets, personally worth nine million dollars. His company is worth forty five million if he were to sell it. I think he can afford to pay your expenses."

Matt looked at his brother in amazement. "Wow, I'm really impressed."

"Not as much as I am with you little brother. Getting a school principal's position at thirty two and handling a staff of over one hundred twenty people and serving our country as well I'm impressed!"

Linda looked at Mrs. Collins. "May I call you Mom?"

"It would be a pleasure Linda."

"Then all I can say to you Mom and Dad is that you have raised two remarkable people. As my father says, 'The apple doesn't fall far from the tree.'"

They finished their meal talking about dates. It was decided that Christmas week was the best time since Matt was off at that time.

"Steve, I'll be bringing a guest to your wedding."

Mrs. Collin's immediately responded. "Oh, come on son. Tell us about her. What's her name?"

"Her name is Beth and she's a Guidance Counselor in my school."

"Oh, she works for you." Steve blurted out.

"I'd prefer it, that you consider her a professional colleague."

"With benefits? Little brother."

Matt blushed. "Oh yeah, with plenty of that. I really like her. I like her a lot. I may even be in love with her."

Linda came over to the back of Matt's chair and put her arms around him. "Leave my future brother in law alone. It's hard enough to get to know anybody in this crazy mixed up world. Matt, give it time."

That ended the conversation at lunch. Matt was pleased that Linda had enough understanding to protect him from more questions. He realized how sensitive a person she was and how lucky his brother was to have her.

That evening Steve and Matt took a walk. "Matt, will you be my Best Man? "

"It would be an honor."

They continued to walk, and as they turned around to go back to the house, Steve took Matt by the arm. "I've got to replace my Associate Director of Human Resources. With your overall supervisory experience and administrative know-how I can really use a man like you. I'm offering you two hundred and twenty thousand a year to start. That includes, stock options, full medical, hospital and dental insurance. Two weeks paid vacation that will build up to a month in three years and I will move you and your significant other lock, stock and barrel. You have a brother who needs you."

"Thanks bro but no thanks."

"What do you make now?"

"One hundred ten thousand. That's based on the Syracuse Principals Schedule. If I go back to Long Island I'll make about one hundred and ninety thousand after six years of service."

"Not bad. Why don't I up the ante. My Director of Human Services makes three hundred fifty grand. I'm offering you three hundred and twenty five thousand per year."

"I love you Steve, but the answer is still no. Case closed."

* * *

Beth's mother knocked on her bedroom door. "May I come in Beth?"

"Oh Mom, I was sure you were going to tell me what's up."

"Beth, I have been diagnosed with multiple myeloma, a cancer of the bone marrow. Its treatable. There has been remarkable progress in its treatment. The oncologist is using a targeted chemotherapy and it is working. My white blood cells are rising and my life expectancy is at least ten years."

Beth took her mother in her arms and hugged her. "What can I do for you?"

"Your dad is wonderful. He is with me almost all the time and on bad days he takes care of me and everything in the house. What you can do for me is to live your life fully and with joy."

Both woman started to cry as they comforted each other, Beth loving her mom so much and her mother trying to console Beth. Her mother left as Beth fell asleep.

The rest of the Thanksgiving holiday was traditional for both families. Aunts, uncles, cousins and children, lots of children, visited on the four day holiday. Both Matt and Beth made sure to call each other every night. The conversations were not long. They realized they would have plenty to discuss when they came back from the holiday. Matt made sure to tell Beth to lock in Christmas week which started December twenty first. She was excited about Steve's wedding. The good news was that Beth would still be able to fly out to see her parents on December twenty seventh.

## CHAPTER 24

Matt drove back on Sunday, the end of the Thanksgiving holiday. He arrived at three in the afternoon. Instead of going straight home he went to his school and checked to see if the custodians and teachers cooperated with each other to have clean rooms. Matt was very pleased. The only room that was a mess was the Art Room. He thought. *Lady, if you are looking for a war you've got it. First thing in the morning I'm writing you up and the hell with your husband and his newspaper!*

Beth was flying in on late Sunday afternoon. He couldn't wait to see her again. Matt wanted to validate their significant relationship. How could he do it? He decided to call Jason Carter. " I hope you and Maggie are doing well. How are you both?"

"She's still shook up about the shooting incident. Every time she hears a loud noise she gets upset."

"I'm really sorry. Tell her to take all the time she needs. I know how she feels. Jason, it will take time. Be patient with her. Give her my best."

"And how was your Thanksgiving?"

"Visiting my family is the best therapy a person could have. I could relate to their love and kindness. It was wonderful. In fact I'm going to be the Best Man at my brother's wedding this Christmas."

"What can I do for you?"

"How do you know I need advice?"

"It's in your voice."

"Okay. I think I'm in love with Beth. I need a way of showing her my love. I want to validate our togetherness."

"Just tell her or write her a poem or a letter or sing to her. Women are pretty smart when it comes to relationships. They know phony from real. Are you up to asking her to marry you?"

"No, not yet. I just want her to know I don't intend to date anyone, only her."

"Well stupid, just tell her that."

Matt was relieved to hear the advice from Jason.

On Sunday evening Matt went to Beth's apartment. Beth was very quiet.

Matt was concerned. "Beth, you don't seem to be yourself. Is there anything wrong?"

Beth rushed into Matt's arms and started to sob. "My mom has cancer. It's treatable, but she's lost weight, she's become grey and is really tired all the time from the chemo. My dad is doing everything. I don't want him to collapse. Perhaps I should take a leave of absence. I feel so frustrated. Oh Matt, why do our parents have to get old?"

Matt held her firmly and rocked her. "My sweetheart, that's the way of the world. We die a little each day, so make sure you have more good days than bad."

"Matt, I need some time for myself. I need quiet time."

Matt was in a quandary. "Alright Beth, you call the shots and tell me when you want me to visit or not."

Beth gently pushed him out of the apartment. "I'll call you when I get my head straightened out!"

On Monday morning school started and Beth called in sick. Matt was concerned since she did not seem sick last evening. Beth called in sick on Tuesday and Wednesday as well. Matt became worried. He tried calling and Beth did not pick up.

He called the Personnel Department and got Beth's parent's phone number.

"Mrs. Andrews, I'm Matt Collins and I'm concerned about Beth. She hasn't answered my calls for the last three days and she called in sick each morning. Perhaps you could call her. She told me about your sickness and was distraught."

"Thank you Matt. When she was a little girl her pet turtle died and she stayed in her room for two days. That's her way to grieve and to get her head on straight. Thanks for your concern. I'll call her. Please don't worry. Beth is very strong."

"Mrs. Andrews, I'm very fond of your daughter and I would do anything for her."

"Matt, the best thing for you to do is let her be. I'll call just to check in. Let's not talk about you calling me. Agreed?"

"Agreed."

Beth called Matt Wednesday in the late afternoon, after the students left the building. "Matt, take me out for dinner. I want Italian food and lots of it. I haven't eaten in two days!"

"You bet my darling. I'll pick you up at six."

"No, make it five. I'm starving!"

* * *

The name of the local pizza restaurant was "The Pizza Place." They served old fashioned Italian dishes as spaghetti with giant meatballs and five layered lasagna. Their garlic rolls dripped with olive oil and fresh garlic.

After a huge green salad Beth feasted on her lasagna and wiped every bit of sauce off her plate with a piece of garlic roll. She ordered espresso and tiramisu for dessert. There was hardly any conversation between them and Matt decided to take Beth's lead. He remained quiet. Beth stood up and took her purse. "I loved every bit of the food. Thank you Matt for not pushing it. I love you! I really do."

As the couple stood up Matt couldn't help it. He took her in his arms and kissed her. She kissed him back! They left the restaurant arm in arm.

There was silence in Matt's car as he took Beth home. He seemed to sense that Beth was in a different place. It seemed to him that Beth was in a state of sorrow. Sometimes there are no words to say about death or being close to death.

He remembered a mission in Afghanistan where he commanded ten Rangers. They encountered heavy fire and two of his men went down. The mission was successful, although he lost one man and had a seriously wounded Ranger to care for through two kilometers of enemy fire.

After the mission he and his men were debriefed by The United States Army Intelligence and Security Command (INSCOM). His men were mourning the loss of one man and they were more concerned about the injured soldier than reporting. The officers of INSCCM were angry at his men for poor reporting and not cooperating.

Matt picked up his M82."light fifty" semi automatic gun and pointed it at the INSCOM officers and commanded, "Get the hell cut of this tent and this Unit. Come back when you show respect to the man I lost and the man I'm going to lose."

The officers ran out of the tent and out of the zone. They filed a report against Matt.

Later in the week Matt was called into his Colonel's office. He expected to be court-martialed. Instead he was lauded by his Colonel who stated that he would have done the same thing to support his men. They were close. A band of brothers!

The same INSCOM Unit came back a few days later and everyone of the officers apologized to his men. They were new on the job and never faced combat. When you never faced death you just don't understand. When one of your team dies you die a little and go into a state of sorrow. Matt understood Beth's behavior quite well.

Matt escorted Beth to her apartment door. "Beth, I'll wait for you to call me. Perhaps we need time to really cement our relationship. Why don't we focus on the good things in life."

"Thank you Matt. I need time to understand my mom's condition. Next week I'm going to take a personal day on Friday and fly back home to talk to my mom and her oncologist. I'll be back on Monday with more information. Hopefully!"

They kissed and held each other for a long moment. Matt understood. Time was really needed. Beth had to get more information. She had to internalize the situation and find hope and peace within herself.

* * *

Jerry Jackson sat at the bar in Jackson's Tavern. Although it was his brother's business, Jerry would always throw a few dollars on the bar to cover expenses. After his third beer he opened up his wallet and left five dollars on the counter. "Take care Bill. I'm going home."

"You certainly are quiet tonight. What's wrong?"

"What's wrong is Matt Collins. This guy is the genuine article. I don't think I could have faced a kid with a gun and do what he did. Jesus, man. This son of a bitch is really a hero."

Bill Jackson thought for a moment. "He may be a short timer. If he's so good he'll be out of the District in a year or two and find a richer District. Perhaps he'll go back to Long Island or Westchester County. They pay big bucks there. That might give you a chance right in your home town."

"Maybe. Nevertheless I'm going to help this guy. He's treated me with more respect than any other boss I've had!"

* * *

The Superintendent called Matt. "Report to the Board Room tomorrow morning at nine. The Arbitrator will be issuing her report about the grievance filed by your teachers. Don't forget that this is binding. I'm going to be out of town at a conference with my Assistant. I guess you will be there alone. No, our School Attorney will be there, that is if he can make it. "

Matt knew the way cowards operated. They never wanted to face the music and would find all sorts of ways to get out of situations. There was no problem for him to be alone.. He thought, *I don't think having the School Attorney would help at all.*

"No problem. I can handle it." He hung up right after that.

* * *

The next morning he arrived at the Board Room a few minutes before nine and had a cup of coffee with a donut hole. Five minutes later a large woman came into the room followed by Jennifer Stanton, President of the Teachers' Union and Sam England her associate.

"I'm Mrs. Rolanda Williams, Certified Arbitrator, chosen by the District and the Union. I have had ten years of experience and try to be as understanding and fair as possible. I was a teacher for five years and a principal for three years. Then I got my law degree and set up my own practice. I understand both sides."

Mrs. Williams placed a tape recorder on the table and turned it on. "Rolanda Williams, final decision on case number 2154. Present are Mr. Collins, Principal of the George W. Bush Middle School who is representing the District, Jennifer Stanton, President of the Teacher's Union and Sam England, Union Steward of the aforementioned school. According to the contract all of my decisions are binding. Do you understand that?"

Matt and both teachers simultaneously said, "Yes."

"Item one. All paper off the floor, except paper measuring two inches or more in diameter will be picked up by the teacher or her designee. Perhaps a student or Teacher Assistant. Affirmed. Any questions?"

All parties shook their heads.

"Item two. All audio visual equipment and computers locked away. Affirmed. Any questions?"

Sam England spoke up. "What happens if the equipment doesn't fit the closets?"

"Then the Administration will find adequate storage place. Is that acceptable to the Administration.?"

Matt quickly responded. "Yes it is."

"Item three. Plan books locked in the teacher's desk so a substitute can use them. Affirmed. Any questions?"

"Many of our teachers work on their plan books during the weekend." Jennifer Stanton remarked.

"Then may I suggest you use duplicate plan books. In my experience three days of plans by the teachers were more than adequate for the substitutes. Other arrangements could be made."

Matt looked at the teachers. "I'll stipulate that a minimum of three days of planning or the plan books to be locked in the teacher's desk for substitutes."

Mrs. Williams laughed. "I think Mr. Collins has given the teachers a break. Alright, let the record show that a minimum of three days ahead for plan books be placed in the teachers desk. Any questions?"

Jennifer Stanton looked at Matt. "Thank you Mr. Collins. The teachers will be glad to hear about your flexibility."

"Item four. All chalk boards will be washed and ready for the next week. Negated. It is not the job of a Middle School Teacher to wash the boards. The custodians can do it. Any questions?"

Sam England rose up from his chair. "Mrs. Williams, sometimes teachers put items on the board at the end of the week for the students to see when they come in after the weekend. How will that work?"

"Then you opt out of the custodian doing your boards and you do it. Its all or nothing in this case. Do you understand?"

"Yes. If the teacher wishes to use the board then he opts out of the custodian doing the board."

"That is correct. You will have a copy of this meeting in a week or so. Any questions? "Thank you. Case number 2154 is resolved."

Matt wrote up the results of the arbitration, had another cup of coffee and left.

CHAPTER 25

Dear Mrs. Higgins:

I have observed your classroom numerous times and find that it does not meet minimal standards of cleanliness. You did not even try to clean your room before the Thanksgiving holiday.

You are directed and instructed to do the following each day:

1. Take all jars of paint, cap them and store them on the shelves under the windows.

2. Take all art paper and sort them into correct sizes. Store the paper in the closet.

3. Take all paint brushes in cans and store them on the counter by the windows.

4. Take all crayons, pencils, and marker pens off your desk and store them in baskets on the back table of your room.

5. Pick up large pieces of paper each day from your classroom.

You are directed and instructed to follow through with the above directive. If you wish to discuss any part of this please make an appointment through my secretary. You are invited to bring a Union representative to the meeting in order to clarify any issues.

Very truly yours,

Mr. Matt Collins, Principal

CC: Teacher's personnel folder

Maggie came in with the letter for Matt's signature. "The shaving cream will hit the fan with this letter."

"I'm doing what other principals should have done years ago. If necessary I will write up a 'Bill of Particulars' to send to the

Superintendent and then to the Board for action. It could lead to either suspension, fines or dismissal."

"What's a Bill of Particulars?"

"Simply stated in law, it's a written statement of claims or charges. It's written formally to be used in civil litigation."

"Gee, you don't fool around do you?"

"Not with bad teachers or blowhards."

"Ask Jerry to come in."

Matt wrote a note for Jerry. It read, "Inspect room 208, the Art Room on Monday, Wednesday and Thursday. I'll inspect on Tuesday and Friday. Keep a log in terms of my instructions.

"You wanted me, Boss?"

"Please read this letter to Mrs. Higgins. Then follow through with my instructions."

Jerry read the letter. "Wow, you are really after her."

"No, I'm after getting a clean Room 208. Your log and mine may be used in a legal hearing against Mrs. Higgins, so make sure you are accurate."

Since it was the first week of December the rest of the week included conversations with Otto about snow clearing. Matt asked the Team Leaders to develop a new snow phone chain in case of school closings. Maggie was asked to do a new phone chain for all the Specialists in the school.

The PTA held formal meetings on different topics. Not too many parents came to them. The September meeting was "Meet the Teacher" night. Tonight's program was "How to Discipline Your Teenager." Beth Andrews, Eighth Grade Guidance Counselor was the guest speaker.

Beth called Matt. "Matt, I'd like to go over my notes with you before my talk with the parents tonight. Can you come over my apartment about five. We'll have a light dinner and you can listen to my speech."

* * *

Matt knocked on the door and Beth answered. She was wearing a robe. "Are you alright?"

"Yes, I'm perfectly fine. Oh, the robe. I didn't want to get any food on my dress that I'll be wearing tonight. See."

She opened her robe and Matt stared at her beautiful body. "Oh I see. I really can see."

"What are you going to do about it soldier?"

Matt took her in his arms and lifted her up. He carried her into the bedroom and gently placed her on the bed.

"Oh my darling. I've missed you so much. Please, come to me. Now! Right now. I need you and I want you now. Please!"

Matt complied. In fact he complied over and over again. Finally they lay side by side. Both of them were filled with quiet joy.

Matt whispered. "I'm going to take a quick shower."

Beth got up. "I'll join you. We have just enough time to get to the school."

Beth's talk to the parents was outstanding.

* * *

On Wednesday morning Maggie buzzed. "Nancy Briggs, attorney on the phone."

"How may I help you Ms. Briggs."

"Mr. Collins. I'd like to take you out for lunch. Nothing more than some conversation about Harold Daniels. Is the Main Street Diner at one alright?"

"Better make it at noon. That's better for me."

"Done. Noon time at the Main Street Diner. My treat."

"No thanks. Dutch is better all around."

* * *

Nancy Briggs was wearing a designer dress with black and white panels. She seemed different today. Softer in her makeup and in her hairdo. She got up from the table when Matt approached and he could see a magnificent figure underneath the dress. Matt thought. *What is she after? Her clothes and makeup will attract any man.*

They both ordered salads and coffee. "Matt, may I call you Matt? I'm trying to get Harold Daniels to a Syracuse court instead of a County Court because the judges are more lenient in Syracuse. I want him tried as a juvenile. If he goes into the County system I'm positive he will be tried as an adult. That means attempted murder and probably a very harsh penalty."

"What do you want me to do?"

"This kid is emotionally disturbed. His father abandoned them and his mother is sleeping with men all over town. The stress of being bullied by kids in the school because he stutters and being disciplined by Mr. Jackson set him off. Do you understand?"

Matt had a choice to make. It was an easy choice for him. "Not only will I write a letter recommending him for Family Court, I think I can have Miss. Andrews, his Guidance Counselor do the same."

"Wow. I thought I would really have to sell this to you. I could have come in jeans and a tee shirt."

"Nancy, may I call you Nancy? Just because I was a Ranger in the United States Army as well as a principal doesn't make me a hard ass. I'm here to help kids, not punish them."

"Thanks Matt. You're one of the good guys. If I can help you in any way or for any matter call me. I'll be available to you."

She grabbed the bill off the table, stood up, kissed Matt on the cheek and walked out of the diner.

Matt let out a long whistle. He thought. *She's one cool gal.*

* * *

Beth called Matt on Thursday evening at his house. "My mom argued with me about coming home for the weekend. She told me everything is under control. I told her that I want to speak to her oncologist and that I'm really worried about her. She told me she understands although the disease is treatable. Well, anyway finally, she agreed. I'm taking the seven thirty plane out of Syracuse tomorrow morning. Mom will introduce me to her doctor late afternoon on Friday. Then I can spend some alone time with her. What do you think?"

"I think you are doing the right thing. Get more research about her disease from the doctor and then make your own decisions about your mom's situation. May I suggest you speak to your dad about his physical condition. Can he handle the house by himself? Does he need respite?"

"Oh thank you Matt. I never thought about that."

"I'm here for you. Don't forget that."

"When I get back let's talk. I want to bring our relationship up a notch."

"Thank God. I'm ready for that as well. Safe trip."

"Good bye my love."

On Friday Matt and Jerry continued their observations of teachers and added a new element to the surveillance of Mrs. Higgins' Art room. Both administrators took pictures with their smart phones annotating it with times and date.

On Saturday the weekend edition of the local newspaper came out. The banner headline read:" Who Are These Newcomers?" There was a scathing article about Matt. The article claimed he was a dictator and was after middle aged women. They had quotes from psychologists knocking his Code of Conduct. Finally the last paragraph demanded that the Superintendent and the Board of Education fire Matt immediately.

Matt read it and it reminded him of typical tabloid papers. The articles were full of innuendos and misinformation. However he knew that the Board of Education and the wimp of a Superintendent would become frightened.

At noon on Saturday Matt received a call from the Superintendent. "The President of the Board has sent you this message. I'll repeat his words exactly, "Fuck Theodore Higgins and his newspaper. Keep up the good work."

Matt was stunned. "How about you Dr. Hull?'

"I listen to the Board. If they support you then I support you as well."

As soon as Matt hung up he called Jason Carter. "Jason, the Board is supporting me. What's up?"

"I spoke to the Board President this morning. Then Vincent Green, the Supermarket owner called and praised you as well. The Board received dozens of calls from parents praising you. Matt, just keep on doing what you are doing. You are making a difference!"

"Thanks Jason."

The next phone call came from Sharon Silver, a reporter from the Risenburg News. "Any comments about the article?"

"No comment. You may contact the Central Office if you wish."

"Mr. Collins, may I speak to you off the record?"

"Okay."

"I think Mr. Higgins is a pussy whipped husband who listens to his crazy wife. Almost the whole town likes what you are doing. My daughter is in sixth grade and she idolizes you and likes the school. Screw the bastard!"

"Thank you so much. Coming from you it means a lot."

Matt spent most of the weekend writing mid year evaluations of the non tenured teachers. It included "Teacher Improvement Plans" which were very detailed. There was one teacher who he thought would have to be let go in her second year. Matt never wanted to keep a teacher for a third year and then deny tenure. That seemed cruel.

On Sunday evening Beth called. "Matt, I'm home and I'm okay."

"How was the flight?"

"Boring, but that's okay. I read a great deal about my mom's condition. After speaking to her oncologist I know she's in good hands.'

"That's great."

"When are we going to your brother's wedding?"

"I thought we could leave on Saturday, December twenty second and return to Risenburg the next Saturday the twenty ninth. Steve and Linda are getting married on December twenty fourth."

"No, that won't work for me. I'll leave California on the twenty sixth and fly to Florida to be with my parents. That will give me five days with them. Thank God it's a very long holiday this year."

"I'm disappointed Beth."

"Sorry Matt, my parents come first. We haven't committed to each other and told each other that we can't date or do other things. We're not up to that level yet."

"I thought we were. Aren't we?"

"No."

Matt remained silent for a few seconds trying to process Beth's answer. "I've been thinking that we shouldn't date other people and become a couple."

"No Matt. I'm not up to that as yet. Perhaps later, but not now. I know it's different because I need to be with my mother not you. I'm sorry, but that's the way it is."

Matt's response was in anger. "Perhaps you shouldn't go to the wedding and just spend the whole Christmas holiday with your parents."

"Is that what you want Matt?"

Matt hung up the phone without answering. He was angry and hurt. In fact he felt as if he never should have opened up to her so much. Matt muttered, "Shit!" He felt offended and irritated.

Matt thought. *I really love her, but I don't like her now.*

Matt started to sweat and shake. His anger about the situation was causing him to lose control. He felt waves of anger and sorrow come through him like spears!

The phone rang. Beth was sobbing. "Oh God, Matt I'm really torn. Please don't feel that way. Please. I met you half wayI mean I was going to the wedding." there was more sobbing on the phone.

"Beth, I'm not going to do this on the phone. Let's talk tomorrow after work. I'm not sure I can handle this conversation after the events of this weekend."

"What happened?

"Buy the local paper!" He hung up.

Matt tossed and turned and finally gave up sleeping at three in the morning. He decided to work out at the local gym that opened at five every weekday morning. Perhaps a good workout to relieve the stress would be good for him.

Matt shaved, showered and got into his gym clothes. He zipped up the essentials in his gym bag and hung his suit, shirt and tie in the car. Breakfast consisted of a fruit smoothie and a granola bar.

He arrived at exactly five in the morning. Matt immediately started his stretch exercises and then went into a heavy workout. Perhaps it was his frustration with Beth or his anger about the newspaper article that led Matt to push the limits of his skills. He bench pressed two hundred ten pounds. The norm should have been no more than one hundred eighty pounds for a male at the age of thirty two with the weight of one hundred and sixty five pounds. It was one hell of a workout!

Matt arrived at the school at six fifteen. He was in his office working when Otto knocked and walked in. "Mr. Collins, thank you for your help. My men are cleaning the rooms better and know that the teachers are cooperating. Mr. Jackson showed me your letter to the Art Teacher. I'm really very proud of you. Tell those newspaper people to shove it up their well you know what I mean. You're the best!"

Matt felt much better after hearing Otto. He just had to figure out what to do with Beth. He had to make a choice about this relationship.

## CHAPTER 26

The next few weeks were devoted to observations, teacher conferences, District meetings and evening PTA events. Matt established a routine of working out at five in the morning. He felt energized after the workouts and was surprised when he weighed himself after two weeks. Without even trying he lost six pounds and hardened up his body core.

There was only one problem. Beth was civil to him and he to her, although they did not make much eye contact. It seemed to him that she was over-reacting to her mother's illness. However he thought, *Perhaps I over-reacted to her.*

The bell for the last period of the school day sounded. Immediately after that Maggie buzzed. "Shelly Katz to see you."

Matt learned over the past few months that Shelly Katz was one of the most respected faculty members of the school. She was an outstanding counselor and teachers did go to her for their own personal problems. Mrs. Katz opened the door and immediately sat down at Matt's small table. "Mr. Collins may I speak to you off the record. I mean from a place that's in my heart to a place that is deep in your heart." Her voice resonated with passion.

Matt was stunned with her tone, articulation and demeanor. She seemed very much in control of the total situation.

"Yes." That was the best he could say.

"Beth is in a very bad way psychologically. She can hardly perform her duties because of this rift both of you have had. There are mornings she comes in red eyed from crying. There are days she doesn't want to eat at all. There are days that she is just a total non person. I think you better get on the ball if you love her because she's ready to turn in on her self and that means bad trouble. She has told me all. I'm telling you all because I think you are one hell of a man who I respect and I think Beth is a noble woman who loves you passionately and loves her family passionately!"

Matt's expletive came out rapidly. "Oh shit! What am I going to do?"

"You go upstairs now, and take her off the school premises! Now, both of you go to a secluded place and make peace with each other! Do it now!"

Shelly Wax slammed her hand on the table, turned around and left Matt with his mouth wide open.

"Maggie, tell Central office that I will be leaving right now and I will be off tomorrow for personal reasons. Let Jerry know as well."

As the kids were going downstairs to their buses Matt was marching upstairs to the Guidance Office. He got to Beth's office, opened the door and quickly closed it. He proclaimed "Beth, I love you, I miss you, I need you and I am truly sorry for being such a stupid man and"

Beth shut him up by kissing him long and hard. She continued to hug him. "Shut up and kiss me again."

* * *

They ended up in Matt's apartment because it was closer than hers. "I just didn't get your real message. That overall distress about your mother. The word 'treatable' caused me to think that everything would be alright. However I didn't visit your mother and see her condition. I was just an ass thinking about my needs, my schedule, my wants. I was stupid! I am so sorry. I regret my actions."

"Okay Matt. 'I' statements only. I didn't think you would mind me visiting my mother during the Christmas break. I thought that you probably would do the same with your mother if she was ill. I didn't think that the timing was right for moving up our relationship to become a couple. I was wrong about that. I now realize I hurt you. I hurt you badly. I want us to be a couple. I want to spend all my time with you. Matt, I love you with all my heart and soul, I love you."

They embraced and held onto each other. "I'm taking off tomorrow. I'd like to go back to Mrs. Williams' B&B where we spent happy times. Is that okay? Tomorrow is Friday. We can have three days to work on our relationship. Beth, please say yes."

Beth took her hands and placed them on either side of Matt's face. Her eyes were streaming tears as she said, "Yes!"

* * *

Mrs. Williams was more than happy to have Beth and Matt as her guests. There were no other parties booked since it was a week before the Christmas holiday. "I'll let you have the run of the house. The refrigerator is stocked and if you want to cook your dinners here it's okay, as long as you clean up and invite Richard and me. He's not here now because he's going to play a basketball game at his high school."

Beth looked at Matt who nodded. "Mrs. Williams, can we go and cheer Richard and his team."

They had a wonderful time at the game. Richard scored eighteen points and his team won. Matt suggested, "I'd like to take all of you out for a victory dinner. Richard, you name the place."

"Let's go to the China Palace Buffet. I love Chinese food!"

They had a marvelous dinner sharing many stories and many laughs.

That night Matt and Beth devoted themselves to each other. It seemed to them it was a spiritual commitment that would lead to marriage. Beth asked Matt to stay as close to her all night as humanly possible. They managed to do that.

They woke up and showered together. After breakfast they were on their way on the tandem bike going towards that very special little town where they had previously visited. Matt had an idea.

Matt and Beth entered 'The Celtic Shoppe." "Beth, I'd like to buy you a ring that matches your pendant. The Claddagh symbol means a great deal to me."

"I'll wear your ring if you let me buy a matching ring for your finger."

"I would love that!"

It took time to select the matching rings and more time to size them. The owner of the store suggested they go to lunch and that he would have the rings sized by three in the afternoon.

They decided to eat at the one and only pizza restaurant in the village. After lunch they walked to the end of town and back. At three they entered "The Celtic Shop."

"Oh, just in time. I've got your rings."

Matt took Beth's ring off the counter and put it on her right hand, third finger. Beth did the same. They looked at each other and gently kissed.

There was a stream and a lovely patch of grass behind the shop. Matt and Beth held hands and sat down on the grass.

Beth held Matt's hand and squeezed it gently. "Matt, we know each other four months. Now we are wearing promise rings. What do you think will happen next?"

"We are committed to each other. No dating other people. We are trying to become a couple who eventually will become engaged and then married. That's what it means to me."

Beth said nothing. They went back to the front of the store and bicycled back to the B&B. She just continued to smile all the way back.

The couple arrived at six in the evening and heard Mrs. Williams from the kitchen. "We're having hamburgers tonight. Yes or no?"

Beth and Matt yelled, "Yes!"

After saying their goodnights to Mrs. Williams and her son they decided to go to bed before ten. Beth was very passionate and filled with intense desire. She exhibited uninhibited pleasure and let herself have all the exquisite sensations over and over again. Matt wanted to please her so much. He was not a skillful lover although he knew enough to make her happy. This night was magical since he kept strong control over his mind and body. He was thrilled with their union and continued to make sure that he was pleasing his lover.

Finally she urged him on. "Please Matt. Oh my baby, please, do it."

Matt groaned in ecstasy as he fulfilled his mission.

* * *

Late Sunday evening Matt tried to get Beth plane tickets to San Francisco, but all the airlines seemed to be booked for the holiday. He called Steve, "I cancelled Beth's ticket two weeks ago. We had a bit of an argument, but now we're okay. The problem is I can't get a ticket for the twenty second."

Steve chuckled. "Give me your ticket number and I'll see what I can do. I'll e-mail you the information."

Just before going to bed Matt checked his e-mail. He was surprised. Steve had bought them first class tickets to San Francisco. Matt was thankful. He copied down the necessary information to get them boarding passes. Matt called Beth. "Is this too late to talk?"

"Never too late for you and me."

"My brother was able to get tickets for us on the twenty second."

"I'm still trying to get tickets from San Francisco to Orlando on the twenty sixth. I'm on standby on three airlines. I'm sure something will break.'

"Oh I'm sure. Should I call Steve to see what he can do?"

"No, not yet. I love you Matt Collins. You gave this girl the best time of her life this weekend. Thank you."

"The pleasure was all mine."

Matt slept peacefully and missed his five in the morning workout. He did manage to get to school on time.

CHAPTER 27

Matt cancelled his faculty meeting. Instead he wrote a separate holiday letter to all of his staff wishing them a wonderful winter break. He worked intensely throughout the week making sure that all the loose ends of closing down the school would be in place.

As he checked his mail he was surprised and delighted to receive many Christmas cards from his staff and parents throughout the community. He read all the supportive notes and best wishes and felt validated. Perhaps the nicest note was from Shelly Katz, his Guidance Counselor and Beth's friend. It read: "Thank you for putting on your big boy pants and saving Beth's life. I feel blessed to have a person as you leading this school. I am in your debt. Almost all of the staff members feel the same way about you. Of course the slackers have had a problem with you and that's great as well. If you ever need my services, as a professional or as a friend please do not hesitate to call me.

With love and respect, Shelly Katz."

Matt smiled and felt an inner glow radiating throughout his body. He went to his car and brought back three large bags that had gifts for special people on his staff. It was time to play Santa.

"Maggie, please come in and bring your pad."

"Okay Mr. Collins, I'm ready."

He wrote a letter of commendation for Otto, his Chief Custodian. "Maggie, please have this ready within the hour."

"Okay Mr. Collins." She started to leave and Matt waived her down. "I have one more to write. To Personnel Department, cc. Mrs.

M. Carter I wish to commend Mrs. Maggie Carter, Secretary of the George W. Bush Middle School for her outstanding and superior work, attitude and service to the total staff and to me. New paragraph"

"Mr. Collins, you don't have to do this."

"Oh yes I do. The paper record is very important and Maggie, you are so important to me. As my Secretary, but also as my friend and advisor."

Matt finished the memo and handed Maggie a beautifully wrapped box. "Merry Christmas Maggie." He then, very gently kissed her on her cheek. Matt thought. *I hope she likes the designer handbag.*

"Maggie, please ask Otto to come and see me as soon as you finish his memo."

Otto knocked on the door and walked in. "You wanted me Boss?"

"Otto, I want to personally thank you for all the work you have done for the school and for making me look good." Matt handed Otto his commendation.

Otto read the complementary memo and wiped his eyes. "Mr. Collins, I have respect for you. You are a man! I mean you are not like the other principals I've worked with I mean you know what I mean. Thank you sir."

Matt gave Otto a large gift wrapped box. "Watch out, it's heavy."

"Thank you Boss. Merry Christmas."

Matt thought. *I hope he likes the individual coffee maker that uses K-cups.*

Matt called Jerry. "Can I see you for a minute? Right now."

Jerry Jackson, Assistant Principal walked in. "Yes sir, what can I do for you?"

"Jerry, I wanted to wish you a very merry Christmas and give you this." He gave Jerry a small gift wrapped box.

"Thanks Mr. Collins. Its been a very interesting year. I learned a lot from you. When I become a principal I'm going to copy everything you do!"

"Thanks for the compliment Jerry."

Matt thought. *I hope he likes the Italian leather tri-fold wallet. That rag of a wallet he uses has to go.*

Matt took a shopping bag full of gift wrapped chocolate candy and started distributing them to certain staff members. His Office Clerk, the Manager and Assistant Manager of the cafeteria, the Guidance Secretary, the School Nurse and to the three Team Leaders of the school. There were two more boxes of candy left. He would make sure to walk outside to deliver them to the School Crossing Guards who serviced the school. He had spent close to seven hundred dollars in gifts for his staff and he was pleased that he did.

Beth called him at his office. "Matt, I still can't get any flights out on the twenty sixth from San Francisco to Orlando. I even checked first class flights. I checked for the twenty seventh and I still can't get any. Will you call your brother and see what he can do."

"'Okay. I'll see what he can do."

Matt called Steve. "Are you anxious about the wedding?"

"No, in fact my jeweler just delivered the wedding bands that you're going to keep in your pocket."

"Steve, thanks for the flights. You're terrific. Beth has a problem. She can't get a flight from San Francisco to Orlando on the twenty sixth or the twenty seventh. She even checked on first class. Do you have any pull to get her a ticket? She's on standby for three airlines."

"I promise you that Beth will have a flight. Trust me she will have a flight!"

"Thanks big brother. See you on Saturday. Love you."

"Right back at you kid!"

Maggie buzzed. "There is a delivery for you. The messenger told me he has to give it to you personally."

"Okay. Send him in."

A young man in his early twenties came into his office. He looked familiar. "Mr. Collins, on behalf of Mr. Vincent Green and his family we extend to you the very best and Merry Christmas. This is a gift for you." He turned around and left.

Matt recognized the young man as an assistant in the supermarket. The basket was made out of wicker and it was huge. It was wrapped in red and white cellophane with a small note attached. It read. "Merry Christmas from the Green family. If you need anything please call me." There was a phone number written as well. Matt viewed the contents of the basket and he saw all forms of cheeses, sausages, crackers and candies. He smiled and was pleased.

Maggie buzzed. "There is a very pretty seventh grader who wants to see you Mr. Collins. I suggest you see her."

Patricia Collins walked into his office. She did not have a wart or blemish on her face. She looked lovely.

"Mr. Collins. Thank you for getting me a doctor to get rid of my warts. No one laughs at me anymore. I have three friends now and my mother is so happy. This is for you."

She gave Matt a purple silken bag. Inside there was a beautiful rosary. The beads were silver with a beautifully sculptured crucifix. "Oh Patricia, this is lovely."

"They were my grandfather's and my mom and I thought it should go to you."

"Thank you Patricia. Merry Christmas to you."

Matt was touched. He called Anita O'Dwyer, his School Nurse. "Mrs. O'Dwyer, Patricia Mullen just walked in. She looks lovely. How did you get a doctor to help?"

"My first cousin is a plastic surgeon in Albany. I called him and he took the case, pro bono. She is a happy girl."

"And I am a happy man. Please give Maggie his name and address. I would like to write him a thank you letter."

* * *

Beth made dinner on Thursday night. They were going over to the Carters for some mulled cider. Beth had made Christmas cookies and placed them on a beautiful holiday platter. "I'm sure they will love these cookies. It's my mom's recipes."

They shared a lovely time with Jason and Maggie. Beth showed Maggie her new Claddagh symbol ring. Matt raised his hand as well. "This is a promise ring. I promise more to come."

Beth went to Matt and kissed him sweetly. She looked at Maggie and laughed. "Oh yes, much more to come!"

Friday was getaway day for the staff. Matt had suggested to the Team Leaders that the day should be filled with joy and happiness. He asked the Music Teacher to supply the newest songs that the kids loved. Otto piped it into the cafeteria as the kids were eating. The kids loved it!

Matt stayed in the outer office as the staff departed. He personally said his goodbye to each and every staff member. They were a happy group of people who would have a consecutive thirteen day holiday due to the uniqueness of the calendar for this year. He looked at Maggie and his clerk. "Go home. I'll cover the school. I'm sure you have many things to do for the holiday!"

Jerry came out of his office. "Jerry, go home to your family. I'll cover."

"Thanks Boss. Merry Christmas!"

Beth came into the office. "What time will you pick me up tomorrow morning?"

"I'll pick you up at eight fifteen. Oh, Steve told me to tell you that you will have a flight from San Francisco to Orlando on the twenty sixth. His exact words were, 'I promise you that Beth will have a flight on the twenty sixth.'"

"When do you pick up your tuxedo?"

"Steve arranged to have it delivered to his house. It will arrive a day before the wedding so if there is a fitting problem they can fix it."

"What are you wearing?"

"I'm not telling you, although I may have other men after me when they see me in my gown."

"I'm looking forward to that."

* * *

The non stop seven hour and fifteen minute flight from Syracuse to San Francisco was made in comfort. Matt had never flown first class. He was surprised by the attentiveness of the flight attendants. The breakfast and lunch meals actually tasted good. Beth and Matt enjoyed the wine and beverages throughout the flight. However luggage retrieval was a nightmare. They waited forty five minutes to get their luggage. Walking out of baggage they saw a uniformed chauffeur with a sign, "Matt Collins."

"I'm Jack. I work as your brother's driver and steward."

Matt looked at the small man. "What are your duties?"

"If Mr. Collins asks me to go to the wharf to get ten lobsters I do that. If Mr. Collins asks me to help him hang Christmas decorations in the house I do that. I'm more of a house assistant and overall helper. I live in a separate wing of the house and have my own apartment. I love my job."

The trip became a joy as the limousine worked its way out of city traffic and onto the road. "The trip will take about forty five minutes to an hour. Just enjoy the bar and the music selections." The chauffeurs voice sounded calm and collected.

\* \* \*

They arrived and Matt looked at a gorgeous two story high end house. "Wow! "

Jack interrupted him. "Your brother asked me to give you the tour. He'll be home later."

When Steve Collins told his parents he built himself a nice "cottage" in Palo Alto, California it was the biggest understatement of the year. The house was a mansion with high-end designer touches  It was light, fresh and airy with many windows. The floor plan was excellent with a guest suite on the first floor. The suite had huge walk in closets and an er. suite bathroom. There was a lanai attached to the guest suite with a table and chairs to eat outside if one wished. A huge dining room, a smaller living room and a large family room were tastefully furnished. The gourmet chef's kitchen would hold ten people at least. There were elegant lighting fixtures and almost all the rooms were tiled. Stylish area rugs were placed strategically through out the house.

Upstairs had a master suite with a balcony and three more bedrooms with private bathrooms. In total there were five bedrooms and five bathrooms not counting Jack's apartment which was on the other side of the kitchen.

Jack escorted them to their downstairs suite. "I'll have the luggage inside in two minutes."

He was true top his word. "Have a restful time. Flying from Syracuse is exhausting."

Matt whistled after Jack left. "My brother told my parents and me that he built a 'cottage' here in Palo Alto. What a cottage!"

Beth took off her shoes and stripped down to her underwear. "I'm going to take a shower." She came back in a moment with two white Turkish terry cloth robes. "Your brother doesn't miss a trick. Care to join me?"

Matt took off his shoes and quickly entered the bathroom.

Later, Steve called Matt. ""Look Matt, I'm stuck here for awhile.

I'll catch up with you for a late dinner."

"No problem big brother. Beth and I will keep busy!"

CHAPTER 28

Matt and Steve's parents stayed in a hotel Saturday night since the flight from Long Island was delayed. Jack, Steve's steward, picked them up and they settled into Steve's house in the late morning. The plan was for every one to meet at one in the afternoon for lunch and conversation.

Matt introduced his parents to Beth. His mother hugged Beth "I hope you are keeping him in line. Every once in awhile I had to swat his bottom."

Matt flushed with embarrassment. "Oh Mom, it was only when you could catch me."

Beth turned around and faced Matt's father. "You have a remarkable son Mr. Collins. He has managed to tame a school in just four months after three principals could not do it."

"He tamed some of those terrorists over in Afghanistan as well!"

Beth smiled. "Matt doesn't talk about his service. He just wants to move on."

"He never told you that he won the Silver Star, the Bronze Star and the Purple Heart over there."

Beth looked at Matt as tears started to stream down her face. "Oh Matt, oh Matt, I just didn't want to push it."

There was anguish in his face. "That's in the past. A long time ago. Dad, let it go. Please!"

Just then Linda came in with her parents. "Mr. and Mrs. Collins, may I introduce my parents."

The Kerseys and the Collins greeted each other warmly. What

followed was a joyful scene. Both sets of parents seemed to get along very well. There were some jokes and much laughter. Matt looked at them and realized that they worked very hard to achieve the American dream. Blue collar or white collar, the parents wanted their kids to have more and do better than they did.

Steve Collins made his entrance wearing a chef's hat and apron. He went over to Linda and gave her a hug and kiss. "Okay everyone. We're eating out on the patio today. I'm barbecuing short ribs and chicken. Come and get it!"

During lunch the wedding was discussed. Linda proclaimed. "Tomorrow night we will have thirty people at the rehearsal dinner. The restaurant is a fabulous steakhouse with a view of the harbor. Steve has arranged that we will have limousines as our transportation. Wear your dressy dresses and men, jackets and ties are required"

Steve interjected. "The same limousines will take us to the church for the wedding. Don't tip the drivers since they have all been taken care of!"

Ice cream cake was served as dessert. There was a picture of Linda and Steve on top of the cake. They were kissing each other.

"Linda and I have some last minute items to take care of in terms of the wedding. Enjoy the pool, the Jacuzzi, the grounds. If you want to go into town for anything last minute shopping, let Jack know. He'll drive you into town."

Since the house had five bedrooms and five bathrooms there was no problem housing everyone. Matt was astounded with the casualness of Steve and Linda as they approached their important date.

Mrs. Collins approached Beth. "I really did not expect such an elegant restaurant for the rehearsal dinner and I'm afraid my dress is not as dressy as I would like. Beth, will you go into town with me and help me choose one that might be more appropriate ?"

"It would be a pleasure. I'm sure we can get something just right for you. Why don't we freshen up and meet in an hour."

* * *

Beth and Matt walked together through the large garden in the back of the house. "I'm going into town with your mom. She needs to find a dress for tomorrow night. I really like your mom. She is gentle and caring. I'm so sorry that your dad made you feel uncomfortable. The truth is I knew you were a very special man when I met you. I'm very proud of you serving our country and being a hero."

"Beth, I lost some men on missions. They are the real heroes. I was lucky to get out of it alive. When you lose even one man you've lost a brother."

"I can't understand or even have empathy for your feelings in the war. It must have seemed you were in a different world. How could you do it?"

"Believe me Beth, it was a different world. We did it by living only day to day without thinking too much about our future."

Beth squeezed his arm and moved as close as she could as they walked through a beautifully tended flower garden. She wanted to nurture him and comfort him as he talked about the war. Beth realized he was just beginning to open up to her. She thought. *Be very slow and careful asking him about the war. Be very slow.*

Matt turned to her and held her tightly. He whispered into her ear." I'm so happy you are here with me. Thank you."

Beth disengaged. "I've got to run. I'll be with your mother for the rest of the afternoon. See you later."

Matt returned to the house and spent quality time with his brother at the pool. "Steve, I'm really impressed and happy for your success. Better than that, Linda is a great gal. You are lucky big brother!"

"I was in the right time, at the right place and I knew just enough to make it big. It could have gone the other way. My values haven't changed. I don't try to screw anybody whether it's the entry level programmer or one of my hot shot salesman."

"Our parents taught us well."

"How serious are you with Beth?"

"We have promise rings and the next step, after I meet her parents, will be engagement. I have to make sure that it isn't just lust combined with love. Sort of a mixed up affair."

"I know how you feel. You will definitely know when you're ready. It's magic when it happens."

As they were walking back to the house Matt thought about Beth's flight to Florida. "Steve, how is Beth going to get to Florida on the twenty sixth?"

"I've arranged my jet, really it's a shared jet with two other guys. Anyway, Beth will be flown to Orlando and a car will take her to her parents. You can tell her tonight."

"The pleasure will be all mine."

*  *  *

Jack took Beth and Mrs. Collins to town. They visited a few shops and had fun shopping together. A beautiful dress was found by Beth for Matt's mother. It was understated yet dressy in a sophisticated manner.

When Mrs. Collins took the dress to the cashier the young lady at the register scanned it. "This has been paid for by Mr. Steve Collins. I was told you would understand."

Mrs. Collins dried her tears as they entered the limousine. "How did Steve know where I was going to purchase my dress?"

Jack responded. "That was my job. My boss gave me his platinum credit card and told me to take care of business. He loves you very much."

In the limo Mrs. Collins held Beth's hand. "Beth, Matt may seem to be tough with people. Let me tell you as his mother, he is kind and caring on the inside.

Beth realized that his family was a loving, affectionate, and devoted family.

CHAPTER 29

The restaurant at the rehearsal dinner was spectacular. The warm wood walls were highlighted by elegant crystal chandeliers. Each table had a fabulous place setting with tall crystal wine glasses and water goblets glistening.

Filet mignon was on the grill and special sauces highlighted the fish dishes. Right before the dessert Matt stood up and tapped on his glass with a spoon. "Okay gang, quiet down, I have a few things to say. I'm Matt Collins, Steve's little brother and Best Man. This has been one of the most pleasurable times I've had in my life." He lifted his glass and looked at Steve and Linda, then Mr. and Mrs. Kersey and finally his mom and dad. "Here's to the parents of Linda and Steve. They have set an example of hard work and superlative values. Our parents have laid the foundation for these two super people. Now a bit of a toast taken from the land of saints and scholars."

Every body started to applaud. There were whistles and a few tables started singing "When Irish Eyes are Smiling."

"Settle down, settle down. You're ruining my moment!" People laughed, but they settled down. He looked at Steve and Linda, lifted his glass and began. "May you be poor in misfortune. Rich in blessings. Slow to make enemies. Quick to make friends, but rich or poor, quick or slow. May you know nothing but happiness from this day forward!"

Steve hugged his brother and whispered. "Do you have one for tomorrow?"

"You bet. I've got a great one."

Beth got up and hugged Steve. She kissed him affectionately. "Thank you for flying me to my parents. This will not be forgotten. Matt told me earlier today. Let me quote something from my psychology professor who loved Henry James. 'Three things in human life are important, the first is to be kind; the second is to be kind; and the third is to be kind.' And that fits you!"

\* \* \*

Matt's tuxedo fit perfectly. He had a tailor from a men's shop measure him in New York. He then sent the measurements to Steve's chosen tuxedo store. The cut was tailored and Matt was pleased that he worked out and remained slim.

Beth walked out of the bathroom and she looked spectacular. Her magnificent gown was Christmas red and form fitting. The neckline was low, in fact décolleté, yet elegant. "You look marvelous in fact stunning!"

Beth smiled. "I hope my neckline won't embarrass you."

"Your gown fits you perfectly. It says that you are sophisticated, stylish and classy. Only a woman who is sure of herself and mature could wear a gown as yours."

"Matt, I'm so happy you have a good vocabulary!"

They both laughed.

\* \* \*

The church wedding was smooth and many of Steve's employees attended. Matt thought. *That's certainly loyalty to my brother.*

Beth and Matt sat in the limousine with the newly married couple. "Linda, what name are you going to use?"

"In our business I'm going to continue to use Kersey. In private I'm thinking of using, Mrs. Linda Kersey Collins. It has a nice ring to it."

"I like it!"

"Why don't you try a name that you may like?"

Beth smiled and hugged Matt. "How about, Mrs. Beth Andrews Collins?"

Matt looked at her intently. "You can start practicing the name only after I meet your parents."

Beth kissed his cheek. "Sounds good to me!"

They all laughed as they drank champagne supplied by the limo bar.

There was an easy transition from the limo to the reception hall. As planned, Linda and Steve would make a grand entrance after they freshened up. Matt would act as the host of the reception.

The bar was already crowded as Beth and Matt walked in. Matt's mother dragged Beth away to discuss something as Matt headed to the bar. He finally got his drink and headed to the head table. Matt was interrupted three times with servers presenting hot and cold appetizers. They were delicious.

The music being played by a five piece band was from Steve's era. Some alternative punk rock played in a softer manner as well as songs from the Kinks and The Beatles. Once in awhile the band played slow music to dance.

The Band Leader announced that the couple will be coming into the hall in one minute. The crowd quieted down. "May I introduce Mr. and Mrs. Matt and Linda Kersey Collins." The crowd applauded and yelled congratulations.

Beth joined Matt at the main table. She noticed that Linda had changed into beautiful long lacey gown, shedding her wedding dress completely. Beth thought. *I like the idea of another dress.*

The food was really good considering they were serving two hundred people. Matt saw the Band Leader point to him, "Ladies and Gentleman please raise your glass as Matt Collins, the Best Man gives the toast." Matt stood up and raised his glass. "Friends and relatives so fond and dear tis our greatest pleasure to have you here when many years this day has passed our fondest memories will always last. So we drink a cup of Irish mead and ask God's blessing in our hour of need."

The applause was thunderous and there was spontaneous singing of "When Irish Eyes are Smiling."

Matt grabbed Beth around her waist and sang with joy and happiness. Beth looked at him and knew that he was the man she wanted to spend her life with for eternity. She joined in and hugged Matt continuously.

* * *

Both the Kersey family and the Collins family spent Christmas day celebrating their new found friendship. Mrs. Collins invited the Kersey's to come to Levittown during the summer. Matt viewed a strong bond happening between both families.

When it came to Christmas presents it was previously decided that the maximum gift per person would be no more than ten dollars. Matt received a small rechargeable flashlight from Beth, a diary book from his parents, a key chain with his name on it from Steve and Linda, and a small picture frame from the Kersey's.

Beth received a silken jewelry travel case from Matt, a diary book from the Collins, a deck of cards and a book of card game rules from the Kersey's, and a box of painted personals with envelopes from Linda and Steve.

Other similar gifts were distributed with squeals of joy, groans of disappointment and lots of fun throughout the exchange of gifts. All knew that tomorrow Linda and Steve would be going on their honeymoon and Beth would be flying to see her parents in Florida.

Many hugs, kisses and goodbyes took place as Linda and Steve flew to Hawaii for their honeymoon. Matt's parents left in the afternoon and Matt would be leaving on the twenty seventh to New York. Matt thought. *I'm going to Florida. I think it is time now. I'm going to Florida and ask for Beth's hand.*

* * *

Flying on standby can be a pain. Matt waited from eight in the morning until one in the afternoon, but was able to get a flight to Orlando. It took five and a half hours non stop. He arrived at six thirty in the evening and called Beth. "Hi Beth, what are you doing?"

"Just about ready to sit down with my parents for dinner."

"How long a drive would it be for you to pick me up. I'm in the Orlando Airport."

Beth started to giggle. "I'll pick you up in forty five minutes. Wait outside at baggage claim. We'll set another place for you and hold dinner. Love you!"

True to her word, she picked him up at the airport. Beth looked at him, kissed him, kissed him again and said, "My God, you've been away for a day and I missed you so much! Oh Matt, thank you."

Matt was determined to ask for Beth's hand in marriage. He knew it was short notice, but he could not wait. When Beth and Linda were talking in the limousine about names and Beth said "Mrs. Beth Andrews Collins" that did it. He wanted to marry Beth.

There was nothing more important than his relationship with Beth.

During their drive back to Beth's parents he thought, *I never had such strong feelings for any person in my life. It's overwhelming and yet calming in the same manner. God, I love her so much!*

CHAPTER 30

Matt had no problem at all getting a ticket from Orlando to Syracuse. He and Beth went through security and had time enough to have a pastry and coffee before boarding.

Matt took Beth's hand. "When we get back let's go to some jewelry shops in Syracuse before we go home. I want to buy you an engagement ring."

"Oh Matt, I'm so excited that if you gave me a rubber band to wear around my finger I would still show it off!"

"I was so excited asking your parents for your hand. I know it's old fashioned, but I wanted it that way. They liked the idea, except your mother who wanted us to have an engagement to last until we knew each other for at least a year. I understand her concerns, but I would like us to get married right after the kids leave school. How about a late June wedding?"

Beth leaned over and kissed him. "I always fantasized being a June bride. Yes! June is great! I'll talk to my mom. She just doesn't want me to get burned."

"Okay. First we get the ring and then I want you to pick a date and check things out with your mom."

"That's a plan!"

* * *

Since they didn't have to get back to work until the second of January the couple decided to stay in Syracuse for another day. That would give them enough time to shop the jewelry stores and exchanges.

Matt had an idea. He called Mrs. Williams whose B&B was close to Syracuse. "Mrs. Williams, this is Matt Collins. I've asked Beth to marry me and I want to get her a ring in Syracuse. Any ideas?"

"Oh Matt, that's wonderful! I'm sure I can help you. My first cousin is an owner of a large booth in a group of stores in West Syracuse. The name of the group is 'Twenty Jewelry Stores Under One Roof.' His name is Charlie Patterson. I'm going to call him and ask him to give you the scoop and not to, pardon the expression, screw you."

"Oh, how kind of you."

"Matt, when you and Beth attended Richard's basketball game and rooted for him and his team I knew you guys were special. If you can drop by to show me the ring I would be thrilled."

Matt checked the address of Mrs. William's cousin and the next morning they drove to a large building. The big sign read, "Twenty Jewelry Stores Under One Roof." Instead of seeing Mrs. Williams cousin they decided to shop around and look at rings and prices.

"Beth, do you know what you want?"

"Oh yes Matt. I know exactly. The most fashionable and the best is called a halo."

"Halo?"

"Sweetheart, it's a ring covered all over with diamonds. There are different type of cuts that surround a larger stone. It's really elegant. I'll show you."

Beth and Matt looked at many rings as they moved from booth to booth. Matt noticed that Beth never went over six thousand dollars at any time. The price seemed to modulate in terms of the total carat weight plus the size of the center stone. A number of jewelers indicated the price could fluctuate depending on the quality of the stone. In about an hour they received quite an education about engagement rings.

They headed over to a booth that was staffed by a large man. Over his head was a sign that read, "Charlie Patterson Fine Jewelry."

Matt approached him. "My name is Matt Collins and this is my fiancé Beth Andrews. We're friends of Mrs. Williams."

"Oh yes. Beatrice called me. You both are school teachers."

Matt answered. "Yes, we're in education."

"I'm just pulling your chain. Cousin Beatrice told me you are a hot shot principal and Beth is a guidance counselor. Okay, down to business. Matt, without trying to upset you please give me a range you want to spend. How much?"

"Between six to seven thousand dollars. We looked around at some of the rings the other vendors had before coming to you."

"Matt, you are such a child. Those are haggling numbers. You never pay retail in jewelry. Never! Beth, what do you want."

Beth went on to explain in detail about the style of ring, the total carat weight, the size of the stone in the middle.

"Do you want white gold or platinum?"

"Platinum."

"Beth, you are a class act."

Beth selected an extraordinary halo ring with a one point one diamond center and a total weight of three carats. It was stunning. There were intricate cut diamonds all over the ring in a lattice pattern. The web of small diamonds brilliantly enhanced the center diamond.

"Okay Matt. I'm making fifteen percent on this deal. That's all. Take this ring to any booth that reads, 'Certified Appraiser' and get it checked out. Don't tell the appraiser where the ring comes from. It will cost you a fee. I'm offering you this ring for six thousand one hundred dollars complete with sizing."

The appraisal came in at eleven thousand two hundred dollars. The appraiser gave them a nod of approval., "If you were to sell this to me I would offer you about sixty five percent of its value. I would buy it for seven thousand two hundred and eighty dollars." Beth and Matt were stunned.

It took about thirty minutes for the appraisal paper work to be finished. Matt and Beth smiled at each other, but said nothing. They took the ring back to Charlie.

As Charlie sized the ring Matt called his credit card company to alert them about the dollar amount for the ring. He didn't want to take a chance that the sale would not go through. He was thrilled.

Matt slipped it on Beth's hand and hugged her. "We are official!"

"Oh Matt, I love you so. Thank you for this beautiful ring. Thank you Mr. Patterson."

"Indeed. This is my pleasure as well."

\* \* \*

They stayed for an early dinner with Beatrice Williams. Mrs. Williams insisted on a first name basis. Upon seeing the ring Beatrice clapped. "Oh Beth, it is stunning. We never had such beautiful settings when I got engaged. The pattern and the stones are exquisite. Did my cousin Charlie give you a good deal?"

Beth looked at her ring and smiled. "Oh, he was wonderful!"

Matt nodded. "We had the ring appraised and we were amazed. He gave us a wonderful deal."

Matt and Beth left after six and got back to Risenburg close to nine in the evening due to a slowdown because of an accident. The trip would have been tedious, but the couple did not care. They talked about their future goals as a couple. Both Matt and Beth were very happy. This was a magical moment for both of them.

Matt dropped Beth at her apartment. He kissed Beth goodnight. "I'll see you at work tomorrow. Will you please show your ring to Maggie first. She'll love it!"

"Of course. Good night Matt. I love you."

As Matt was driving back to his house he started to think about his family. He resolved to call his folks tomorrow. Since Steve and Linda were on their honeymoon, he hoped he could get a message to Steve through Jack, Steve's all around man.

\* \* \*

There is a certain tone in a school as students and teachers get back after a long vacation. The nature of this feeling is one of slowness. This is combined with a quietness that permeates in every classroom, even the cafeteria. It is up to the administration to nurture their staff and to move slowly. There should be caution presenting new policies and projects. Teacher observations should start two weeks after a long vacation. Overall it is up to the principal to set the tone. Matt's weekly newsletter reflected this as he wrote reminders of previous policies and helpful hints for his staff.

Beth came in early to see Maggie. She put out her left hand in a dramatic manner and Maggie jumped out of her chair. Both women hugged. "Oh Beth, I'm so happy for you. Matt and you were destined to be a couple. The ring is spectacular. Oh, it must have put Matt in the poor house."

"He is so sweet. I sort of guided him into a range of rings I was interested in. We had a recommendation from Beatrice Williams, the B&B owner. Her first cousin is a jeweler in Syracuse. We bought from him. He really gave us a great buy. I'm thrilled!"

Jerry came out of his office when he heard both women talking. Again, Beth put her left hand out. "Wow, congratulations."

Matt came out of his office and hugged Beth. "We hope to have a late June wedding and both of you and your spouses are invited. Hey, we better get to work!"

Five minutes later Maggie buzzed Matt. "Jason Carter on the line."

"Congratulations Matt. Maggie told me the good news. We want you over for dinner tonight to celebrate. Is that okay with you?"

"I better check with Beth. Since we truly are an engaged couple I can't make the decision without checking with her."

Jason laughed. "Get used to it Matt. From now on this will happen to you for a lifetime. Get back to Maggie."

Matt called his Assistant Superintendent and Superintendent to tell them about his engagement. They were cordial and congratulatory. He called John Bird, the Purchasing Manager to tell him the good news. John and Matt had gone out to lunch a number of times. There was a strong bond between them because of their military service. He decided to tell all the principals at their next District administrators meeting.

Matt called his parents. They were elated.

"Matt, I really think Beth is a marvelous person. We got to know her at Steve's wedding and she is the right girl for you. Love you!"

"Thanks Mom. Beth sends her love."

During period two, Beth was in her office doing some paper work. Shelly Katz came in to discuss a case when she noticed the ring. "Oh my God. Beth Andrews tell me right now"

Beth cut her off. "Matt and I are engaged. Look at what he bought for me!"

The two women hugged. Shelly went outside and motioned the remaining staff of the Guidance Office to see Beth's ring. They were thrilled for her.

Beth felt so happy that her colleagues responded in such a

marvelous manner. "Thank you all. We plan a late June wedding. There are no plans other than that as yet."

CHAPTER 31

Matt picked Beth up at her apartment to go to dinner at the Carters. He had purchased a bottle of champagne for them to celebrate the engagement. As they started out, the snow came roaring down in an avalanche of white swirling color. "We better make this a short evening if this weather continues. I'm not sure we'll have school tomorrow."

Upon arriving Maggie and Jason hugged and kissed Beth. Matt stood aside and glowed. It was then Matt's turn. He thought. *How wonderful to have such warm and loving friends.*

The champagne was a big hit. Jason lifted his glass. "Even though Maggie and I don't drink, this is a special occasion. May you have a life filled with pleasure as your union grows each year."

After eating a wonderful meal of roast lemon chicken and the trimmings Matt rose and lifted his glass. "May our friendship continue here or anywhere."

Maggie got up and looked out the window. "I think you better be getting home. I doubt if we're going to have school tomorrow."

Beth and Matt said their goodbyes and left.

\* \* \*

Matt was awakened at five in the morning by the High School Principal. "Okay Matt, institute your phone chain. School is officially closed for today."

Matt called his three Team Leaders to start the classroom teacher phone chain. He then called his School Nurse to start the school teacher specialists phone chain. If all went well it would take less than ten minutes to get every person notified. There was a rule that if the next person on your phone chain did not pick up you were to jump to the next person on the list. Then you were to try to contact the missing staff member two times in a thirty minute period. If that didn't work you were to call the principal.

About forty five minutes later Matt got a call from his Music Teacher. "I tried calling Mrs. Higgins, the Art teacher three times. "No answer at all."

"So noted, thank you."

* * *

The blizzard kept the school closed for two days. Matt drove out to the school on Thursday to inspect the sidewalks where the students would walk. They were adequate, but not up to Matt's expectations. Standing outside Matt used his cell phone and called Otto's office. "Otto, get more pellets onto the area where the students come in from the buses. Please keep your eyes open and continue to apply pellets throughout the day."

That strategy worked well as the magnesium chloride in the pellets did their work.

Matt received a call from the Director of Transportation that there would be early dismissal and school would be closed on Friday. He had forty five minutes to prepare the school Matt got on the school microphone and said, "Attention, attention our buses will arrive in forty five minutes. All students will go to their homerooms immediately to await bus instructions. School is cancelled for tomorrow!" He heard loud cheers from the kids. They were going to have a winter three day weekend. He smiled and turned to Maggie. "We're going to have a three day winter vacation!"

Beth called him. "I want you to pack a bag and spend the weekend with me."

"Will you protect me from the elements?"

"I'll protect you. I promise to cover you with my whole body to protect you. I'll make sure. Wait and see!"

Matt looked forward to some quiet time with Beth. There was a great deal to discuss and plan.

He heard Jerry calling bus numbers on the loud speaker. Only one bus was delayed by fifteen minutes. After all the students left, Matt lifted up the microphone. "Attention, attention the total staff is to leave now. Drive safely. Hope to see all of you on Monday."

Otto walked to Matt's office. "Thanks for the tip to continue to apply pellets on the sidewalk. Last year a kid fell and broke his arm. I really thought the pellets would have lasted longer. Good call Boss!"

Matt looked at the weather report on his smart phone. The blizzard would be through Risenburg by Saturday evening. Matt contemplated snowboarding or ice skating for Sunday.

* * *

Matt went home to quickly pack for the weekend. He arrived at Beth's apartment at five in the evening. She was wearing a robe and her hair was put up in a scarf. She looked fresh.

He kissed her and she smelled wonderful. "Love you!"

Beth patted him on his rear. "Take a shower and get into something casual. A tee shirt and shorts would be okay."

"Sounds good to me."

When Matt came back into the kitchen he saw Beth lighting a new candle. She waved him to the table. Beth kissed him gently on the lips. "Dinner will be ready soon. Have some wine."

"I don't want wine. I want you."

"But dinner

"I don't care!"

"Good I don't care either."

When they got back to the kitchen table the candle was well used up. They ate with enjoyment and were delighted with just the idea of being alone with each other.

Matt helped Beth clear the table and put items in the dishwasher. She turned to Matt, put her arms around him and pressed as close as she could to him. She whispered in an intimate manner. "I like you touching me. I like me touching you. I'm yours, mind, body and soul. Oh Matt, you make me so happy. I feel grateful that you are in my life."

Matt whispered into her ear. "I am truly happy because you are in my life. I vow to be the best partner and husband I could be. You are my life's blood. I love you! I exist for you."

Beth started to slowly shake and her body collapsed against him in sheer pleasure. After a moment she pushed back against him and looked into his eyes. "Oh my God Matt, I only thought one could have this special moment in romance novels. You made me move the earth. Thank you darling."

They continued to make love well into the early morning hours. Each partner doing their best to satisfy every need of their lover. Beth and Matt fell asleep near three in the morning.

They slept away Saturday morning. Matt looked outside and saw that the snow was tapering off. He turned on the TV and the weather forecast indicated clear skies for the early afternoon and for Sunday as well. "Beth, when the snow ends do you want to go snow boarding?"

"I want to build a funny snowman and put a carrot in his face as a nose."

Matt was pleased to see her so happy. He thought. *Beth can be so funny and warm even with the pressure of an on coming wedding.*

"I'll use your cork coasters. It will really be a comical snowman!"

And so it was!

## CHAPTER 32

On Monday, Matt asked Mrs. Higgins to see him immediately after school as they returned from the extended snow weekend. "Mrs. Higgins, when it came to your phone number on the teachers phone chain there was no answer. Have you changed your number?"

"No."

"Thank you. That's all."

"Are you insinuating that I chose not to pick up my phone?"

"No Mrs. Higgins, I didn't even think of that. If you were out of your house that's your business."

"I think you are harassing me."

"Well then you can do two things, ask for a transfer or get a restraining order."

The Art Teacher stood up, opened the door and slammed it as hard as she could.

Later in the day the Dr, Hull, the Superintendent, called. "Mr. Collins I just got a call from Mrs. Higgins' attorney. He states that you are harassing her."

"If you mean I'm doing my job then I'm doing my job!"

"Don't be so glib with me young man!"

"Dr. Hull, this teacher has been a thorn in the side of this District for a very long time. The President of the Board indicated he doesn't care about her husband's newspaper. Why are you so concerned?"

"I don't like to go to court and defend your actions. You are a first year principal and I am evaluating you. On the surface you are doing a great job, but your diplomatic skills need improvement."

Matt was really pissed and counted to five. "Either you back me up with this teacher or I'll talk to the President of the Board. You can dismiss me if you wish. That would be the fourth principal in nine years. Sounds as if you can't provide the right leadership!"

"Now just a minute. I didn't mean it that way. It's a troubling situation. I think I have an administrative answer. I'll get back to you later in the day."

Matt called Maggie into his office immediately. He wrote a memo to himself in terms of his talk with Mrs. Higgins and the Superintendent.

Maggie looked concerned. "Are you going to leave us Matt?"

"I really don't know."

The Superintendent called back in an hour. "Mr. Collins, I'm transferring Mrs. Higgins as of tomorrow to Northside Elementary School. It seems they have a first year Art Teacher, Ms. Janet Sharpe who is certified for all grades. Mrs. Higgins is certified as well. There is nothing in the contract that prohibits transfers of teachers. I'm sending a courier over with my official letter. Will you please make sure she gets the letter."

"Thank you Dr. Hull. I think your administrative solution will work out."

Matt asked Jennifer Stanton, the Union President, Jerry and Maggie to witness the meeting with Mrs. Higgins. It took place immediately after school.

"Mrs. Higgins, here is a letter from Dr. Hull, the Superintendent of Schools."

She read it and in a shrill voice yelled, "You can't do this. I'm being transferred tomorrow to an elementary school. Jennifer, tell them."

"I'm sorry Mrs. Higgins. There is nothing in the Teachers' Contract that concerns transfers."

"But I'm a senior teacher. Doesn't that count?

"No it doesn't."

Matt looked at Jerry and at Mrs. Higgins. "Mr. Jackson, you are directed to go to the Art Room and make sure that Mrs. Higgins only removes her personal property. Otto can help in moving any of her items. Mrs. Higgins you are directed and instructed by me as your principal and a surrogate of the Superintendent of Schools to report tomorrow morning at eight in the morning to the Northside Elementary School."

Everybody in the room focused their attention on Mrs. Higgins. There was complete silence in the room. Mrs. Higgins put her hands to her face and wiped away some tears. "I'm being demoted."

Matt looked directly at her. "Are there any questions?"

Mrs. Higgins slowly rose from her chair. She looked at Matt. "No sir."

Jerry followed her out and Maggie left the room as well. Mrs. Stanton remained.

"Thank you Mr. Collins. It is a pleasure to have you as our leader."

Matt smiled after she left. He realized that getting rid of this thorn would sit well with his teachers. Matt felt, for the most part, most of the teachers worked very hard.

The next two weeks of school ran as routinely as a Rolex watch. All the conferences with the teachers about their observations were finished. A few teachers worked with Matt and the High School's Department Chairmen on Teacher Improvement Plans. There seemed to be no acrimony within the school.

* * *

The third Monday of January was Martin Luther King Day. Beth and Matt planned a ski weekend at Labrador Mountain. It was located about thirty minutes south of Syracuse and had a large family ski area. There were six lifts and many different winter activities. Beth loved the idea.

They rented a small A frame cabin that had all the essentials. Electric heat, a small combination family room, two burner stove and a microwave. A small TV set hung from a wall in the family room as well. The bathroom was located in the rear of the kitchen area. Upstairs there was a queen size bed and a large cabinet. It was cozy and comfortable.

Matt was a beginner skier and Beth was an intermediate skier. There were easy trails for Matt. Beth joined him. They departed from each other to take lessons from different instructors. Matt was intent to learn and practice. He was cautioned not to overdo it the first day.

They ate dinner in a small café about ten miles away from the site.

Matt was aching. He was sore in his lower back and his thighs felt as if they would burn off. Although he did not like to use many medications he accepted some ibuprofen from Beth. Matt started to feel better half way through his meal. "I thought my working out would help me in the skiing."

"You weren't working out specific muscles for this activity. Tomorrow I'll show you some stretching exercises that will help you."

"I'm afraid I'm going to be useless tonight."

"Don't worry sweetheart. I'll work something out."

The weekend was wonderful. Matt improved his skills greatly and he took the intermediate trail on his last run with Beth. He was thrilled with his improvement.They arrived home on Monday in the early evening and stopped at the Main Street Diner for dinner.

Nods of approval, an occasional hello and waves greeted them. The couple seemed pleased and happy with their reception. They realized that the community at large was comfortable with their relationship. Both he and Beth were pleased.

Matt and Beth them ate heartily and vowed to return to Labrador Mountain. The weekend was a great success.

CHAPTER 33

Matt's faculty meeting with the staff focused on the next four weeks before the Mid-winter Recess. There were a few administrative matters and calendar changes. These took less than fifteen minutes to cover. "This is our time to make sure our students are targeted on learning. Introducing new concepts and reinforcing them for four successive weeks will certainly give them a boost up. Any questions?"

Shelly Katz stood up and looked at Janet Sharpe, the new Art Teacher. "I've gotten word from some of my kids that they just love going to art. That's quite a change from earlier in the year!"

There was instantaneous applause from the staff. Matt pointed at Ms. Sharpe. "Ms. Sharpe please tell us your overall strategy to have the kids love art."

Janet Sharpe was twenty two years old. She looked like a teenager. Some of the eighth grade girls who put on makeup looked older than she did. "I don't know what I did, although I haven't had any trouble at all. If I ask a young man to cool it he usually does it quickly. I have no idea, but I'm enjoying the older kids. I can do so much more with them and for them and I have found some very talented artists in the school. I would like to start an after school Art Club."

Matt regretfully informed her. "We have no budget for that."

"I'll do it pro bono. I really like it here."

"Any reaction from the Teacher Union. Let's hear it now."

Jennifer Stanton stood up to answer. "Mr. Collins, a breath of fresh air is in the school. Let's not quash it with any rules right now."

The total staff applauded again.

Matt quickly responded. "I'll make sure that the school provides Ms. Sharpe with all the art materials that she needs! Any questions?"

There was silence from the staff.

Matt smiled. "Our meeting is over. Safe drive people."

Beth sat in the rear and observed all the teachers. She realized how Matt had galvanized them in such a short time. He displayed much courage as he handled one problem after another. Matt had an inherent quality to lead. No wonder his men followed him into the jaws of hell during the war. She loved him more each day she was with him.

The following day a peculiar incident happened in his office. Maggie buzzed. "A Mr. Evan Johnson, Special Agent of the FBI to see you."

A large man entered and Matt ushered him over to his small table. "May I see your identification, please?"

"Sure, good thinking Mr. Collins."

Matt read the blue letters of his name on a white background. There was a gold seal on the left side of the card. Underneath the name was an identification number. A badge was attached to the bottom of his identification case. "What do you want Mr. Johnson?"

"We are investigating Nick Decanio, father of Julius Decanic, a sixth grade student in your school. We know he and his family left the school during the Christmas vacation. Did you send any school records to a school in the United States?"

"Why do you ask?"

"We want to catch up with him!"

Matt looked at the man very carefully. He was wearing a suit that must have cost five hundred dollars and his shoes were Italian leather. The agent seemed very slick. "Will you please wait outside on the bench in the outer office. I have to check on your credentials."

"Listen Mr. Collins, do I have to get a subpoena and call your superiors?"

Matt stood up and took the agents arm. He escorted him out of his office. Then he called the Syracuse office of the FBI and the Albany office of the FBI. They had no record of an FBI agent called Evan Johnson. Matt called Maggie. "Please tell the FBI agent to wait."

"Sorry Mr. Collins. He ran out of the office quickly."

"Okay, no problem." Matt thought. *This impersonator probably worked for the mob and was trying to locate one of their runaways.*

"Phone call for you, Mrs. Linda Collins calling."

"Hello Matt. Congratulations on your engagement."

"Thanks Linda. How was your honeymoon?"

"Fabulous. Hawaii is a great place to visit. Listen Matt, Steve wants to give you an engagement gift and he doesn't know what to do. Would you mind if he sent you a check?"

Matt understood why Linda called. "Linda, I'm neutral on the idea. Why don't you bounce it off Beth. She's smarter than I am on these things. I'll get you transferred."

Fifteen minutes later Beth called Matt. "We are getting matching Movado watches. I've always admired the designs, but they were too expensive. Linda and Steve want to do something special for us. She is a very persuasive person. I asked her to keep to the basics and she promised she would do that."

"Beth, I just didn't know what to do. The etiquette is beyond my pay grade."

"I'm changing the agenda. We have to talk about the Mid-winter Recess. I'd like to fly to see my folks."

"Ouch, I'd like to see my folks."

"Let's talk about it tonight. How about if I bring in some pizza and we can have dinner at my place?"

Matt cleared his throat. "Okay. This will always be a problem. How will we split our time with our loved ones?"

"Sweetheart, I'm sure we can figure something out."

They decided to continue to see their parents individually for holidays until their marriage. Then it would be a matter of swapping off vacation periods and holidays. Matt thought. *Being a couple brings on challenges that I never thought of. I'm glad Beth is flexible.*

* * *

The following week Matt received the New York State testing schedule. English and Math would take place the first and second weeks of April followed by a week of Spring break. He called a Team Leader meeting.

"Mr. Jackson and I will be monitoring you and your teachers during the testing periods. I intend this to be held to the strictest rules of testing. Make sure to tell the teachers that any cheating will be dealt with in the harshest manner. The students will have to follow the explicit rules as promulgated by the New York State Education Department and the Office of State Assessment. Any questions?"

Team Leader Julia Lovell raised her hand. "Last year we had twelve students opt- out of taking the tests. Where do we put them if they come to school?"

"The auditorium will be a study hall for those students. Luckily I found out from the PTA that most of the parents approve of the testing program. Obviously the Core Curriculum has been politicized by some."

Team Leader Tim Franklin spoke up. "Should we let our ESL students take the test?"

"No. They are to take the New York State English as a Second Language Achievement Test. The ESL Teacher will administer it."

Team Leader Sam English immediately asked an understandable question. "Mr. Collins, we have made accommodations for our students who are anxious about testing. We provide them with quiet rooms and we try to have our Counselors available. Should we continue to do this?"

"We must follow New York State guidelines. Those students previously identified as handicapped will have extended time or whatever their Individualized Educational Program provides. The student who just seems anxious or asks you for help will be reviewed by me. If this pattern was seen before, as in normal tests throughout the year, I would accommodate the student. If it suddenly comes up during New York State testing I probably would not. Am I clear?"

All the Team leaders understood the policy.

Matt thought. *I will watch you like a fox watching the hen house!*

CHAPTER 34

The first week in February started off well. There were only some slight snow flurries and all the buses came in on time. Matt asked Jerry to come into his office. "Jerry, here is your half year evaluation from me. Please read it over and let me know what you think. You have helped me tremendously and I wish to thank you again."

Assistant Principal Jerry Jackson stood up and shook Matt's hand. "If you were to go to another school I'd ask to be transferred with you. You are a great boss!"

Matt was ready to go to the cafeteria to check on student noise when Maggie buzzed. "Mr. Collins, please pick up. Some really bad news."

"Mr. Collins, this is Head Nurse Bradford calling from the hospital. Mr. Eric Wall has died. I believe Mrs. Wall is a teacher in your school. Will you please let her know and ask her to come to the hospital."

Matt was stunned. Mrs. Hope Wall was a seventh grade social studies teacher who was excellent. She had only taken a few days off during the new year because her husband was ailing. He had congestive heart disease. Matt thought. *Do I tell her or should I just send her to the hospital?*

"Maggie, have a Teacher Assistant cover her class for the day and send Mrs. Wall down to see me."

Mrs. Wall came into the office looking strained. "Mr. Collins, is everything alright?"

"Mrs. Wall, please sit down."

She continued to stand. "Please tell me."

"Hope, your husband passed away at the hospital. I just got the call."

She collapsed into Matt's arms and started to whimper. He held her gently, "I'm so sorry for your loss. So sorry."

This lasted for almost a minute. Then she separated from him and wiped her eyes. "I've got to go. I won't be back for at least a week."

"Let Maggie know about the details." He walked out with her to the front office.

Mrs. Hope Wall left his office in a dignified manner. She even signed out at the front register.

Matt thought. *This was just as bad as death in the service. It always hurts.*

"Maggie, make sure to get the information about Mr. Wall. I want to attend the funeral and I'm sure some teachers would want to go as well. Make sure Jerry gets the news and find Sam England, Seventh Grade Team Leader. I want to talk to him."

Matt notified Mr. England of the situation and called substitute procurement for one of his regular substitutes to cover for the week. The school had a group of excellent substitutes who Matt called "regulars." Some of them were originally full time teachers who chose to raise families. There were several who were trying to get full time employment in the District. He had a good handle on most of the substitutes.

Beth stayed with Matt in his office after school was over. "How are you doing?"

Matt looked at her and answered as he shrugged. "I'm okay in one respect, that is the school is running well. I'm not okay with my meeting with Mrs. Wall. It hurt. It really hurt!" He lowered his head and when he raised it tears ran down his cheeks.

Beth hugged him. "Death is something most of us don't even want to think about."

"I thought about it for two years in the Rangers. I thought about it every day."

"Sweetheart, let's go home to my apartment. Please stay with me tonight."

Matt thought. *God bless her. She is a comfort!*

Beth reflected on Matt's overall condition. She recognized that he was suffering from Post Traumatic Stress Disorder. The syndrome would come up quite often in talk about death or in death of a friend or loved one. The result is usually situational depression. She recognized Matt's situation and vowed to have him talk to her about his war time experiences. Catharsis is one of the best tools available. It is the process of letting go or releasing. In this manner it provides relief from strong or repressed emotions. You don't have to be a psychotherapist to listen. Just give your loved one the gift of listening.

* * *

The couple had chef's salads for dinner followed by some fresh fruit for dessert. Matt ate sparingly and Beth did not mention it to him or encourage him to eat anymore.

She realized that he was down and food wasn't the highest priority for tonight. "Hon, why don't you turn on the national news for tonight while I finish up. I'll be through in a few minutes."

Matt started to watch the news and fell asleep. When Beth came in she covered him with a light blanket and decided to read. At ten thirty she made sure Matt was still covered and went to bed.

Later, she felt his warmth and the awareness of his body. He spooned her and she was happy. Beth wiggled to make sure they had a tight fit. She loved him and his body. They fell asleep that way until the alarm woke them at six in the morning.

* * *

Later in the week Maggie heard from Mrs. Wall about the funeral. There would be a viewing from nine to ten thirty in the morning and a mass at the Catholic Church at eleven. Matt asked the Team Leaders to work out a schedule with the teachers. He would make sure that there would be four extra substitutes that day.

Matt and Beth went into the funeral home with a group of teachers. Hope Wall was overjoyed to see them. There were many hugs and many tears. When Matt and Beth approached her, she greeted Matt with a warm hug. "Mr. Collins, thank you for making sure my friends from the school are able to be here with me. You are a very special man and I'll remember your kindness forever."

Beth heard her and realized that her man was so very special. He went out of his way to make sure Hope Wall would have plenty of people to be with her as she mourns. Beth's eyes filled with tears as she thought of the sorrow that Hope was feeling.

The Catholic service was beautiful and very comforting. Matt looked around and realized that the Team Leaders made sure to have Catholic teachers covered by substitutes or Teacher Assistants for the service. He thought. *They did a good job and I'll let them know.*

Matt held Beth's hand and prayed. He prayed for help with his depressed feelings about the war. He prayed for a good life with Beth. He prayed for deeper understanding about his life's journey.

Beth prayed for wisdom to help Matt get over his painful feelings of depression. She prayed that the wedding would be great. She prayed that their life together would be wonderful.

The teachers returned to the school by one in the afternoon. Matt called Jerry on his cell phone. "Jerry, I'm taking Beth out to lunch in the country. You've got the school for the rest of the day!"

CHAPTER 35

Matt and Beth looked at each other over a low fresh flowered centerpiece. Jason Carter recommended this restaurant to Matt. He remembered Jason's words. "If you ever want a restaurant to really relax and chill out its called 'Bryan's Café'."

They served only organic and vegan food. The menu was quite different. They ordered a watermelon and baby kale salad with grilled mushroom for a starter. Then the Chef, Bryan, prepared a barbecued smoked tofu with tomatoes, scallions, and steamed green beans. Bryan came to the table with his roasted corn gravy and gently poured it over their main meal. "Enjoy my organic vegan style feast! You will love it!"

They both loved it. The couple topped it off with a sticky pecan pudding for dessert. There were absolutely no wheat products in the dessert. Bryan guaranteed it.

"Beth, what are we going to do about our Mid-winter vacations?"

"Let's look at our options. Either we separate, we go together, we don't go at all, or we split our time."

"Great options. We have to eliminate we don't go."

"And we have to throw out splitting our time."

"So its really down to either together or separate."

Beth looked at Matt and realized he needed her. She could nurture him and get him to talk a little more about his PTSD. She remembered how he molded himself into her body as if needing protection. This is the man she would spend the rest of her life with and she made a decision. "Matt, I'm going to go to Long Island with you. All the wedding arrangements can be done between my mother and me through the phone and the internet. We have time. Our week's recess starts the third week in February. I'm going home with you!"

Matt took her hand and squeezed it. " I love you."

"I love you and we're partners. Right!"

"Damn straight!"

* * *

Beth put her luggage into Matt's trunk and they took off to Levittown. The drive from Risenburg to Levittown would take about four hours. She put on her seat belt, squeezed Matt's arm and kissed him on the cheek. "Let's get going. We have a lot to discuss on the way to Long Island."

"What's the issue?"

"Money for the wedding. Let me give you some history. My dad was a corporate accountant in a medium size company in Pennsylvania. He made a good living, but nothing special. My younger sister died of leukemia when she was thirteen. I was nineteen and in college. Even though the insurance paid for most of the expenses there were thousands of dollars to pay doctors and hospitals. It drained them and they were close to exhaustion when she died. I'm telling you this because you have to understand my position."

"Did you pay for your undergraduate degree?"

"Smith College gave me a free ride. They were looking for talented, verbal, scholars who excelled in sports. I was a softball pitcher with a twenty six and four high school record. I was on the Debate Team and had a three point nine average. My Guidance Counselor, Mrs. Prince, called Smith and they told me to apply."

"How did you do in sports?"

"I made it as an All-Star to the Eastern College Athletic Conference Division Three New England Softball League. Go 'Pioneers!' Anyway my father's company was moved to Syracuse and he moved with them. He joined the Syracuse Republican Club. A few years later they needed a live body to run against the incumbent State Senator. My father, at the age of fifty four, volunteered and he won because the Post-Standard newspaper found out that the Democrat was stealing money from his campaign funds."

"Wow. That's really unique."

"My father served six two year terms and loved every bit of it. Now he has a State pension, Social Security and my mom has Social Security. They live a nice life, but they really don't have big money."

"What's your point?"

Beth moved closer to Matt. "I want to pay for most of the wedding. I've saved thirteen thousand dollars. There will be at least one hundred and twenty people invited. At about one hundred dollars a person that's twelve thousand dollars. I still need a wedding gown, shoes, veil etcetera."

"Are we a couple?"

"Of course."

"I have most of my money tied up in pension funds, but I do have nine thousand dollars after paying for your ring and I have thirty five hundred in U.S. bonds. Let's split the cost of the wedding!"

"Are you sure?"

"You bet I am. That's a done deal! Beth, I want you to get the wedding gown of your dreams. You're not going to do this over again so make it right!"

\* \* \*

Matt's mother had connected with Beth's mother after Matt told her about his engagement. They became close phone friends, talking almost every other day about the wedding.

Mrs. Collins hugged Beth and laughed. "I'm so pleased with your parent's attention to detail. The last Sunday of June for the wedding sounds marvelous to us. We've discussed a number of things such as wedding invitations, flowers, grooms men gifts, bridesmaid gifts, limousines, the rehearsal dinner, the wedding cake, and our dresses for both occasions and"

"Wait Mom. Beth and I are going to pay for the wedding."

Matt's dad spoke in a quiet voice. "We know our limitations and I promise you we will not go into hock for all of these things. Beth, your mother told us that you would pay for the reception, your gown, and other costs."

"Mr. Collins, Matt and I are splitting the costs. We are partners and between us we can handle a great deal of the expenses. I spoke to my mother a few weeks ago about the wedding and she is searching for an appropriate hall. I just didn't realize that you guys were so close."

"We really like your folks, Beth. They are good people."

Beth rushed into Mr. Collins arms and hugged him. Mrs. Collins was next as the family laughed and cried at the same time. It was joyous.

The week went very fast. Matt and Beth spent one day in New York City seeing a show and checking on new styles of wedding gowns. Beth liked one particular gown and asked the saleswoman the price. It staggered both of them.

"If this is the New York City price I'm sure I can get it in Syracuse at a forty percent discount. Everything is more expensive in the Big Apple."

Matt introduced Beth to some of his friends on Long Island who would be groomsmen.. There was a great diversity among them a banker, a golf professional, a teacher, and a shop owner. Beth was pleased because she had planned on four bridesmaids.

Matt hooked up a video camera for his parents computer. They established a link with Beth's parents and were able to see each other as they talked. It was decided that the Collins' would fly down to visit the Andrews' in a few weeks. Both sets of parents were excited to help plan the wedding.

"Mom and Dad, please don't break the budget."

Matt's mom hugged him. "Son, this is thrilling. We are eager and happy to be part of this wedding. Beth's parents are marvelous. I predict we will become very good friends."

The last day the couple spent on Long Island they drove to Montauk Point Lighthouse. They walked up about one hundred steps and moved to the balcony. The view was fantastic. Even though it was February and cold it was worth it. Long Island Sound had a dark blue color and it glistened under the winter sun. They saw some fishing boats, large sailboats, two ferries, and one huge yacht coming into port.

Matt took Beth to one of his favorite restaurants in Montauk. It had been established in the eighteen eighties as a whaling station and morphed into a restaurant.

The outside wooden walls were weather beaten and had an antique quality about them. Inside there was a huge horseshoe bar and tables placed along massive windows so anyone could enjoy a great view of Long Island Sound.

Later they ate Manhattan clam chowder, steamed mussels in white wine sauce, and soft shelled crabs with chips. It was a feast that one could only find in special places. "I used to go here with my buddies and have a few beers. The management kept pretty good control of us. I wanted to show you some of my haunts when I was growing up."

Beth was so happy that Matt was loosening up. He seemed more relaxed and really in his element. "Do you plan to go back to Long Island?"

"That would be my wish, but only with both of us agreeing. When I said we are partners I truly meant that."

Beth looked at Matt across the table and realized that he seemed centered and happy right on his home turf. She resolved to support his wish of returning one day. Beth downed her coffee and looked at Matt. "I love this place. Perhaps we can come back to it. Perhaps return to Long Island on a more permanent basis."

Matt recognized her affirmation of his inner wishes. "You are so insightful. When we are married, how am I ever going to hold anything back from you?"

"You're not supposed to do that?"

"Even if it's a special gift."

"Well, maybe once in awhile."

They laughed loudly as they left the restaurant, both knowing, in a distinctive way, that there was a bright future ahead.

The trip back to Risenburg was uneventful except that it started to snow when they passed Albany. "Oh, I hope we'll be able to start school tomorrow. You never can make up lost instructional days. The kids really need more time in school."

"Matt, I've worked with a few principals, and you're the only one who seems truly interested in educating the kids. The others were just administrators. I feel exactly the way you do."

"When you are committed to a mission and the leader, you have to really focus all your energy to the mission. It sounds almost military, but it works in civilian life as well."

## CHAPTER 36

Matt's faculty meeting during the first week of school, after the vacation, focused on instructional time. "Ladies and Gentlemen, we have six uninterrupted weeks of school. The last two weeks are centered on New York State tests. The Team Leaders have organized schedules that will be distributed to you. I have received approval to hire two extra substitute teachers for weeks three and four. They will be used for 'prep for tests.' Identify your students who need extra help and assign them to the substitutes for tutorial aid. Perhaps some of our marginal kids who just miss the State norms can reach up and get a few more answers correct. My gift to you will be a hold on faculty meetings during the next six weeks. Your time is valuable. If I need to discuss items I will do so on a group basis, not the total faculty."

There was a positive response to his words. He saw it in their faces and a few teachers spoke to him thanking him for thinking of the kids before anything else. Matt felt validated as an educator. He remembered the heavy work load in terms of curriculum that New York State expects of their students. The teachers had a weighty problem of time management, preparing for tests, and covering all the necessary curriculum items.

Later, Maggie buzzed. "Attorney Nancy Briggs on the phone."

"Mr. Collins, will you be able to appear in court this coming Friday? Your student's case, Harold Daniels, is coming up for determination."

"Just give me the time and place and I'll be there."

"I'm driving to Syracuse for the case. Why don't I pick you up at ten at your school. Is that okay with you?'

"No problem. Should the School Attorney attend?"

"I've already spoken to him. No problem. He will rely on your judgment."

Later in the day Maggie brought in a small package. "UPS told me I have to sign for it. I did. It was addressed to you and Ms. Andrews."

Matt called Beth. "Can you come to my office."

"I'm with a student. How about in twenty minutes."

They opened the package together. The black velvet boxes contained beautiful Movado watches. The card read, "Happy engagement to a great couple. Love, Steve and Linda."

The watches were superb. The distinctive black faced "Museum dial" had a gold dot and the two-tone bracelet was striking. Matt knew about the Swiss quartz movement and the accuracy of the watch. "They're beautiful. Your brother and sister in law know how to pick them."

"Wow, I'm overwhelmed. They are beautiful time pieces."

Beth showed Maggie her watch before returning to her office. Maggie walked in to Matt's office. "Well, may I see your watch?"

Matt lifted his arm and showed Maggie the gift. "Oh Matt. The matching watches are exquisite. Your brother is a class act."

"I think my sister in law is the class act, but we'll just say both of them are!"

Matt was picked up by Nancy Briggs on Friday. She drove a late model German car that announced prestige to all who could see. He sat down next to her and looked closely at her. Her cream complexion and striking dark eyes presented a remarkable picture of beauty. She down played her looks with a minimum of makeup and a dark blue business suit. Nancy smiled, "You can sit closer so we can talk. I promise not to bite you."

Matt shifted a few inches towards her, but kept his distance. "Do you live in town?"

"I live just past the town's border. I own a working apple orchard with about two hundred acres of trees. New York State is a high producer of apples. I have a manager and in a good season I could net close to ninety thousand. In a bad season, if blight and disease hits us, I can lose up to ninety thousand. So far I've been very lucky."

Matt thought. *She is quite independent and strong.*

"How did you get the property?"

"It was my deceased husband's farm. He died of a sudden heart attack five years ago."

"I'm very sorry. I didn't know."

"Forget it Matt. May I call you Matt?"

"As long as I can call you Nancy!"

They both laughed and the rest of the drive to Syracuse was easy. He told Nancy about Beth and their engagement. She told him about kissing a lot of frogs to find a prince.

Again they laughed together.

\* \* \*

The court building was old. Matt read the corner stone eighteen ninety nine. Nancy took his arm and steered him into a waiting room. They sat on a wooden slatted bench. "Matt, just tell the judge your opinion as an educator and an expert who understands children. Tell the judge why Harold Daniels should be tried as a child. Don't even use the word 'family court' or anything legal. Leave that up to me. Okay?"

"You're the boss. It sounds pretty simple to me."

The bailiff asked them to move to the courtroom. It was just a large room with a small desk resting on a platform no higher than six inches. They were quickly seated. "All rise for the Honorable Kathryn Jergins."

Judge Jergins looked at Nancy Briggs and a tall man wearing a brown suit. He had a small beard and a spotted tie. "Who are you?"

"Nancy Briggs, Esquire representing Harold Daniels."

"And you?"

"Daniel Silver, representing the State."

"Mr. Silver, I read the case file this morning. What are your recommendations?"

"Since this happened in a public school in New York State we want this case to be determined through criminal court. No one has the right to come into a school to attempt to murder teachers or personnel. This is a simple matter of charging Harold Daniels as an adult."

"Ms. Briggs, your statement."

Nancy Briggs stood up and moved slightly to the right of the judge. This caused the judge to look away from Mr. Silver. "Harold Daniels is an emotionally disturbed youth just fourteen years old. His father abandoned the family and his mother is just getting by. Harold is suffering greatly and I submit into evidence the State's psychiatric report as well as our own psychological report. The conclusion, based on both reports, is that Harold was out of his mind when he took a gun into the school to cause harm. I'm not a psychologist so I use the vernacular in this matter."

"Who is this man sitting next to you?'

"May I introduce Mr. Matt Collins, Principal of the George W. Bush Middle School. Harold is one of his students."

"Mr. Collins would you wish to make a statement?"

"Yes Your Honor." He stood up and approached the judge. Matt stood nearly three feet away from her and looked up. "Your honor" he was cut off.

"You're the person who disarmed the student. Am I correct?"

"Yes Your Honor."

"I want to hear that story first."

Mr. Silver stood up. "I object. That's irrelevant."

Judge Kathryn Jergins looked at the State's attorney, "Overruled."

"Mr. Collins, tell me what happened."

"I was in my office and I heard some shots. I'm familiar with that noise since I had a few tours in Afghanistan. I ran out of my office and disarmed Harold. He was not in his right mind."

"Specifically how did you disarm him?"

Matt looked at Nancy Briggs. She nodded. "I was trained as a Ranger so I closed the gap between Harold and myself as quickly as I could. Then I rolled up to him and karate chopped his neck to keep him quiet. I then took the gun and threw it into a corner."

"Since you certainly have a vested interest in this case what would you recommend?"

"I would counsel you and the court to look at Harold as a child. He needs emotional help. He doesn't need a juvenile detention center or youth jail. This emotionally disturbed child needs help. The brain of kids who are fourteen are in a developmental stage. They are developing the abilities to think, to reason and to learn. Their intellectual, physical, emotional, social and maturational stages are in conflict with each other. Harold Daniels had so many negative things happening to him that he just lost it. Your Honor, give this kid a chance to get well. Please!"

"Mr. Silver. Any comments?"

"Your honor, he shot a gun in a school. He was out to murder teachers. It seems to the State that this a pure criminal act."

"Ms. Briggs, comments?"

"Your honor, after listening to Mr. Collins I can only say, I agree with Principal Collins."

"And so do I. The case of Harold Daniels is to be remanded to Family Court for determination. Case closed!"

* * *

They drove back to Risenburg immediately after the hearing. "Sorry to rush you back, but I have a client waiting for me."

"That's okay."

"Matt, I owe you one. You were great in the court. I've never seen a judge make that quick a decision."

"It was just the truth. Nothing more or less about it."

"I want you and Beth to come out to my farm over the weekend. Nothing to do with business. I don't have many friends in town, but I certainly would like to be your friend."

"I'll check with Beth and I'll call you."

"Beth better be very good to you because if I met you first I would keep you from meeting any women."

"The problem would be defacto. I work with close to ninety percent women. As their boss I'm always involved professionally. There are times I am their minister, there are times I am their father, there are times I am their therapist, and at times I am their friend It goes with the territory. My job is to get the best teaching out of them. I want to see kids learn. That is my true passion!"

Nancy looked at Matt with an admiring glance. "How long are you going to stay in our town? I think you are a big leaguer who came to the minor leagues for some experience. I'll bet you are back to lower New York in a few years. Maybe Westchester County, perhaps Long Island, a place that will pay you a hell of a lot more than you're making now!"

"Right now I do my job to the best of my ability. No bullshit Nancy. I don't screw around when it comes to my profession. I give it one hundred and ten percent."

"I know more than you think Matt. Jason Carter and I are friends. I know Maggie and she thinks you just about walk on water. Your service record is safe with me as well. I know exactly what you did in the war and I am really proud to sit next to you."

* * *

Matt lifted his piece of fried chicken that came out of a round box and chewed it. "This is really great. I'm not going to count the calories tonight."

Beth took her plastic fork and dipped it into her mashed potatoes and gravy. She quickly finished it. "Thanks for being flexible tonight. I just didn't feel like cooking. How did it go in court today?"

"Harold was remanded to family court. I'm sure the judge will make sure he gets the proper treatment. This kid really screwed up. Psychotherapy and even heavy duty drugs might help him. It's a crap shoot."

"Did you speak to the judge?"

"I got my five minutes in. The judge seemed to understand the case. Let me tell you that the State's attorney seemed ineffective. He was unsuccessful in convincing the judge of anything."

They threw away their paper plates and boxes and retired to the living room. "Let me show you a few pictures of some wedding gowns I found on the internet."

The rest of the evening they huddled at Beth's computer looking at different style gowns, tuxedos, possible groomsmen gifts and bridesmaid gifts. Matt was amazed that there were so many options and so many different prices. He thought, *I guess this is the most important event of our lives. Let's try to make it as perfect as possible!*

"We have more research to do. I'm tired and want to take a shower. Tomorrow is Saturday. Do you want to go into Syracuse to check on gowns?"

Matt smiled, "I'd like to try Albany first. After all, it is the State's Capital. Any way I know of a pizza place there that is terrific!"

"Okay. It looks like your stomach wins over Syracuse."

Matt grinned, "I'm going to shower first. Okay?"

Beth nodded and continued to work at the computer. She was happy that Matt was a true partner in their wedding plans.

As Matt showered he saw Beth's figure through the opaque door. She stepped into the shower and hugged Matt. "Are you really tired?"

He lifted her off her feet. "Not that tired!"

The water flowed all over them as they laughed and scrubbed each other clean. Then the fun really started!

## CHAPTER 37

Matt and Beth visited Albany. They went into four stores that carried wedding gowns. The good news was that they were all located on or around Central Avenue. Beth tried on many and asked Matt his opinion. "Hon, I'm prejudiced. Everything looks great on you."

"Okay Matt. You're no help at all. Next time I'll ask Maggie and Shelly to go with me."

They turned around and headed back to Risenburg. Matt put his hand on his head. "Oh shit, I forgot to call Nancy Briggs. She invited us over to her farm for the weekend."

"Do you have her number?"

"No. Not with me, but Maggie knows it."

Beth obtained the information. "Hello, Ms. Briggs, this is Beth Andrews, Matt's fiancé. I know it's a bit late, but may we visit you tomorrow?"

Nancy excitedly responded. "Wonderful! Plan to come about noon so we can have lunch together. I'm off Route Five going north. The sign reads Briggs Apple Orchard."

* * *

They arrived a bit late. Beth wanted to bring a small gift. The couple settled on an indoor plant that flowered almost all the time.

Nancy greeted them warmly. She was wearing an old leather jacket, jeans and her hair was made up in a bun. The attorney wore absolutely no makeup and she looked youthful and vibrant.

Matt looked through the eat-in-kitchen's large bay windows. "You have quite a spread here."

"My husband and I were expecting to buy some nearby property to enlarge our business. Then he died. It was sudden."

Beth looked at her and nodded. "It must have been awful. I'm so sorry."

"I'm over it. It took awhile, but I'm over it."

Matt placed his coffee cup down. "No, I don't think you can get over it. You can repress your sorrow, you can sublimate your sorrow, you can rationalize your feelings you just can't get over it!"

Nancy Briggs shook her head negatively. "Oh Matt, I think you're really wrong. I have faced my fear and I have come to terms with my husband's death. There's no set time schedule for this. People mourn in many ways and it takes a great deal of psychic strength to finally be at peace with yourself."

Beth quickly changed the subject. "What kind of apples do you grow?"

"I grow only one kind. McIntosh! It's the United State's most well-known apple. Did you know that we in New York State produce the largest number of McIntosh in the States? They are available starting in the middle of September through early October. Our apples have such a wonderful flavor. We are even known in Europe."

"How do you farm and keep up with your law practice?"

"Beth, I have a wonderful manger who handles almost everything. He makes a good salary and a percentage of the crop."

Matt nodded. "That's a great incentive."

"Let's get into my truck and I'll show you around."

Matt thought. *She drives a prestige car to work and a beat up truck on the farm. Quite a paradox.*

\* \* \*

"I like her. She is a strong woman who is centered. Her home is warm and inviting plus she has a great personality."

Matt continued to look ahead as he drove. "I think she was just fooling herself about her husband's death. It's not that easy!"

"Perhaps it was easy for her. People are different. That's why many go to grief counselors. They have to talk it out and express their feelings."

"Bull! I spent three months with this woman who was a certified grief counselor. Hell, nothing worked. I still feel the same."

"Perhaps she wasn't the right counselor for you."

Matt quickly looked at her. "Perhaps you're right."

The rest of the drive the couple remained silent. When Matt dropped Beth at her apartment he did not accompany her to the door and remained in the car. "I think I'll go home now. That lunch was huge. I'll make something at my place tonight."

When they kissed Beth felt a slight pullback from Matt. She thought. *He is in a bad place right now. A really bad place!*

\* \* \*

It was March fifteenth. "Beware of the ides of March!" Matt remembered his undergraduate world history professor talking about the significance of the date. It became famous as the date of the assassination of Julius Caesar in 44 BC. Some people think bad things happen on this date.

Matt returned from an emergency Administrators meeting at four in the afternoon. It seemed that one of the schools had their roof cave in from the weight of snow. Luckily the kids were already out of the school. A plan to spread the youngsters throughout the District was developed. Matt's school would have to house eighteen fifth graders. He knew that the school could absorb them easily.

Matt went through the front office and knocked on Jerry's door. He was anxious to develop a plan for the new kids. Matt opened the door and saw Jerry drinking out of a small metal container. He smelled whisky. "Oh Christ Jerry, what the hell are you doing?"

"I can explain Boss. Please."

"Jerry, get out of this school now. I'll see you tomorrow morning at seven. Got it at seven!"

\* \* \*

Jerry Jackson finished his Mexican beer and motioned to his brother. The owner of Jackson's tavern finished serving a customer and moved to his brother. What's up little brother?"

"I'm so screwed up. It's really bad!"

"What the hell are you talking about?"

"Matt caught me drinking in my office."

"Christ man! What a dumb thing to do."

"He told me to see him tomorrow morning at seven. Boy, was he pissed."

"Listen. Tell him you've been under a lot of stress. Beg him for his forgiveness. You told me he's a good guy. Play the game on his kindness. Cry if you have to. God, you are so stupid!"

"Is there anything you can do?"

"I'll think about it. Go home and stop drinking. God, you are a stupid ass."

"Please Bill, help me. What can you do for me?"

"I told you, I'll think about it. Go home Jerry."

\* \* \*

Matt got into work at six in the morning. He set up the coffee urn in the utility room and in less than fifteen minutes he was drinking his first cup. Matt saw Jerry coming into work and glanced at his watch. It was six thirty. "Come into my office now Jerry. We might as well get this over with right now."

Before he sat down Jerry started to talk. "Boss, I've been under a lot of stress. That's why I drink. I've got marital problems and financial problems. I don't sleep well and I think I have a real stomach problem. Please, Mr. Collins, give me a chance. I promise I'll never do that again."

Matt looked at Jerry and with as much compassion as he could muster he began, "I hear you Jerry and I can't help you with all your problems. There may be a way to help you with the most important problem you have right now. Jerry Jackson, you're a drunk and need help."

Jerry put his hands to his face and sobbed. "I'll do anything, but please don't tell the Superintendent or the Board of Education. That will ruin my career."

"I want you to take a week off and consider the following. One, go to a rehab facility that will help you with your drinking problems. Two, consider going to A.A. Alcohol Anonymous runs a meeting right here in town."

"I can't do that. People will know me."

"There is a certain trust members in A.A. will have. They won't tell any person about you. You will be anonymous."

"No, I can't do that."

"Then go out of town. Perhaps in Albany or Syracuse. But you must get help."

"No."

Matt stood up and stared at Jerry. "I'm calling Central Office and telling them you will be out for this week due to illness. Come back next week and give me your decision. Now, get out of here before the teachers see you leave."

When Maggie came in Matt called her into his office. "Please cancel any appointments and meetings I have for the week. Mr. Jackson will be out for a week. I'll have to carry the school without an Assistant Principal."

"How sick is he?

"I think he is very sick. End of conversation Maggie."

Matt had to spend half of his day coordinating the move of eighteen fifth grade students to his school. Matt planned to convert a Science-Nature room into a self contained fifth grade classroom. The students were due in on Wednesday morning.

He developed a small task force utilizing Otto and his men for the physical layout. Mrs. Sangria, the fifth grade teacher assigned was very cooperative. A Teacher Assistant was placed with her to help with the transition and movement of books and materials. All specialists had to absorb the fifth graders into their sixth grade classes. They weren't happy, but it was an emergency. The new section of the roof on the elementary school would take at least six weeks to finish.

Matt checked with the guidance counselors to make sure that they would be supportive if some of the fifth grade students needed help. They set up a program and called it a "Mini Orientation" to show the kids around and about the school. Mrs. Sangria was thrilled with the cooperation of the staff.

Mrs Sangria came into Matt's office. "Thank you for all your help Mr. Collins. You and your staff have made me feel that everything will be okay."

" I can guarantee that you and your kids will have a good

experience. I have assigned some of my best eighth grade students as buddies. They're going to take your kids from the bus platform into the cafeteria. I'll greet them with you and then you'll take them up to their classroom. I'm sure the counselors will have fun with the kids as they give them their orientation to the school."

"Thank you sir."

"If there are any problems, you are to see me. My secretary, Mrs. Carter has been told to give a high priority to your needs."

* * *

On Tuesday night Matt had a meeting with the PTA Executive Board. The meeting ended at nine thirty in the evening and Matt went back to his office to check on a few things. At about ten Matt approached his car in the school parking lot. Two large men approached him. "Can I help you guys?"

The largest man came up against Matt and pushed him. "The Jackson family doesn't feel kindly about you spilling the beans about Jerry. If you know what's good for you forget about doing anything. Or else!"

Matt became pissed. He went into combat mode. "Or else what?"

The man threw a right hand punch at Matt who used a judo move breaking the man's wrist. He went down in pain. The other thug rushed him and Matt spun away and hit him as hard as he could in the kidneys. As he went down Matt kicked him in the face and knocked him out .

The big man got up and staggered towards him with his right hand dangling. Matt finished him off with a punch in the throat and knee in the groin. He took off their belts and used them to tie their hands behind their backs.

When they were conscious he looked at them. "Listen you shit-heads. I'm letting you go instead of calling the police. Tell whoever sent you that if I'm harassed at any time I will call the police and spread Jerry Jackson's name all over the town. Got it!"

They hobbled as fast as they could out of the parking lot and got into a white van. The noise of screeching rubber from the tires made Matt chuckle. He thought. *I don't know why I feel so good. I could have been murdered.*

Matt slept well that evening. He did not have any ghastly dreams, sweats or bad thoughts at all. The incident at the parking lot last night was not in his thoughts at all. He woke up refreshed and ready to work.

The rest of the week seemed relatively easy, even though Matt had no Assistant Principal to help him. There were no incidents with the fifth grade students. He stopped in once to see if everything was okay. Mrs. Sangria was a fine teacher and the kids seemed comfortable.

Matt called Maggie into the office late Friday afternoon. "Maggie, thank you for helping me run the school while we were short handed. I really appreciate it."

"Matt, I appreciate you. Have a great weekend!"

## CHAPTER 38

Matt and Beth had a Friday night take-in pizza party. They drank bottled beer and pigged out on a pepperoni and mushroom topped pizza.

Beth informed Matt that she would be busy all day on Saturday. She was driving to Syracuse to look for a wedding gown. Accompanying her would be Maggie Carter and Shelly Katz. "Matt, I need their opinion. They will be straight with me."

"How about dinner when you get back?"

"No thanks. I'm taking the girls out to thank them for their help. How about meeting me for lunch on Sunday at the diner?"

"Okay. Sounds like a plan to me."

"Noon time. Don't be late. I love you sweetheart."

Matt kissed her and she kissed him back. "I'm going to bed Mr. Matt Collins and I expect you to be on time."

He laughed out loud. "Ms. Beth Andrews, I accept your offer and I will be on time. I promise."

They both giggled as they raced into Beth's bedroom.

Two mature loving people, as they were, enjoyed love making which included sex. Matt enjoyed cuddling and kissing as much as Beth. He felt safe, secure, sheltered and at times empowered. Beth guided him to slow down and have fun. Matt began to realize that sensuality really pleased him mentally as well as physically.

He had experiences as she had. Matt was old enough and wise enough to know the difference between lust and love. They fit together beautifully. Matt knew how to please her. At times she guided him and he was a fast learner. There was nothing that was out of bounds for them. He loved her with his mind, his body and his soul!

Beth muttered "Matt" almost all the time. It was part of her nature. She loved his body, yet she loved his values even better. Never in her life did she meet a person who had such strong positive ethics. It had nothing to do with his religion. It had everything to do with his view of doing the right thing for people. He could be working for his brother for three times his salary and living a very prosperous life. Matt chose to help educate children. The man she loved was a patriot and had the physical and emotional scars to prove it.

Beth realized that he had emotional scars from the war. Maggie told her that he was a true hero with a chest full of medals to prove it. He had been to hell and back. Matt grieved for the men he lost. She recognized the dynamic of guilt for surviving, since some of his men did not. Matt needed professional help. Beth could not be his counselor. She prayed that she could guide him to go to one.

\* \* \*

The trip to Syracuse was successful. Beth had read about wedding gowns for brides in their thirties. She stated to her friends that she was looking for a more cosmopolitan look a style made for the city. She did not need fluff as chiffon. Beth wanted a gown that would express her personality.

Shelly articulated Beth's wishes as they were driving to Syracuse. "Beth, you have to find a gown that will make your statement. I look at you and I see restrained elegance and you will need a dress that has to be elegant, not overstated. Am I right?"

Beth looked at her friend with amazement. "Are you reading bride magazines? It sounds as if you are."

"Hon, you need a dress that will show off your body, but in an understated manner."

Maggie spoke up. "Beth, you need a dress that has to combine the best of natural fabrics to emphasize your beauty."

"Oh, I wish Matt could be here to listen to you."

\* \* \*

Jerry Jackson was besides himself. His brother called him. "Jerry, you are on your own. I sent a couple of my old buddies I knew when I was serving time to see Matt Collins. They were supposed to convince your principal to lay off. Well, to make a short story even shorter, he took them on and beat the shit out of them. They told me he used some military moves that surprised the hell out of them."

"Oh shit, what am I going to do?"

"Why don't you see Reverend Mitchell. He was always a good guy who helped us when we were teenagers. Who knows, he may have a solution for you."

* * *

The Methodist Church was in the poorest area of Risenburg. The building was built in nineteen twenty and it had it never changed. Jerry remembered going to church with his parents. He saw a sign that gave the hours of service and the ministers name. Reverend Mitchell was a young minister in his late twenties when Jerry was a teenager. He was still there.

A tall grey haired man greeted Jerry. "How can I help you?'

"I'm Jerry Jackson and I used to go to this church when I was a teenager."

"Do you have a brother called Bill?"

"Yes sir."

"I remember both of you. You were two cut-ups if I remember."

"Yes sir. My parents decided it wasn't worth the trouble to go to church with us."

"Well Jerry, come on into my office and we can talk."

They walked side by side into a large room that smelled of pine. The minister waived him to a chair. "Okay, what's troubling you?"

"I'm the Assistant Principal of the Middle School and my Principal caught me drinking in my office."

"That's quite serious!"

"Yes sir. He told me to take a week off and consider going to rehab or A.A."

"That's good advice."

"I can't have people knowing that I go to A.A. This town isn't that big. People will find out. That will ruin me."

The minister stood up and looked through some windows located on the side of his office. He turned around and stood over Jerry. "Do you know anybody in East Syracuse?"

"No sir."

Every Wednesday at seven thirty in the evening there is a closed A.A. meeting."

"Closed?"

"Closed meetings are for A.A. members only. If you have a wish to learn about the program you would be able to attend."

"Yes sir. I want to stop drinking. I have to stop drinking."

"Alright Jerry. Pick me up next Wednesday at six thirty. You can drive me to the meetings. My eyes aren't as good as they used to be."

"Are you an alcoholic?"

"Yes. I've been clean and sober for fifteen years, but I go to my meetings."

Jerry felt a sense of relief. He would tell his Boss. It was a start!

* * *

Beth and Matt sat in a booth in the back of the diner. "I'm declaring this a no calorie zone for this lunch. Beth, order anything you want."

"Thanks Matt. I'll stick to my two poached eggs on an English muffin. I feel righteous when I order it."

"A synonym for righteous is virtuous. Do you feel virtuous?"

She giggled. "Oh shut up. I'll order a rash of bacon on the side as long as you help me with it."

Matt ordered buttermilk pancakes. When their meals came out he spied five slices of bacon on a dish beside Beth's eggs. He put two on his plate and cut another slice in half. "Okay partner. An even rash of bacon!"

Beth looked at him. She felt really good about the engagement. She thought. *He will be a great husband and perhaps, an even better father.*

After a second cup of coffee they left the diner and took a ride going towards Albany. They spotted the first sign of spring on the side of the road. The forsythia bushes were in bloom. The bright yellow flowers were a pleasure to see after a rough winter.

Beth pointed the flowers out to Matt. "Spring is here by the calendar. Now I know it's here because of those flowers. Just a few more months and we'll be married. I'm so happy."

They drove north of Albany and spotted a farm stand. A large hand painted sign read, "Apples cider jam juice pie apple butter." Matt bought some apple butter for Maggie and Jason. Beth bought some jam for Shelly.

As they drove back to Risenburg Matt declared. "I'm looking up some certified therapists to help me get over some of my grief."

"That's wonderful Matt. Is there anything I can do for you."

"Just explain things to me, psychologically, if I don't understand what the counselor is getting to."

"I'll do the best I can Matt. I don't want to hinder you in any way."

"No, I need you to help me understand my feelings if I don't get it from a session."

"The only way I can do that is if you give me permission to speak to your counselor."

"I trust you Beth. I trust you with my life!"

Small tears ran down her eyes. She nodded, but said nothing.

They returned in the early evening to Beth's apartment. After a small salad for supper Matt decided to go home. "I'm tired. Perhaps the week took too much out of me."

Beth hugged him. "Get to sleep early. It will be a busy week at work."

Matt put on his jacket and turned to face Beth. He thought. *Should I tell her about last Tuesday night's fight.* "I had a little confrontation with a few toughs last Tuesday night. Nothing serious."

"What was it all about?"

"Work related. A confidential case that was blown out of proportion by the other side."

"Did you call the police?"

"No, I felt that the people involved would suffer even more."

"Matt did they try to hurt you?"

"Yes."

"Did you hurt them?"

"Yes."

"How badly did you hurt them?"

"Enough for them to keep away permanently!"

"Good. I hope you taught them a lesson."

"I sure did!"

He drove home in good humor. Perhaps a new grief counselor would help him get over some of his bad feelings. He prayed that would happen.

## CHAPTER 39

Matt drove into the school parking lot at seven in the morning. He saw Jerry's truck and realized that this was the decision day for Jerry. "In a tentative manner Matt spoke up. "Good morning Jerry."

"And the top of the morning to you Boss."

Matt poured a cup of coffee. "Let's go into my office and talk."

Jerry poured himself a cup of coffee. "With pleasure. I've got a lot to tell you."

Matt chose to sit behind his desk. He wanted to establish authority and some distance between himself and Jerry. "Okay, shoot."

"I'm attending the A.A. meetings in East Syracuse. Once a week on Wednesday evenings. I've gone to one meeting so far."

"What did you learn?"

"I've been an alcoholic since I was sixteen. Matt, I never knew that it could be so addictive. Anyway I learned one expression that will help me."

"The slogan of the day: 'Insanity is doing the same thing over, and over again and expecting different results.'"

"Sounds good to me. I'm proud of you Jerry.Keep going and keep learning. You don't have to drink to enjoy life."

"Thanks Boss."

"One more thing. I'm sure you weren't responsible for the little conference I had with two hooligans last Tuesday night. Whoever thought that was going to help your cause was dead wrong. If it ever, and I mean ever, happens again, you are dead in the water. Got it!"

Jerry stood up. "Yes sir. Loud and clear. Thank you."

When Jerry left the office Matt finished his coffee and called Maggie. "Please pull the folders for the last three years of testing results."

Matt reviewed the testing results and developed a presentation to be reviewed by his staff for their next faculty meeting. He had to go to the Media Room to scan in all the data. After that he developed a Powerpoint presentation.

Matt called John Ward, the High School Principal. "John, may I come over today to show you a Power Point presentation on testing that I will be presenting to my staff."

"Come on over at two."

"John, will you have the ninth grade testing results available for me to look at?"

"No problem Matt. I think I know what you're up to. Let's talk."

Matt buzzed Maggie. "Tell Jerry that I'll be with John Ward at two. Don't expect me back to school."

* * *

Matt presented his findings to John Ward. The New York State testing results for the Middle school did not correlate at all. The scores were too high. "John, it just doesn't make sense. Look at the standard deviation."

"I've got a better idea. I'll add to your Powerpoint presentation the ninth grade scores. They are right on target with the State. It correlates beautifully."

"John, would you present your high school finding to my staff"

"It would be a pleasure."

* * *

The faculty meeting covered only one item New York State testing. The Team Leaders presented their schedules. Matt presented modified specialist schedules. Students needing special help were covered, as well as students who opted out of the tests.

At that point John Ward showed up. "Mr. Ward, please join me up front."

There was an excited buzz from the staff. The appearance of the

High School Principal was highly unusual. "Mr. Collins, Ladies and Gentlemen, I have been invited by your principal to discuss testing statistics with you."

Matt waved to a teacher who closed the lights. His computer was attached to a port that sent its signals to a huge screen in front of the staff.

"I'll just cover one item. The term is called standard deviation. Many of you have been out of college for awhile so I'll give you a simple explanation. Standard deviation is the mean of the mean. If we keep in mind that mean in this case means average, then this definition is fairly accurate."

A teacher from the back of the room yelled, "I don't get it."

Matt raised his voice a bit. "Standard deviation measures how much, on average, individual scores of a given group vary or deviate from the average or mean score for this same group. In other words, standard deviations ferret out peculiarities and results that don't seem to be within norms."

The same voice yelled, "Thanks Got it!"

"Now let me show you the last few years from the George W. Bush Middle School test results. Matt marked the deviations in red. He continued to show all the grade levels. The pattern was the same. The significance was a mind blower. "Either we have super kids, super teachers or both. Now let me have Mr. Ward present his findings."

"Ladies and Gentlemen, let me show you that my ninth grade testing results correlate with the New York State testing statistics. Further when we break out specific tests that measure math and science the correlation becomes very murky. In other words, are my teachers less proficient than you? Or are the kids you sent to me not learning as well as they have in your school? Mr. Collins and I cannot prove anything except it sure looks fishy."

The staff exploded with all sorts of noisy statements. Finally, the President of the Teacher's Union, Jennifer Stanton stood up and came to the front of the room. "Mr. Collins, Mr. Ward, are you accusing us of cheating?"

Matt came to within two feet of her. "I wasn't here for last years testing nor the previous years. I only know what Mr. Ward and I have come up with is quite unusual. We plan to look further into the matter."

The Union President shook her head in disgust. "I plan to look into the matter myself."

Matt called out. "Okay, sit down and quiet down. I promise you that testing papers this year will be examined very carefully. If I see, or Mr. Jackson sees, too many erasures and cross outs then there will be an inquiry. This meeting is over."

The faculty walked out shocked. Some had their heads hanging low while others talked excitedly with each other.

"John, thanks for your presentation!"

"Matt, it is my pleasure to know you. You are a true educator."

By the time Matt returned to his office there were two calls waiting for him. The Superintendent of Schools was calling as well as the Assistant Superintendent of Schools. Matt decided to call Eric Bolt, the Assistant Superintendent. He heard a distraught person on the line. "What kind of riot did you have at your faculty meeting? I've gotten calls from some senior teachers who don't like your attitude and your insinuations."

"My allegations come from a statistical study that John Ward and I did. Why don't you come over and visit. I'll show you all the scores and the gross standard deviation units that came out of the study. I think that if you were to visit the school it would be the second time in seven months. I would love you to visit."

"I'm much too busy to visit. Send me a memo with the statistical results. Keep it simple. Good bye!" He slammed the phone down.

Matt then called the Superintendent of Schools. His secretary delivered the message that he was to deal with Eric Bolt over the faculty meeting situation.

Matt thought. *What a bunch of chicken shit leaders in this District.*

Jerry came into Matt's office. "Boss, about the faculty meeting. Last year I collected and looked at the kids testing papers. I thought it was kind of fishy, but I just didn't want to confront anybody. That means I'm as guilty as the Team Leaders."

"Why do you say the Team Leaders?"

"Because as soon as the tests are over they collect the papers immediately. The teachers don't have a chance to even see if any kid's name is on the papers."

"You are taking responsibility and I like that. Listen Jerry, I can't prove that a Team Leader changed a test result. I only have control over this year's testing. I want it legitimate and following all the State rules. Perhaps I'll have a talk with the Team Leaders."

\* \* \*

Theodore Higgins, owner and Managing Editor of the Risenburg News sat in his large leather executive chair and took a puff from his cigar. "Sharon, you are the best reporter I have. I'm putting you on a special assignment. I want you to get everything you can on Matt Collins."

"Mr. Higgins, do you want me to do a hatchet job on this man?"

"No, not at all. A hatchet job is a maliciously destructive critique of a person. I just want to know everything about him bad and good right and wrong constructive and destructive."

"I know that your wife was targeted by Mr. Collins. Is this going to be pay back?"

"No, not at all. He thought. *I'll write the fucking piece myself. By the time I finish with him he'll be railroaded out of town.*

"Mr. Higgins, my son goes to the Middle School and the school is run well. Mr. Collins seems to be the most effective leader the District has right now. The PTA loves him, the staff respects him, leaders in the community are happy with his actions. Why do you want to go in-depth?"

"If what you say is true then he'll be a hero, but don't forget only Jesus walked on water!"

'I'll do it in as fair a manner as I can. Do you have a budget for me?"

"Don't worry about costs. I want to know about his childhood, his schooling, his family, his love life, his service record, and his current affair with a guidance counselor in his school."

"It's not an affair. They are formally engaged."

"Whatever." He waved her off.

She left the office upset with her boss. He always had a hidden agenda on big stories. Obviously this was going to be big. Sharon Silver was a long term resident of Risenburg and did not want to tarnish any of the leaders of the town, unless they deserved it. She thought. *I will be as good a reporter as possible, without making value judgments.*

## CHAPTER 40

Jerry Jackson sat in the back of a meeting room at the Unitarian-Universalist Fellowship in Syracuse. It was seven thirty on a Wednesday evening and he was listening intently to a corporate president who was presenting to the A.A. Group. This was sort of a mission statement type of speech. He learned that Alcoholics Anonymous is an association of men and women who share their experiences with each other. They share common problems and help others to recover from alcoholism. The goal is to stay sober and the only requirement for membership is the desire to stop drinking. Contributions are voluntary and most groups are self supporting. For the most part churches and other institutions offer on a pro bono basis their meeting rooms to support the mission of A.A.

There is absolutely no affiliation with any denomination, sect, political party, organization or institution. There are no causes that A.A. endorses. The only task is to stay sober and help others in A.A. as you follow the Twelve Step Program.

The speaker ended his talk with this, "Sobriety is a journey not a destination."

Jerry felt really good since he had not had a drink for three weeks. He reached in his pocket for the silver chip given to him at the first meeting. It represented hope and desire to stay sober. In one more week he would get a red chip indicating one month of sobriety. He thought. *One day at a time. I have to do it one day at a time.*

He had not seen his brother in three weeks because he did not want to tempt himself walking into the bar. Jerry decided to see his brother on the way back. He felt determined and resolute to stay sober.

* * *

Jerry arrived at Jackson's Tavern at ten thirty. Bill greeted his brother. "Well little brother, haven't seen you in a few weeks. How's it going?" He poured a beer for Jerry and placed it in front of him. "Drink up, the evening is late and you have to catch up!"

Mr. Jerry Jackson, Assistant Principal of the George W. Bush Middle School stood up and pushed the beer back to his brother. "Please pour me a ginger ale. I'm on the wagon and I hope to stay that way."

"Come on little brother, don't you want to drink with me?"

"I'll drink ginger ale, diet soda, water, tomato juice or any other liquid. The only requirement is that it contain absolutely no alcohol at all!"

"Do you really mean it?"

Jerry walked over to a trash can and poured the beer into it. "Damn straight I mean it!" He pivoted and walked out of his brother's tavern.

* * *

Mrs. Celia Jackson, Jerry's spouse, grew up in the hills of Appalachia in West Virginia. She graduated with good grades from Wheeling Community College. Her degree was in Culinary Arts. Celia immediately got a job at a local diner as an assistant short order cook. She worked there for five years and finally became the head short order cook.

One day a man came into the diner for dinner. He ordered liver, onions and bacon. Celia cooked the order and as she slid it out to the waitress she spotted the gentleman. He had reddish brown hair, brown eyes and seemed well dressed. Obviously he was not a regular.

Peeking through the pass where orders are picked up, she saw the man enjoying the meal. Not knowing why she did it, she put on a clean apron and walked out to the dining room. "How do you like the liver?"

Jerry Jackson looked up and wiped his mouth. "Absolutely great. You can cook for me anytime!"

Celia touched his shoulder and squeezed it. "Thanks. You must say that to all the cooks."

"No, I meant it. What time do you get off?"

"I'm out of here at ten thirty tonight."

"I'll pick you up in front of the diner."

Six weeks later they were married. Jerry was a teacher in a place called Risenburg, New York. He was just passing through on a month's vacation touring the Appalachian Mountains. Jerry was struck with her openness and honesty. He liked her from the moment he saw her. There was a certain quality he saw in her that made him feel that he was the only one she cared about.

She in return wanted out of the drudgery of working six days a week with nothing to look forward to except more work. Her parents were divorced. Once a year she would get a birthday card from her father with a twenty five dollar check. Her mother slept with any man who would buy her two drinks. There was no communication between mother and daughter except hateful language and insults.

Jerry stayed in Wheeling courting Celia. She did not want to sleep with him because she felt that he would think she was a slut. Previously she had a boyfriend who could not make a commitment to marry. Celia felt as if she wasted three years cultivating and nurturing her boyfriend. In the final analysis all he wanted was sex, more sex and no commitment.

On their fourth date, Celia and Jerry started petting heavily. Suddenly he pulled away from her. "Celia, marry me. I'm just a teacher, but I'm almost finished with my masters degree and one day I'll be a school principal.'

Celia hugged him tightly, kissed him deeply and said, "I will marry you and love you for the rest of my life."

Celia was twenty seven and Jerry was thirty years of age. They were married by a Justice of the Peace in Wheeling, West Virginia. The couple rented a small trailer to carry her belongings. Jerry's truck was good enough to haul it all the way to Risenburg, New York.

Later they tried to have children. The doctor ran all sorts of tests and found that Celia could not produce fully formed eggs. After two years of different chemicals and prescriptions the couple decided that it wasn't for them. They stopped all treatments and resolved to be a couple.

Celia worked occasionally at the Jackson's Tavern for Jerry's brother, Bill. She was an excellent cook and had regulars asking for her. Two years later Bill changed his approach and cut out dinners. The tavern just provided bar food. Celia quit and stayed home as a devoted wife to Jerry.

Jerry at the age of thirty four became the Assistant Principal of the George W. Bush Middle School. He started drinking heavier soon after the succession of new principals into the school. He felt stressed and pressured and wondered if the Board would ever consider him as the principal.

Jerry was thirty seven when Matt came into the school. Here was a thirty two year old bossing him around. Jerry hit the bottle harder and harder. His relationship with his wife went from passive to aggressive. It was really a bad scene.

* * *

When Jerry returned from his brother's tavern he found that Celia was sleeping. He shook Celia's shoulder and she woke up. "What's wrong Jerry?"

"Celia, I'm going to A.A. in East Syracuse. I go there every Wednesday evening."

Celia kissed him and held him. "Oh Jerry, I thought you were having an affair."

"No, I would never do that. I'm just beginning to understand myself and I have a long way to go. I've been sober for three weeks."

Celia smiled and hugged her husband tightly. "If I can do anything to help you, let me know. What can I do to help?"

"I need to talk to you about my day at school. It's a tough job being the Assistant. I'm sort of the clean up guy, the messenger, the tough guy and what ever job that Matt doesn't, do I do."

"Is he abusing you?"

"No, that's not the point. He even works longer and harder then I do. The man is really an honest guy who wants kids to learn."

"And you?"

"Of course!"

"Then both of you are on the same team."

"Celia, I'm sorry for my behavior. I'll try harder to keep our relationship whole."

* * *

The following week Maggie was amazed to see Jerry Jackson dressed properly. His hair was cut short, his suits were pressed and his ties matched the suit. "Jerry, is that a new suit you're wearing?"

"Thanks Maggie. Celia and I went to Syracuse to shop. I had to pay a bit extra, but they did the alterations quickly. I bought two new suits, shirts, ties, a sport jacket and two pair of pants. Celia helped me. She has good taste."

"You look wonderful."

Later Maggie talked to Matt about Jerry. "Jerry seems like a new man. He's bought new clothes, he cleaned himself up, and I haven't heard him use his wife's name in a long time. What magic did you do to get him going.?"

"Jerry is cleaning his act up. This metamorphosis will take time, but it will develop into something beautiful. Wait and see."

"Well I guess he's using you as a role model."

"Thanks for the compliment, but I think this is all Jerry."

"Well, if it is, I think that this school will run even better. Matt, I am overwhelmed by the way you are able to change negative situations into positive behavior."

"Maggie, I love my job and I love being in a leadership position. Sometimes you just have to focus on the mission."

Maggie smiled and saluted. "Thank you sir. I'll follow you anywhere."

"Anywhere? Let me quote an old Irish proverb about leadership."

"If its Irish it has to be profound."

Matt blushed, " May the gift of leadership awaken in you as a vocation
and keep you mindful of the providence that calls you to serve."

"Well," Maggie blurted out, " almost anywhere!"

They both started to laugh.

CHAPTER 41

Sharon Silver called Matt's parents. "I'm Sharon Silver, from the Risenburg News. I'm doing an article about your son. If I know Mr. Collins, he would nip it in the bud so I didn't tell him I was calling you."

Mrs. Collins quickly gave the phone to her husband. "A reporter would like to interview us about Matt."

"Who am I speaking to?"

"I'm Sharon Silver, a reporter from the Risenburg News. I'm doing a piece on your son and I'd like to visit you. Is that alright?"

There was a moment of silence. "Alright. Maybe this Wednesday. Do you have the address?"

"Yes sir I do. Perhaps at one, is this acceptable?"

"Oh yes, one it is."

\* \* \*

The drive to Levittown, Long Island was uneventful. Sharon contemplated her strategy for this interview. She would be straight forward, yet a bit folksy. Yes, perhaps being unsophisticated would be a good tactic. It worked before when interviewing older people.

The Collins' house was painted foam green and had a huge dormer on the second floor. The trees along the street and around the house were huge with new budding green leaves. Spring was just around the corner. Sharon rang the bell and entered a small screened entrance way.

The door was opened by a woman who appeared to be in her early sixties. She had a beautiful head of grey hair and wore little makeup. "Welcome to the Collins' house." Her smile was cheerful and sincere. Behind her stood a tall lanky man who was obviously Matt's father. The resemblance was uncanny. His nose, cheeks and forehead were almost a perfect match to Matt.

"I'm Sharon Silver from the Risenburg News." She took out a business card and gave it to Mr. Collins.

He glanced at it. "Okay Mrs. Silver, what can we do for you?"

"Would you mind if I recorded you. I'd take notes, but my handwriting is so bad I probably couldn't read it."

They agreed. Sharon was ushered into a contemporary furnished living room and placed her recorder on a coffee table. Mr. and Mrs. Collins sat across from her.

"Where did Matt go to school and how did he do?"

Mrs. Collins pointed to a picture on the wall. There was a young boy about ten and a younger boy about seven years of age. They were wearing white shirts and bow ties. "That picture is Matt and his older brother Steve all dressed up for Christmas mass. We are Catholic and Matt was brought up as one. He continues to follow the teachings of Jesus, but I doubt if he goes to church too often."

"Tell me about his schooling."

"Matt went to the Levittown schools. We are a very middle class community, although very proud of our school's achievement. Matt was placed in the honors program early on. He skipped in elementary school and made high school in three years. He was sixteen when he graduated."

"Did he join any clubs?"

"He was Captain of the school's Quiz Bowl Team. They competed against other high schools on Long Island. The competitions were held at three Universities on the Island."

"Did he play any sports?"

Mr. Collins spoke up. "Matt was in Little League, played intramural baseball and basketball in high school. He wasn't good enough to win a varsity letter in sports."

"Of course he won a varsity letter as Captain of the Quiz Bowl Team." Mrs Collins seemed pleased with her answer.

"I understand he was a Captain in the Army. That's what my

paper got from his initial biographical information. The School District released that information when Matt was hired."

"Matt received an ROTC scholarship at Long Island University. He had to sign an agreement that after college he would serve four years in the Regular Army. Every summer he went for officer training."

Mr. Collins added. "He became a Second Lieutenant at the age of twenty. Matt spent four years in the service and ended up as a Captain in the Rangers."

Sharon Silver was on to something. "Rangers?"

"They are the elite of the United States Army!"

"What is their mission?"

"They go on missions that are the most difficult to carry out. If the Army needs the job done they call upon the Rangers."

"Did he go to school to be a Ranger?"

"Oh yes. Ranger School is one of the hardest training courses for which a soldier can volunteer. Army Rangers are experts in leading soldiers on problematical and tough missions. They need rigorous training. Rangers train for two to three months and it's exhausting. There are many dropouts. When you become a Ranger and wear that distinctive cap you are one of the elites!"

"Did he see action?"

Mrs. Collins took a shadow box off the mantle above a fireplace. It contained an American flag folded into a triangle. Beneath the flag were medal slots of medals.

"Matt would never brag, but as his father I have a right to brag about my son. He is an honest to goodness hero. He served in Iraq and in Afghanistan. Those stars are battle stars. Two for each country."

The reporter looked at the shadow box carefully. "I know the medal with George Washington on it. That's the Purple Heart, isn't it?"

"He got that saving two of his men in a fire fight in Paktika Province. Caught some shrapnel in his back."

"That's a Bronze Star."

"He got that for some black ops mission that he would not talk about. All he said was that it was tough. It's still classified. The one next to it is the Silver Star, one of the highest awards"

Mrs. Collins interrupted. "Perhaps Mrs. Silver would like some coffee"

The reporter realized that Mrs. Collins did not really like to hear about her son's exploits. As a mother she understood, but as a reporter she had to ask the questions. "No thank you Mrs. Collins. I really would like to hear about the Silver Star."

"Matt commanded a team of five men who protected the Secretary of State. His team was sent out first to clear any hazards or enemies before the Secretary came through. Well, his team encountered twenty of the enemy. Somehow Matt positioned himself around the Taliban and removed most of the threat. His team finished the job."

Sharon Silver commented. "He seems so mild mannered when I see him at PTA information meetings. He is well liked by the parents and the kids adore him."

"It's getting late. Do you have any other questions?" Mrs. Collins seemed perturbed.

"I know he served three years as a social studies teacher and four years as an assistant principal. Did he have a girl friend?"

Mrs. Collins took Sharon Silver by the arm and escorted her to the door. "That's all we will have to say about our son. If you are looking for things about his social life you are to ask him. That is pushing too hard!"

"Thank you Mr.and Mrs. Collins."

Mrs. Collins closed the door immediately and Sharon felt ashamed. She was investigating an honest to God hero of the United States of America. The question about his social life was really out of bounds and she realized it.

On her interview list was Jennifer Stanton, President of the Teachers Union, Jerry Jackson, Assistant Principal, Maggie Carter, Matt's Secretary and Vincent Green, the father of the child Matt saved earlier in the year. She decided not to talk to the Superintendent of Schools since he would be biased. After all, he hired Matt Collins.

* * *

The week of testing was almost finished. Matt had to attend an administrators meeting on Friday morning. "Jerry, will you be able to handle the rest of testing today?"

"No problem. The Team Leaders have been most cooperative. They have bundled the tests for me and I have checked to make sure the headings are okay. Other than that, it's the way the kids answer the questions and write their paragraphs."

The administrator's meeting was strictly on next year's budget. It was long and boring, yet very necessary to run the schools. Preliminary figures were given to each principal and new categories were added while some were taken away.

There seemed to be less Federal money coming into the District. The Business Manager, John Bird stood up and presented new facts and figures. It seemed Risenburg had lost a great deal of money.

The Business Manager continued in a serious tone. "The Title One money that we used to get has been cut dramatically because of the Federal sequestration. We know that last year we lost fifteen percent and this year we will lose twenty percent. The Board of Education has refused to raise the tax base, so we will have to lose twenty five percent of our Title One Reading Teachers."

The Superintendent of Schools looked around the conference table. "Any ideas on how we will support our poorer readers?"

No one answered.

"Come on principals, any ideas?"

Matt raised his hand. "Our best bet to help our Title One students is to evaluate them as soon as they come back to school in September. Set up a task force of the remaining Reading Teachers to do that. Then take the top twenty five percent Title One performers and assign Teacher Assistants under the supervision of the Title One Teacher."

An Elementary School Principal asked, "Won't that diminish their actual teaching time?"

"With the specific diagnosis obtained from their evaluations an explicit program can be set up. The Teacher Assistants should follow the plan to the letter. It's sort of a mini individualized program."

There seemed to be a consensus that the plan might work.

Dr. Hull thanked everybody for their cooperation. "Matt, may I see you in my office for a minute?

"Yes sir."

Matt thought. *I think he's going to tell me to get another job and I'm through.*

\* \* \*

The Superintendent's office reminded Matt of his Colonel's office when he was in Officers Training School in the Army. It was sterile and showed no personality at all. There was a plaque on the wall that indicated ten years of service to the District. A "paint by the numbers" landscape picture was on the wall behind a large mahogany desk. The Superintendent's chair was of fine leather and had a raised executive back.

"Sit down Matt. How do you think your first year in Risenburg is going?"

"I'm satisfied with it. The teachers, for the most part, are cooperating and I think I have excellent rapport with the community. My observations and evaluations are right on target and I think my Assistant Principal is really helping out."

"Oh, Jerry is doing a good job?"

"He certainly is. For example, he's keeping a very close watch on all the answer sheets on the New York State Testing program."

"I'm glad you brought that up. You caused quite a commotion with the teachers at your last faculty meeting."

"Dr. Hull, may I be direct."

"Of course my boy."

"There really has to be an investigation of the District's last three years of testing. The scores are blown up way out of proportion."

Dr. Hull's face became beet red. "That's not going to happen Mr. Collins. Not on my watch. That would ruin me as an educator. That would put Risenburg into the news as the laughing stock of the State. We would be ridiculed. No way that will happen. Over my dead body!"

Matt got out of his chair and walked to the edge of Dr. Hull's desk. "The truth always comes out. It seems to me you condoned the irregular high scores. Did you know about the testing fraud?"

"How dare you. No I did not. As God is my witness, I did not!"

Matt counted to ten in his mind before he said, "I believe you Dr. Hull. The truth is that it did happen and it will probably not go away."

In a subdued voice Dr. Hull looked directly at Matt. "Matt, as I understand it all you need is your dissertation for your doctorate."

"Yes sir. I plan to write it this coming year. My research is fully finished."

"Did you know that Eric Bolt, my Assistant Superintendent will be retiring next year."

"Perhaps, through the grapevine."

"I like your ideas, like the one you proposed for the Title One Reading Teachers. I think that you would make a fine Assistant Superintendent of Schools in this District. Who knows. I have five years to go. Or you could do two years as my Assistant and then get yourself a Superintendent's position somewhere else. What do you think?"

Matt was stunned. He again, counted to ten in his mind. "Dr. Hull, thank you for the opportunity. I have to think about it. Give me a little time to review all my options."

"You understand what I am saying, don't you?"

"Oh yes sir, I certainly do understand the quid pro quo."

Driving back to the school Matt thought. *My career would be jump started by at least three years. I would be in a great position to improve myself. All I have to do is to remain quiet. The big jump in salary would help when I marry Beth. It sounds like a good deal. All I have to do is live with myself for the rest of my life. Shit. What a choice!*

\* \* \*

Beth made dinner that evening. Matt finished his decaf coffee and placed it on the table. "Beth, I had a long talk with Dr. Hull today. We discussed my future plans in Risenburg."

"Did he fire you?'

"No, in fact he offered me a choice. If I were to keep quiet about the test scores, from now on, he would make me the Assistant Superintendent of the District. It seems Eric Bolt is retiring in one more year. I could finish my dissertation next year and start in Central Administration the following year."

"That's quite a deal. How do you feel about it?"

"Conflicted."

"Why?"

"I don't know why, other than moving my career timeline up by quite a few years."

"Conflicted?"

"Oh come on Beth, I know that it's not honorable. I recognize that the real world works this way. I just don't know if I could live with myself."

"Go home and sleep on it. I'll love you either way."

"Yeah, but will I love myself?"

Normally Matt slept very well. The conflict within kept waking him up. Finally he arrived to the local gym at five in the morning. His workout was intense. At six he saw Beth walk in. She nodded to him and started to stretch. He gazed at her body and smiled. Matt knew every line, every muscle and every crevice.

Beth walked over to him. "Hey Mister, stop leering at me or I'll call the police."

"Okay. I won't stare anymore."

Beth patted him on his rear. "Good boy!"

They both started to laugh simultaneously. He felt his tension break and he became less anxious. He thought. *I certainly know what to do now!*

CHAPTER 42

Matt called the Superintendent, "Dr. Hull, I wanted to let you know that I do not wish to advance in this District unless I earn it. As far as I am concerned I have tightened up the testing procedures in my school and I am satisfied."

"Are you sure this is what you want young man?"

"Yes sir."

"Well Matt, then this issue is finished and we can move on together. Do you agree?"

"Yes sir."

Matt called Beth and told her about his phone call with the Superintendent. "I'm really pleased. I feel like celebrating."

"Well, why don't we?"

"Okay, I'll pick you up at seven. We're going to the Black Swan."

Soon after Maggie buzzed. "Mr. Collins I have a problem that only you can decide on."

"What is the problem?"

"Susan Sullivan's Grandmother, Mrs. Rodgers, is here to pick her up. She's not on the official list for child pick up. I tried calling Mrs. Sullivan, but could not get an answer. When I called Mr. Sullivan he went into a rage and told me he would be coming to school in thirty minutes."

"Send the Grandmother into my office."

A large woman, about sixty marched into the office waiving a piece of paper. "I have a an official custody order remanding Susan to my daughter."

"Are the parents divorced?"

"They most certainly are and I have an order to pick up Susan! I demand you give her to me now."

"May I see the order?"

Matt read the order. It stated that Mrs. Sullivan, the mother, would have temporary custody until a new court case would be convened next week. There was no mention of the grandmother.

"Call your daughter and I will certainly release Susan to her. I cannot release the child to you."

"But I'm the grandmother. My daughter told me to pick her up."

"Silly as it seems Mrs. Rodgers, if I release Susan to you, Mr. Sullivan can take out kidnapping charges against you. You could also be charged with interfering with a custody case. Try calling your daughter to come to school to pick up Susan."

"How dare you! I'm going to sue you and the School District. Wait and see, you are in real trouble."

"Please go outside and sit on the bench. Try calling your daughter to pick Susan up. If not, Susan will go home on her bus just like any other day." Mrs. Rodgers stormed out of the office yelling. "I'm going to sue you!" Some ten minutes later Maggie buzzed. "Mr. Sullivan is here and he's screaming at Mrs. Rodgers." Matt went out to the outer office and stood between both antagonistic adults.

"Please come into my office. Stop yelling. This is a school, not an arena!" Both of them stopped and followed Matt into his office. "Mr. Sullivan, are you aware of this order?"

"Yes. It starts tomorrow."

Matt was aware of alcohol on the man's breath. "May I see the order?" Matt read the order and it stated that the starting date would be the next day. "Mrs. Rodgers, you are a day too early."

"Susan doesn't want to go home with him. He's a drunk! And he hit her!"

"That's a fucking lie." Sullivan blurted out in anger.

"Call Susan. She doesn't want to be with her father."

Matt called Maggie. "Have Susan Sullivan come to my office."

A few minutes later Susan was ushered into Matt's office. She was petite and had red hair and a bruised face. When she saw her father she cowered and hid behind Matt.

"Susan, you're not in trouble. Do you want to go home with your father?"

The little girl started to shake and cry. "No, He hurt me. He's bad when he drinks!"

Mr. Sullivan took the girl's arm. "I've got a legal right until tomorrow so butt out everybody."

Matt stood up and blocked the angry man. "You're not going anywhere."

Sullivan pushed Matt, trying to move him. Matt countered with a judo leg drop move that put the man on the floor. "Stay down there."

"Maggie, call the police and get me Child Protective Services. We have a problem!"

Every time Mr. Sullivan tried to get up Matt told him to stay down. It was obvious that the man was drunk and out of control.

Matt spoke to a case worker. "I'm reporting child abuse and need you at the middle school to sort things out. Will you please come?"

It took less than five minutes for a patrolman to get to the office. "What's the problem?"

Matt pointed to both of the adults. "We have a domestic problem concerning custody of Susan."

"I've called CPS and they are sending a social worker over. Mr. Sullivan seems drunk and his daughter doesn't want to go home with him. He pushed me and I had to defend myself. Mrs. Rodgers is the Grandmother, but we don't have her on a pickup list. The mother cannot be found. I need you here to watch Mr. Sullivan and to be a witness to this civil matter."

The officer whose name plate read "Officer Sherman" shook his head in disgust.

"I hate domestics. Everybody seems to lose. Okay, Mr. Sullivan come outside with me and sit on the bench in the front office."

Matt nodded. "Mrs. Rodgers, please remain in my office. Try calling your daughter again."

Matt called Shelly Katz. "Mrs. Katz I need you down here right now to help Susan Sullivan, fifth grader. I need you right now!"

Mrs. Katz came into the office and saw Susan. "Hello sweetheart. Are you okay?"

Susan ran into her arms and started to cry. The Guidance Counselor took her in her arms. "We're going to hang out in Mr. Jackson's office for awhile." Fifteen minutes later the social worker from CPS came in. She was dressed in a black business suit, about forty years old, and had a no-nonsense attitude. "I'm Anne Gonzales. Tell me the story."

Matt pointed to the small table. "Mrs. Rodgers will you please go outside and see how your Granddaughter is doing. I'll call you back in a few minutes."

"Who is she?"

"That's how the problem started. Mrs. Rodgers is the Grandmother of Susan Sullivan. The Sullivan's are divorced and the mother got a temporary custody order starting tomorrow to hold onto the child until a new court case comes up. Well, Mrs. Rodgers is not on the school's pickup list and the order is dated for tomorrow. We called Mr. Sullivan and he came into the office drunk. His daughter came into my office with a bruised face and told all of us that quote, "He hurt me. He's bad when he drinks.' She ran behind me very afraid of her father. Mr. Sullivan pushed me and I had to sit him down. He smells of alcohol and is angry and aggressive. We cannot contact Mrs. Sullivan. That's why I called you."

"Okay. It seems to me I have this alternative. Release the child to the Grandmother or take the child into protective custody. Since the Grandmother is not on the list and Mr. Sullivan does have a legal right to the child, but is incapacitated, I choose to take the child into protective custody until the mother picks her up."

"I'm sure you can explain it to Susan. She's in the Assistant Principal's office with Mrs. Katz, her Guidance Counselor."

"I'll make it very clear. As soon as Susan's mother sees me I will release her. That's the best I can do."

"Thanks Ms. Gonzales. I'm on record on filing a child abuse report against Mr. Sullivan."

The adults met in Matt's office again. Ms. Gonzales lectured all of them about responsibilities and the reason she would take Susan. Upon hearing the decision Mr. Sullivan placed his hands onto his face and started to cry. Officer Sherman took him out of the school. "I'm putting him into the drunk tank for the day. Maybe he'll get the message."

Mrs. Rodgers was flustered. "I'll get my daughter as soon as I can. I'm going to drive to her business. It's an hour away, but I'll get her back!"

Matt looked out of his office window and saw all of the parties leaving the school. He felt saddened by the event and thought. Alcohol is so addictive. *It ruins a lot of people.*

When they left Maggie came in with a cup of coffee. "Hey Boss, I think you need this!"

Matt took a sigh of relief. "Thanks Maggie, I sure do."

* * *

The Black Swan restaurant catered to cultivated people. There was no snob appeal, although when you entered you felt as if you were in a palace.

Beth looked around the room. "Oh Matt, the crystal chandeliers are stunning the oil paintings are superior the drapes and decorations are so luxurious it's perfect!"

Matt smiled and looked directly at her. "You are stunning, you are superior and you are perfect."

"Oh Matt, you say that to all your girls."

They toasted each other with some fine white wine. Beth's eyes shone brilliantly in the subdued light.

The waiter came to the table to prepare their Caesar salad. "With anchovies or without?"

They simultaneously said, "With!"

"My mother spoke to me last night. The count for the wedding has increased to about two hundred people."

"Wow, we planned on one hundred twenty."

"It seems that many of our cousins and their spouses or significant others want to come."

Matt laughed. "I do have four aunts and uncles."

"And I have three."

"Between both of us we have a twenty five thousand dollar budget. That won't make it."

Beth reached over, took Matt's hand and replied. "I know your folks and mine are pitching in, but I think we will be short at least ten thousand or so."

"We can't plan on receiving expensive wedding gifts. Think about what it will cost for guests to come in. There's air fare, motel costs, food and car rentals."

"What should we do Matt.?"

"I'll go to the Teacher's Credit Union and take out a loan for ten thousand dollars."

"Don't you mean we'll take out a loan?"

The lobster thermidor arrived and it was served with finesse. The creamy sauce accented the wonderfully subtle flavor. They both enjoyed the meal immensely.

Matt started to laugh. "You better enjoy this meal because for the next year or so we will be on a Ramen noodle budget."

"Oh I think I know how to make chili, franks and beans, and spaghetti and meat balls."

"Beth, I love your attitude. I wish I could contribute more."

"We're partners. Right!"

"We certainly are." He lifted his water glass and the couple clinked their glasses in a toast. "To a great wedding!"

Beth responded. "Amen!"

"I'm looking forward to visiting your parents. One more week and I'll be swimming with you in Florida."

"I hope my mom has the strength to put us up. Her chemo treatments keep her weak. My dad does his best to take care of her. I plan to work at cleaning up the house a bit better than my dad and to do some organization. I already spoke to my mom about it."

"Is there anything I can do?"

"If you could keep my dad busy on the days I tell you it would really help."

Before he could answer, the crème brûlée was served. The couple enjoyed their dessert and left.

On their way back they resolved to get specific dollar amounts for all the wedding expenses. The hall, the caterer, the band, the bar and all of the extras for the wedding.

Matt thought for awhile as they continued their drive. "Is there a way to cut costs for the rehearsal dinner?"

"Well, perhaps a buffet instead of a sit down. That saves on personnel. We can control the buffet menu."

"I don't want to short change them, but isn't the wedding the most important?

"No Matt. It's the whole experience."

"Okay, we'll work it out."

They made love later in the night. Beth did not want him to let go of her. She felt that she needed his touch, his aura and his reassurance. They held each other in a close embrace. Matt felt their souls were melding as they drifted off on a journey with no destination. They were at peace that night.

CHAPTER 43

Maggie came into Matt's office with his newsletter for the teachers. "There is a conflict for the faculty meeting on May first."

"Sounds funny. I mean the word May. One more day until spring break. Okay I'll take a look at it

Jerry rushed into Matt's office . "Fire, there's a fire in rooms two ten and two twelve."

"Pull the fire alarm and get the kids out of the building. I'll call nine one one. Let's do it now!"

Maggie came back. "The teachers in those rooms just called. They evacuated as soon as they started seeing smoke coming out of the electric outlets. Looks like it's something in the electrical system."

"Jerry, call Central and tell them what's happening. Tell them help is on the way."

Matt called Otto. There was no response. He rushed into the Main Boiler Room and pulled the largest electrical box handle he could find. Then he pulled all the other small box handles. He thought. *Perhaps I could stop the fire by cutting out the electricity.*

Otto came into the Boiler Room. "Good thinking Matt. I was going to do that."

"Go outside and speak to the Fire Chief and tell him that my teachers saw smoke coming out of the electrical outlets."

Matt rushed back to his office and took a bullhorn out of his closet. He went outside to the front of the school. "Will the teachers and students walk to the rear of the school and join the other classes. I'll be making an announcement in a few minutes." Since most of the teachers and kids were out on the playing field he decided he wanted everyone there.

The Fire Chief, Brandon Casey approached Matt. "Looks like an electrical fire. There are four rooms that got hit pretty bad."

"What rooms Chief?"

"Two hundred eight through two fourteen. The odd number rooms on the other side are safe. Perhaps a bit smelly, but safe."

"Thanks Chief. Can we turn on the circuit breakers?"

"No way. Do you want to start another fire. We need to get a master electrician in to check out everything. Right now the school is unsafe. Who pulled all the breakers?"

Matt nodded. "Yeah, I couldn't find Otto so I did it."

"You saved the school and perhaps injuries to some kids Mr. Collins. Good catch and smart move!"

Since all the land lines in the school were out due to no electric power Matt used his cell phone to call the Superintendent. "There are no injuries to any student. We have four rooms out of service until a master electrician comes in to figure out what happened."

"What do you suggest Matt."

"I have my bullhorn. The teachers and I will organize the kids back into home rooms on the field. Then I'll sit the kids down in the bleachers and on the grass. Very slowly and in simple sentences I will explain to them what happened. I'll tell them that they can go with their teachers to their lockers and homerooms to collect what they need. The kids in the four rooms that had the fire will only be allowed to their lockers. But the big news will be that they are off tomorrow."

"What about after the spring break?"

"Dr. Hull. Depending on what the electrician says either we fix the rooms or we will have to go into split session or a modified school day. I'll stay on and work with Mr. Bolt to get letters out to the parents and kids."

"Eric Bolt left for Europe yesterday. I guess you and your Assistant will have to work over the spring recess."

"I'll need my secretary, Maggie Carter."

"Whatever it takes Matt. I'm putting you in charge. Use Mr. Bolt's office and facilities."

"Thank you sir." Matt thought. *This guy is afraid of his own shadow and really is stupid about how schools really run. He is a first class bureaucrat!*

"Jerry, call transportation and tell them to send the buses to the school at two o'clock. This time the high school will have to wait for us."

Matt went onto the field. "Attention, attention. Calm down and let me talk to all of you."

The noise from the kids and their excitement was loud. Matt used a booming voice. "Cool it! Cool it! Cool it!" The kids quieted down. "Will all the teachers who have home rooms go to the far wire fence. I want the students to see you."

That took a few minutes. Beth came over and whispered in his ear. "Can the counselors do anything?"

"Keep alert for kids who are frightened. Tell all the counselors to be prepared."

He lifted up the bullhorn. "Now young ladies and gentlemen, make me proud by walking to your home room teacher. Line up behind your teacher. Please do it now."

It took about ten minutes to get it right but the kids came through. Lifting the bullhorn Matt projected his voice into it directly. "Okay, listen carefully. The seventh and eight grade classes will march to the bleachers and sit down. Do it now!"

After another ten minutes Matt talked to the sixth graders and one fifth grade class. "Go to the grass part of the field and sit down."

They did very well and Matt was ready to talk to them. "Young Ladies and Gentlemen, there was an electrical fire in rooms two hundred eight, two hundred ten, two hundred twelve and two hundred fourteen. A master electrician has to come here and find out what the problem is. Therefore the whole school is off tomorrow."

There was a great cheer and whistles. "Cool it. Cool it!" The kids quieted down. "Your parents or guardians will get a letter from the Superintendent and me letting you know if we need to change your hours or keep you on vacation or go into a modified split session. That means some grades would have to split their time while other grades will stay in school the whole day."

Some noise erupted and Matt again repeated, "Cool it. Cool it. The teachers will receive letters as well. The assignments may be different, but this is an emergency. I'll be available after the buses leave to speak to any staff member."

This time there was noise from the staff and Matt repeated his famous words, "Cool it. Cool it. Young ladies and gentlemen, we will let you into your home rooms and lockers to take things home. Only lockers for the students of the damaged rooms. Be careful because the light are off. You will have fifteen minutes to do this."

Jerry came to Matt. "The buses are standing by."

" I repeat again, those students in the rooms affected by the fire will only be allowed to their lockers. The buses are in. Will all the teachers help monitor the students all the way to their buses after they picked up their stuff. Counselors will be on duty if any student or teacher needs to talk to them. Okay. Let's do it!"

After the kids left and the teachers signed out Matt, Jerry, Maggie, Otto and Beth sat in the outer office. "Maggie, will you be able to work with me in Central office. I'll be in Mr. Bolt's office. He's in Europe."

"I'll be there."

"Jerry, tomorrow in Central, start assembling labels for envelopes to our parents. In fact make the labels duplicate. If anybody gives you a hard time tell me who that person is."

"Anything you want Boss." *He thought. I don't know if I have the stuff to do what Matt did today He is in command.*

"Otto, make sure to get the electrician in as fast as possible. I'll need a number of scenarios to review. One: Is it fixed and can we go back to school? Two: Are the damaged rooms not ready, but can we go back to school?" Three: Can we go back to school at all? I'll be working through the spring break so let me know as fast as possible. No later than Wednesday night. I have to get letters out on Thursday morning as well as having the town paper give information to the public."

"Yes sir. Will do."

"Beth, I'm so sorry. I can't go with you."

Beth walked over to Matt and in front of everyone hugged him. "You amaze me. I am dumbfounded by your calmness and sense of command. I now understand many things. Come to dinner tonight, We're having franks and beans."

"Okay people. Let's do it tomorrow!"

Otto shook his hand. "Well done. You saved kids today."

Maggie kissed him on his cheek. "See you tomorrow."

Jerry remained quiet. "Are you okay Jerry?"

"Yeah, I've worked for a lot of principals and saw nothing, but with you I learned something: It's easy to talk the talk, but you have to walk the walk. And you do it! Thanks for being my role model." He got up and left quickly.

CHAPTER 44

Matt and Beth ate slowly as they discussed a ruined vacation because of the fire in the school. "Matt, do you think you could possibly fly to Florida by the end of the week?"

"I doubt it. It really depends on the electrician's report. I'm going to design a few plans for the Board of Education to approve."

"The Board of Education?"

"I present to the Superintendent who presents to the Board unless the Superintendent wants me to be there."

"But it's all your work!"

"It really doesn't matter. What matters is that the kids get the best I can do for them. I just want you to have a safe trip and concentrate on our wedding plans."

"I'll do that. Do we have an agreement that any loans from the Teachers Credit Union is shared."

"I agree."

Matt left immediately after the conversation. He had an idea and went back to the school to get the floor plans that gave the dimensions of all the rooms.

\* \* \*

Matt entered the Administration Building on Saturday at eight in the morning. A uniformed guard was on duty. "I'm Mr. Collins, Principal of the Middle School. My staff and I will be working in Mr. Bolt's office for awhile."

"I'm sorry. No one told me about this. I have to call the Business Office and Mr. Bird has to approve you. It's the weekend. He comes in at nine on Monday morning. "

Matt hid his anger and took his cell phone out. He punched in John Bird's number. "John, this is Matt. Will you tell the guard to let me and my people in for as long as it takes."

Matt handed the phone to the guard. "Yes sir, okay Mr. Bird told me that you have the run of the building. Sorry I'm just doing my job."

At that moment Maggie came in followed by Jerry. "These are my people who work with me."

"Yes sir. I've got it!"

The trio walked to Mr. Bolt's office. It had an outer office where his secretary worked. It was small. Bolt's office was much bigger. "Jerry, let's get a rectangular table and bring it in to this office. We'll set up shop right here. Maggie, hunt for some chairs that we can use to sit around the table."

At eight thirty Otto called Matt. "Boss, we have problem. The electricians are out of town and will return on Monday. The Fire Chief called and he will not be available until Monday afternoon. I tried calling Syracuse to get another master electrician. No luck at all. We are stymied until Monday."

He looked at his staff as his eyes looked down. "Jerry, Maggie, go home. We really can't do anything until Monday morning."

Maggie started to walk out and stopped. "I know Phyllis Workfield, Mr. Bolt's secretary. She can be a big help for us. When she comes in on Monday I'll introduce you. She's a good worker."

"Thanks Maggie. We're going to need all the staff we can get." Matt had an idea. He called John Bird again. "John, can you get me a part time clerical worker for Monday maybe from noon to four I have to plan on at least three letters ready to go out to the parents."

"Why three?"

"There will Plan A to shut the school down and give the kids another holiday for the week until we do split session with the high school. Plan B will be a modified schedule in the school having only four and a half hours of school and no lunch period. Plan C will be a room utilization plan where I can substitute different rooms and make up for the destroyed rooms."

"Wow. How the hell did you come up with these?"

"I read a lot books!"

Both men laughed.

Matt and his staff left the building. "I'll see you at eight on Monday morning."

Maggie and Jerry nodded.

Matt's weekend was broken up into four parts: working out, planning, eating and sleeping. He worked out as early as he could and ate lightly. During the late morning and early afternoon he planned for as many contingencies that he could think of in case his plans did not work.

Beth called late Saturday afternoon. "Are you okay?"

"I wish I was with you. Anything new on the caterer and the hall?"

She sounded excited. "We are set for the wedding. The church is set, the flowers are set, the color scheme is set, the cocktail party is set, the meal is set and I love you and want you and need you now!"

"Oh Beth."

"Shut up. I know I can't have you and my wishes. I'm just sharing a feeling."

"Do I have to go to the Credit Union?"

"Not yet. There may be another plan that we have to discuss."

"What is it?"

"It's not clear yet. Do you trust me?"

"Of course I do."

"Then just wait."

"I'll call you tomorrow. What's a good time?"

"We 're going to church. After twelve is okay. Love you!"

Matt felt better after talking to Beth.

* * *

On Monday Maggie set up the temporary office. Matt met Phyllis Workman. She was chubby, wide eyed, happy, and willing to do anything to help the kids."Mrs. Workman, thank you for helping us out."

"Mr. Collins, my daughter goes to your school. She is in eighth grade and has a crush on you. Now I know why!"

Every one in the office laughed loudly. Matt flushed and took a deep breath. "I wrote three letters. On the top of each letter I used magic marker to indicate if the letter is Plan A, B, or C. Don't confuse the letters. They are quite different. Maggie, I'll leave that up to you. Get them printed and ready for insertion into the envelopes. Then recheck the letters and keep all of the different letters separated."

"Got it! Will do Mr. Collins!"

Matt called the Superintendent. "May I come in to speak to you about three plans I'm thinking about. I'm sure the Board of Education will want to know about them."

"Matt, I want you to come to the emergency Board meeting tonight at seven thirty. Make sure you have enough copies for the Board to read. I'll see you at six thirty before the meeting so you can go over the plans with me."

"The plans are complex. Don't you want more time to discuss them?"

"No, this is your show. If I have any comments you will hear them in front of the Board."

"In the service we always prepared for contingencies. Are you sure you don't want to see me now."

"No." He hung up.

Matt thought. *I've met your kind before. You're an ingrate and an opportunist!*

Maggie brought him three letters to the parents that he composed. He scanned them, took a thin tipped magic marker and designated Plan A, Plan B, Plan C on the top of each sheet. God forbid a wrong letter could be sent out.

At one in the afternoon Otto called Matt. "The electricians are in the building now. They had to coordinate with the Fire Chief. I'll know in an hour or so what our situation will be."

"Otto, call me on my cell. I'm meeting with the Board tonight."

The clerical tasks were done in three hours. Maggie supervised every aspect of the operation. Jerry double checked Maggie. Everything was set for a decision.

Otto called. "Boss. They have to pull some wires and check the side of the building. They said they would have an answer by tomorrow."

"Did you tell them that it is imperative. It is an emergency."

"They know. A work crew is being sent in to work tonight in order to get the side of the building opened up. They're bringing spotlights in to lighten the building. They're going to work all night."

"I'm going to the Board tonight. What should I tell them?"

"Plan for the worst and hope for the best."

"Thanks Otto.

Matt called his team together. "The Board of Education will be listening to me tonight. They called an emergency meeting. I have to plan to show the Board how each of the three plans will work. We are going to make up folders for them. The plans will be organized and I want tabs on each plan. I'll have a short written introduction and a summary as well. Maggie knows my style and she can organize the folders. I have to set up some transparencies as well. Phyllis, will you make sure that an overhead projector and screen is set up in the Board Room for tonight's meeting."

Matt called John Ward, Principal of the High School. "John I need a favor. Will your media person make some transparencies for me? I'll send Jerry over."

"Sure, what else can I do for you? I know about the fire."

"I'm making a presentation to the Board and one of the plans involves going split session with your school."

"Holy shit," John exploded, "when the kids come back we only have ten more weeks of school. That would kill motivation for the New York State Regents, clubs, extra curricular activities and upset all the students and staff. That's a rotten idea."

"I have three plans John."

"What the hell are they?"

"I can't tell you now because it depends on the electrician and the Fire Chief giving me permission to open the school."

"Well split session is one and it sucks. How about a modified schedule?"

"That's another."

"How about room exchange or room utilization."

"That's another, but I didn't tell you."

"Matt, I'll be at the meeting tonight. I hope the electricians come through for us."

"Thanks John. See you tonight. I've got to get back to work."

Maggie came in with a cup of coffee and a sandwich for Matt.

"Here, eat this. That's an order." He looked at the clock and it was five thirty.

"Where has the day gone?"

"I don't know. May I go home?"

"Oh, I'm so sorry Maggie"

"Good luck at the Board meeting. Everything is set for your presentation."

Otto called at six in the evening. "The people I've been talking to have told me that they think they can rewire the side of the building. That's in my opinion maybe they can. They just have to visually see the mess. Electrical tests have been done and their special meters indicate the only damage is to the four rooms. They can possibly isolate those rooms to make them safe and during the summer rewire them.:"

"Can I tell the Board that."

"No. It's a guess right now."

"Well, who spoke to you?"

"The master electrician. He's covering his ass with the word 'think.' I'll call it maybe!"

"Otto I can report the maybe situation to them as well. Then I will need their permission to move on it. I don't want to go back to them again."

"Okay, you're in charge."

Matt thought. *Yeah, they'll hang me and no one else.*

He finished his sandwich, sipped his coffee and took the stack of folders. He was happy with the transparencies that were delivered to him and walked towards the Board Room. Matt was going to set up for the meeting. He previously asked that the overhead projector and screen be set up. When Matt got to the room it was not set up. He looked at his watch. It was six fifteen.

Matt called Jerry at his home. "I need you to go to the school right now and get an overhead projector and screen for me. They didn't set it up in the Board Room."

"No problem Boss. I'll set it up myself and attend the meeting."

"Thanks Jerry."

At six thirty Matt entered the Superintendent's office. Dr. Hull looked chipper. He was wearing a dark blue suit with a matching striped tie. Matt was wearing a dark grey suit with a dotted blue tie.

He felt slightly underdressed.

"Tell me your plans Matt."

"Plan A is split session with the high school. We would have to keep the middle school out for an additional week to make the transition. Plan B will be a modified schedule in the school having only four and a half hours of school and no lunch period. The plan will entail having half the school start at eight in the morning and the other half start at one in the afternoon. No lunch at all. Plan C will be a room utilization plan where I can substitute different rooms and make up for the destroyed rooms."

"What did the electricians say?"

"They don't know as yet. My custodian indicated to me, off the record, that they think that they can isolate the four rooms and make them safe. He used the word 'maybe.' Then the kids can return to school and I would use Plan C. Here is your folder. The rest are laid out for the Board. I'll be focusing their attention with a transparency presentation. I'm going to make sure that it is as clear as possible."

"Excellent job. You make your presentation and I will make some comments as well. Please don't think I'm hurting you personally if I disagree with some of your plans."

Matt waited ten seconds to calm himself. "We are on the same team, aren't we?"

"Of course my boy, of course."

CHAPTER 45

Dominic Costello led the Board of Education and the audience in the Pledge of Allegiance. The Board President looked out and saw every one of the forty five chairs filled and some fifteen people in the back of the room who were standing. "We are here to discuss the emergency plans for the George W. Bush Middle School due to an electrical fire that has destroyed four class rooms. Mr. Superintendent, your report and recommendations, please."

Dr. Hull turned his head and looked at each member "I have instructed Mr. Collins to come up with plans for the students of the school. He has worked diligently to achieve the task. I have just received the information and have not had time to fully digest it. Mr. Collins will go through the details and then I will comment on them. Mr. Collins, you're up."

Matt thought. *You fucking weasel. You look good no matter what I do or say.*

"Thank you Dr. Hull. Ladies and Gentlemen, you have a folder describing in detail three plans. One of them will have to be used depending on the report from the master electrician and the Fire Chief. At this moment they are working twenty- four-seven to give us a determination. In the audience is my colleague, John Ward, High School Principal. He can answer questions concerning Plan A that is pertinent to split session using the high school. That means closing down the middle school until summer repairs can fix the school. I have a short presentation using transparencies that will crystallize and simplify all three plans. I would appreciate questions to be held until the presentation is finished."

Dominic Costello, the Board President, thumbed through the extensive folder in front of him. "I agree Mr. Collins. No questions until after the presentation."

Matt very carefully and in specific non-educational terms explained all the plans. His tone was even and his demeanor was statesmanlike. If one never heard him before they would think he was experienced in the art of government and the art of politics. He made no value judgments as he presented, yet presented the pros and cons of each plan. The presentation took twenty five minutes. "Thank you very much for focusing on my presentation and plans. Are there any questions?"

Dominic Costello looked at John Ward. "Mr. Ward, do you think that the high school could do split session with the middle school successfully?"

John Ward rose from his seat in the audience. ""It would be difficult with the Regents testing coming soon, but it can be managed. May I also comment that I have never heard such a clear and concise plan as Mr. Colllins presented."

There was applause in the audience and it was directed at Matt. He looked at the audience and saw Maggie and Jason Carter, Mr. and Mrs. Green, the parents of the child he saved, Maureen Stuart, President of the PTA and her husband, Jerry and Celia Jackson, Nancy Briggs, attorney and apple orchard owner and Sharon Silver, reporter for the Risenburg News.

The Board President looked at John Bird, Business Manager. "Mr. Collins has indicated that it would cost one hundred and fifty thousand dollars to hire extra teachers, reroute transportation, move supplies and equipment to the high school for split session. His other numbers are much less if he uses Plan B and C. Do we have enough money in this years budget to do this?"

"We would have to defer some capital projects and utilize some of the bond money for the repairs on the middle school. Additional money could be shifted for split session. We can do it. I am sure the transfer of funds would be approved because it is a true emergency."

"Dr. Hull, do you have any comments?"

The Superintendent thought. *The applause from the audience supports that young principal.* "I wish to compliment Mr. Collins and his staff for their diligence. Let's pray that Plan C can be adopted."

The Board President looked into the folder then took off his glasses. "Let's talk about Plan B. Mr. Collins. What will it mean for a curtailed four and one half day for the kids?"

"It diminishes all extra school activities including team sports, clubs and intramurals. Our government sponsored lunch program for the under privileged will stop since there are no lunches served. Studies have shown that attendance will drop five to ten percent. The burden to the teaching staff is great. Perhaps the worst is the transportation of students with a four and one half day. It raises costs dramatically."

"Are there any questions from the Board?"

A female Board member raised her hand, "I make a motion to give approval to either Plan A or Plan C. Plan B would hurt the education and the life of students."

There was a second with no discussion. The motion passed easily.

"Dr. Hull and the administration are directed to put Plan A or Plan C into action depending on the report from the master electrician and the Fire Chief. Mr. Collins you are to be commended for your report. This emergency session of the Board of Education is dismissed."

Dr. Hull left with the Board as people surrounded Matt. Jerry Jackson slapped Matt on the back. "Nice job, Boss. Nice job!"

Nancy Briggs grabbed Matt's arm. "You should go to law school. Great presentation."

Vincent Green smiled. "My boy, you can work for me any time. I mean in management, sir."

Jason Carter looked at Matt and shook his hand. "You are a winner. I hope you stay around Risenburg. Your talent is amazing."

Matt went directly to his house. He was emotionally drained. Otto called at eleven in the evening. "Boss, good news. We all agree, the Fire Chief, the electrician and me that we can isolate the four rooms and have the school run its regular program."

"Are you very sure Otto?"

"Here, speak to the Fire Chief."

"Mr. Collins, it's a go. You can inform the kids to come back, of course with different places instead of those four rooms."

"Thanks. May I speak to Otto."

"Otto, I owe you big time. I want you to take tomorrow off and just rest. I'm exhausted and I know how you feel."

"Mr. Collins, it is my pleasure to work with you."

"Otto, sometime next week we will go out and celebrate. Your family, Beth and me."

"That's a date."

It was eleven thirty in the evening. Matt thought. *Should I wake Dr. Hull. Hell yes!*

The voice was weak and sluggish. "Hello."

"Dr. Hull, Matt Collins on this end. We go with Plan C. The kids can come back on Monday to their school. We isolate the four rooms. I'll make all the necessary arrangements."

"Thank you. I'll call the President tomorrow." He hung up.

Matt called the airline and was able to get a seat to Orlando on Thursday morning and a return flight on Sunday evening. He figured that the letters to the parents would be sent out tomorrow morning. The newspaper would be informed. Specific information would be read in the Wednesday morning edition. He would answer any questions on Wednesday and instruct Otto and his team to move the necessary furniture and equipment to make up for the four lost rooms.

Matt fell asleep. His last thought was of Beth and her beautiful face.

* * *

On Tuesday morning Matt met with everyone on his team in the temporary office. "Maggie, you are to destroy Plan A and Plan B letters. You are to mail out Plan C as early as possible. If we get this out to the post office by noon the parents will get their letters on Wednesday. I'll be here to answer any questions on Wednesday because on Thursday I'm going to Florida to join Beth. You are directed and instructed to take Thursday and Friday off. At least you can have part of the spring break. Any questions?"

"Boss, what physical arrangements will you use to make up for the four lost class rooms.?"

"Jerry. Both of us will see Otto tomorrow and give him instructions."

Matt took out four folders from his brief case. They were marked, Jerry, Maggie, Otto and Matt. "Here is the plan. Read it and weep."

Jerry started to read it and said, "Holy shaving cream, this will work."

Maggie read it. "I'll say a prayer tonight for all of us!"

* * *

Wednesday was a day filled with answering questions about the school. Anxious parents called about safety, others inquired about student housing and others did not understand why the District could not fix the problem. Throughout all of the phone calls Matt stayed cool and calm. He made sure that Maggie and Jerry answered in the same manner.

Matt called Sharon Silver. "Thank you Mrs. Silver for your article on the general plan for the school. You're invited to come to school on Monday morning and see what we are trying to do with the students. We will have different rooms to make up for the four lost classrooms."

"What's the specific plan?"

"Sorry. Why don't you come in and report it. I'm sure your followup will be well read. See you in the auditorium at the first period of the day."

"Would you mind if I brought a photographer along?"

"I believe in the freedom of the press to report as accurately as they can. Yes indeed."

In the late afternoon Matt and his crew cleaned up the temporary office returning all furniture and making sure everything was clean. He turned to Phyllis Workfield, Mr. Bolt's secretary. "Please check to make sure everything is alright. I don't want Mr. Bolt to be upset."

"Everything is just fine. Mr. Collins, it has been my pleasure to work with you. If Maggie ever leaves you please consider me for your next secretary."

Matt flushed. "Thank you so much."

Matt called the Superintendent's office and told his secretary where he would be for the next four days. "You have my cell number if there is a problem. Mr. Jackson should be called first since he is remaing in town."

The last call was to Otto. "How are you?"

"I slept ten hours. I'm fine."

"I'm going to Florida tomorrow morning. Check with Jerry if there are any problems. If you can't settle it between both of you call me on my cell."

"Have a nice vacation Mr. Collins."

* * *

The amazing thing about arriving in the Orlando Airport is the happiness of the children and their parents. They are either going to or coming back from "The Magic Kingdom Walt Disney World," "Universal Orlando Theme Park Universal Studios," or "SeaWorld, Orlando." There are more smaller theme parks and enjoyment venues throughout the area as well.

Matt observed them as he was taking a ride on the Monorail from the Airport Gates to the Main Terminal. He thought. *This is the first unofficial ride to the theme parks.*

Beth spotted him coming down the long hallway where the monorail dropped him. He looked tired. There were bags around his eyes and he walked a bit slower than usual.

Matt spotted Beth and sprinted towards her. They met in an impact of love and happiness. "Oh Matt, I'm thrilled that we can have a few days together. I love you so much!"

Beth drove them to her parent's house where he was greeted as part of the family. He noticed that Mrs. Andrews was drawn and pale. She had lost more weight and walked slower. He thought. *Beth was so right in her worries about her mom.*

After a light lunch of sliced turkey sandwiches and salads Beth took Matt into her room. She looked at him carefully. "You look tired."

"I haven't had too much sleep lately."

"Lie down with me and rest for awhile. I'll be here with you."

Beth slipped out of her tee shirt and shorts and went under the covers. Matt took off his shirt and pants but kept his shorts on. They just held each other. There was nothing to say at this time. Within ten minutes Beth saw Matt asleep. She slipped out of the room satisfied that he would have a restful nap. Tears of joy rolled down her face.

Her man was home.

Later in the day Matt joined the family. There was a great deal to discuss about their wedding plans. Beth held Matt's hand. "Hon, we have a problem with the rehearsal dinner. There are so many out of town guests coming to the wedding that a traditional sit down dinner the night before the wedding is not in our budget."

"What are our alternatives."

Mr. Andrews gave a belly laugh. "I suggested a pizza party at a local park and a softball game. The girls nixed the idea."

Mrs Andrews went to her husband and kissed him on his cheek. "I wish we really could do that, but it seems to me the best thing to do is have an open house here. We can be open from one to five and people can pop in when they want to. We can set up a bar and have hors d'oeuvres ."

Matt looked at her and shook his head negatively. "No offense, but I don't think you should have anything to do the day before the wedding except to go to the hairdresser and the manicurist. I have a better idea. Well, it isn't original since I'm taking it from a friend of mine. I was a groomsman a few years ago and the rehearsal dinner problem was solved very easily. I have just one question. How many rooms have you booked at the hotel for the wedding?"

Beth took out a folder and started looking at papers. "We have a block of thirty five rooms reserved."

"That's plenty to have leverage. Here is the plan. We arrange with the hotel management, especially the bar manager, that from seven thirty to ten thirty in the evening the engaged couple will meet and greet family and friends in the hotel bar. The guests can order what they want and pay for it. We will supply endless munchies. After all, isn't the purpose of the rehearsal dinner is to see the couple and talk to them, wish them the best, share a drink with them and laugh with them. This clears a full day for the guests to visit theme parks. They can visit us later that evening."

There was silence in the room. Matt looked around and saw everybody processing his suggestion. "Any questions?"

Mr. Andrews spoke up first. "Yes, who is going to call the hotel manager for a meeting?"

They all laughed. Mrs. Andrews looked at Beth. "You have a problem solver as your future husband."

"Mom, why do you think I'm marrying him. It certainly isn't his money."

Every body howled with laughter. Matt called and set up a meeting with the manager.

Arrangements were very easy. The hotel was used to conventions and corporations meeting and greeting people in their large bar. Mr. David, the Manager told the happy group that there would be a separate section for Beth and Matt with at least four tables reserved.

The Manger took them into the bar area and they were pleased to see a lovely alcove with four tables and at least sixteen chairs available.

Mrs. Andrews sat down in a chair. "What will the cost be for nuts, pretzels, and other munchies?"

"We are pleased that you have reserved thirty five rooms. There is no cost. My bar manager will make sure your guests will have plenty to munch on. I just want to go over the spelling of your names since I will have a sign on an easel right outside the bar. It will read, "Please visit us. Love, …"

"Their names are Beth and Matt." Mr. Andrews loudly proclaimed.

On their way back to the house Beth snuggled in the back seat with Matt. Nuzzling his shoulder, "Oh, what an easy and inexpensive way to have a rehearsal dinner." and then kissed him on his cheek.

Every one laughed again. The money pressure was certainly relieved. They all seemed reassured.

After an early dinner the Andrews told the couple that they were going to play bridge at a friends house and they would return about ten in the evening. Mrs. Andrews hugged Matt. "Take good care of my little girl Matt."

Beth looked at Matt playfully. "I'll race you to the bedroom!"

She beat him and jumped on her bed. Matt slowed down and looked at her. Beth raised her arms to him. "Come to me my sweetheart. Come to me."

Matt complied with vigor, drive and enthusiasm.

## CHAPTER 46

The letter to the parents read:

Dear Parents and Students,

The George W. Bush Middle School is back to the business of educating young minds. The buses and time schedules will remain the same. There will be modifications to the students whose homerooms are 208, 210, 212, and 214. If your children are in these rooms they will immediately report to the auditorium for instructions. We have new home rooms for the students.

The entire School District has worked diligently to make our school safe. The Fire Chief has given approval for us to resume our regular schedule and the Board of Education has approved the school modifications.

We have ten more weeks of school. Let's have a great fourth quarter.

Sincerely, Matt Collins, Principal

cc: Superintendent of Schools

President, Board of Education

There was a memo in every staff member's mailbox directing them to have the home room period extended through period one. The plan called for the following modifications: Room 208 meets in the Music Room

The Music Teacher holds all classes in the auditorium.

Room 210 meets in the Science Room

All science takes place in the classrooms. No experiments or displays allowed.

Room 212 meets in the far south corner of the Learning Resource Center.

The LRC teacher will utilize the far north corner for individualized instruction and student research.

Room 214 meets in the Computer Center

The Center is closed when subject classes are in session.

Note: The lockers may be used by the displaced students.

I will have an assembly with the students and teachers who are affected the first period. All teachers who are affected to attend.

Matt Collins, Principal

The assembly was a great success. Matt stressed the importance of cooperation and flexibility for the next ten weeks. Some questions came up about the potential of books being smelly because of smoke and personal items not being found. Matt replied in a serious tone. "We are lucky that our school is safe. Would you have preferred to go to school from twelve thirty to five thirty every day? We will do the best we can, but I don't expect any grief from either the students of this school or the staff. Assembly dismissed!"

During the assembly Sharon Silver and her photographer took pictures of Matt at the podium and the audience. After the students left she moved to Matt. "Mr. Collins, do you expect any problems ?"

"Not really. Perhaps the normal aspect of kids finding their way around the school from their new homerooms."

Matt reached into his pocket and took out the memo he wrote to the teachers. "Here is the specific information I gave to the staff. Use it as you see fit."

"Thank you Mr. Collins and off the record, as a parent, a double thank you. My son is in good hands."

Jerry and Matt spent the whole day in and out of the temporary classrooms. There were some problems with kids using the computers when they weren't supposed to use them. Another problem was the Music Teacher filing a grievance about her working conditions. The LRC Teacher was unhappy with the kids noise. She claimed she could not do individualized instruction. Further she could not finish the computer classes as well. The Science Teachers wrote a letter complaining they could not finish their curriculum without the Science Room.

Matt, Jerry, Maggie and Otto met in the cafeteria at the end of the day. All the staff and kids were out of the school. Maggie had made coffee and Matt had asked her to buy some pastries. Matt lifted his coffee cup. "Here is to you. The best people in this school!"

Otto countered. "Here's to you Mr. Collins, the best Principal this school has ever had!"

Jerry lifted his glass. "Here's to the best coffee I've had today."

That cracked every body up and the laughter was silly and funny. They were tired and happy. A few bumps, but overall the day was okay.

Jerry stopped laughing and set his coffee down. "I learned an expression last week. "But for the grace of God.' I mean but for the grace of God this school could have burned down and children hurt. Thank you Matt. Otto told me you were the person who shut off all the electricity in the school."

"Jerry, I believe you are right about God." Matt spoke seriously.

Jerry looked at the happy group. "I want to tell all of you something. Matt, not as my Boss, but as my friend, all of you not as co-workers but as friends. I go to A.A. and it really is helping me."

Maggie went to Jerry and hugged him. Otto and Matt slapped him on the back and shook his hand. They were delighted.

Jerry commented as they were leaving the school. "The first step in overcoming mistakes is to admit them."

His staff left but Matt went back to his office. He called the Superintendent's office to report about the day. "My boy, no news is good news. I haven't received one complaint about the your school."

"There are some problems to discuss.

Dr. Hull interrupted Matt. "I'm sure you and Mr. Bolt will take care of it. Nice job young man." he hung up.

Matt called the Assistant Superintendent. "Mr. Bolt's office."

"Hello, Phyllis, it's Matt Collins."

"Oh, how did school work out today?"

"Thanks to the team which includes you and the staff it worked out pretty good. May I speak to Mr. Bolt."

"He's sick Mr. Collins. Mr. Bolt came back from his vacation with a terrible cough. The doctor says it's acute bronchitis. He will be out at least two weeks."

"Thank you Phyllis."

Matt realized that Dr. Hull knew his Assistant was out. This was the old shuffle. He saw it many times in the service. Junior officers were not given the right information or information was kept from them in order for them to fail. Matt thought. *Not here. Not on my watch!*

Matt's cell rang. "Captain Collins"

"Yes, Matt Collins."

"This is Sergeant Major Ed Joyce. Do you remember me?"

"Of course Ed, what's up?"

"Sorry to give you bad news, but Major Jim Clinton has been killed in Afghanistan. I understand you served with him."

"He was my buddy. Jim had my back on a few missions into Indian Country. What are the plans?"

"His mom and dad want you to be a pallbearer in Rochester. The ceremony and service will be held at St. Mary's Church on Friday at noon and he will be buried at Riverside Cemetery, The Veteran's Area."

"I'll be there."

"Sir, in dress uniform please."

"Thank you Sergeant."

Matt immediately called the Superintendent's office and informed the secretary that he will be taking a personal day on Friday..

Ten minutes later the Superintendent called. "I'm afraid I can't give you permission to go. You just put your plan in action and it has to be monitored."

"With all due respect sir. I have Mr. Jackson who is excellent and my Team Leaders. They know what to do."

"Sorry. My answer is no."

"Dr. Hull, a friend and a buddy of mine in the United States Army Rangers has been killed in action in Afghanistan. I have been asked to be a pallbearer. I have to be in Rochester by noon on Friday."

"Sorry. My answer is no!"

Matt waited five seconds. "Have you served?"

"No."

"Then you don't understand. This man was a brother to me on the battlefield. I have an obligation."

"Matt, I have an obligation to the District."

"Well why don't you come down from you high perch and become the principal for a day and take my duty. That would solve the problem."

"Are you being impertinent?"

"No sir. I'm being truthful. You can dock me a day's pay. You can fire me on the spot. You can tell the newspapers that I went AWOL. I'm going to bury my comrade in arms. Why don't you ask the local VFW to give you their opinion? Why don't you ask your Business Manager to give you his opinion? Why don't you ask any veteran who served and the same answer will come up. Dr. Hull, with or without your permission I have a sacred duty and I will fulfill it."

There was silence on the other line. "I didn't know how strongly you felt about this. Certainly you may go."

Matt thought. *I don't think I want to work for this man at all. I'm going to go to my university and start looking for another position.*

* * *

Beth took the day off. She did not want Matt to be alone as he buried his friend. His PTSD symptoms were diminishing and she felt that he might overreact to this situation.

Matt had taken off his blue dress uniform jacket and was wearing a crisp white shirt with a blue tie. His neatly pressed pants had a gold stripe running down the sides. When he picked her up she was amazed at the four rows of ribbons on his jacket and special badges he wore. His officer's hat made him seem much taller.

"We should be at the church no later than eleven thirty. Thank heaven the traffic is light."

"Matt, tell me what to expect."

"The Funeral Director usually runs the protocol. When the hearse comes to the church the pallbearers will march alongside the coffin as it rolls down to the front of the church. The Priest takes over and we have a regular Catholic mass."

"How long will that take?"

"About forty minutes. Then the pallbearers take their places and we march alongside the coffin and bring it back to the hearse. We use our judgment if there are inclines and help move the dolly that is under the coffin.

"I've seen pictures of an American flag on the coffin."

"We usually place an American flag on the coffin before or after the church . It depends on what the family wants. Nevertheless, before the coffin goes into the hearse there will be an American flag on the coffin. We then follow the hearse to the cemetery. Then we give assistance to take the flag draped coffin to the gravesite."

"Is that where they blow taps?"

"Yes. The bugler stays near the gravesite and blows taps. After that a special color guard, probably from a Reserve Unit in Rochester has a flag folding ceremony."

"Does anybody say any words?"

"That's up to the family. I doubt it since we've just come back from mass. Usually the highest ranking member of the military unit presents the folded flag to the widow."

"Do they say anything?"

Matt wiped his bow. "I've had that duty a few times. I usually say: 'On behalf of a grateful nation we thank you for your husband's valor and service.'"

Beth's eyes started to fill up with tears as she looked at Matt driving to his friend's funeral. "There really aren't words, are there?"

Matt glanced at Beth. "No, no words just sorrow!"

* * *

After the funeral, as they were on the way back to Risenburg, Beth remembered seeing the strong, young men in uniform hugging each other and staying close to each other. Yes, they acted like brothers. The church mass was beautiful. Beth noticed Matt stayed on his knees a long time as he prayed. As a Catholic, Matt took communion. Beth was pleased that she attended.

She looked at Matt's drawn face. "You're very quiet. Is there anything you want to tell me?"

"The Superintendent wanted to deny me a personal day even when I told him what it was for. I told him I was going in no uncertain terms."

"You don't care anymore do you?"

"You know me like a book. I'll start looking for another position as soon as possible. Hell, I might take a year off and write my dissertation."

"Well I have to work somewhere. Maybe I'll get out of the school business and become a psychotherapist. It would take another twenty four credits and a psychology internship, but I could do it."

"That's a great idea How much would you charge me?'

"Oh, I'll think of something you can barter." She flushed and Matt laughed.

CHAPTER 47

Bryans Café was on the way home. They arrived at ten in the evening and were pleased that his vegan kitchen was still serving. Since they had become regulars, Bryan greeted them by name. "Ah, Beth and Matt, you look tired."

"We just drove in from Rochester."

"Well Beth, I'm going to make you a dish that will rejuvenate you and your man." He quickly did a perfect about face and ran to the kitchen.

Matt and Beth looked at the far wall where Bryan posted his monthly slogans. It read, "Bryan's is an establishment for detoxing the mind, spirit and body, and we feed you thusly!"

The waitress brought fresh pineapple juice to the tired couple. "This will help you get the fog out of your mind. Drink it slowly and enjoy it!"

On the table was Bryan's special honey wheat bread. Matt spread some home made strawberry jam on a slice and chewed it. "I don't know if I could ever be a complete vegan, but I could come close."

Beth finished her pineapple juice. "That was so refreshing. I wonder what dish Bryan is cooking up for us right now?"

A few minutes later Bryan came in with a creamy avocado carbonara. The pasta was hand made by Bryan and it was delicious.

Beth and Matt started to relax. It was a long day, but an important day. Matt seemed to be doing very well even though he attended his friend's funeral. Beth continually monitored him looking for signs of anxiety, anger, depression or disassociated thinking. None of these behaviors appeared. She was pleased that she came with Matt.

They finished the meal with a mock chocolate mousse that was off the charts. Thirty five minutes later they arrived at Beth's apartment. The couple crawled into bed and within ten minutes they both were asleep.

The rest of the weekend was meant for fun. They picked up local fruits and vegetables from the many farm stands at the Green Market just outside of town. Small farms located within thirty minutes from the heart of Risenburg were typical of many upstate New York communities.

Beth took off her straw hat and wiped her brow. "Matt, I want to look at some of the local art work and I know that doesn't thrill you too much. Why don't we meet at the Hamburger Joint."

They both looked at their watches, kissed and separated. Matt had a cute idea. He didn't know that Beth had a cute idea as well.

One hour later they met at the Hamburger Joint with bags on their arms. "You first," Matt grinned, you first."

Beth took out two tee shirts. The front of the shirts had a large red heart outline and inside was written, "Beth - Bride!" and underneath "Matt- Groom!"

"I love it! When we get to Florida that's the first shirt I'll wear."

Matt took out his surprise. Two baseball caps in red and written on the front was "Beth & Matt" and underneath "Together!"

Beth took off her straw hat and immediately put on the baseball hat. Matt followed her lead. They laughed and ordered hamburgers. Beth chewing on her juicy burger said, "Too much vegan food makes me inert. I want to be lively."

On Sunday the couple went out to the grand opening of a new restaurant outside of town. Maggie and Jason Carter invited them. The owner of the restaurant was one of Jason's clients.

They arrived and found a Tex-Mex restaurant. Maggie looked at Jason. "Did you know about this?"

"Believe me, if I did I would have thought twice about going here."

"What's wrong with Tex-Mex food Maggie?"

"Matt, I love the food, it doesn't love my stomach."

"Let's look at the menu when we get inside. Let me guide you through an easy way to love Tex-Mex."

Matt showed Maggie that she could have a simple chicken dish as Mexican Lime Chicken breast with yellow rice. It would not hurt her system, yet it was tasty.

"Just hold the refried beans and you will be in great shape"

"Where did you learn about Mexican food?"

" I was stationed in lower Texas for a few months. They serve a lot of Tex-Mex food there."

The all ordered flan for dessert and they loved it!

That night Matt slept well. There was no stirring around, or waking up with a start, or moaning. Beth had observed all of this during the time they were together. She thought, *Thank God he's getting better.*

Matt slept peacefully. She fell asleep happy, contented and dreaming of a beautiful wedding.

## CHAPTER 48

Matt called Professor Francois Lebo, his mentor at New York University. "I think this District is stuck with a Superintendent who is always covering his tail and an Assistant who is never around. I've had to do the heavy lifting by myself."

"Tell me about it. I have time."

Matt laid it all out. He had kept a log for each day and used it as a guide. When it finally came to the personal day incident his mentor was stunned.

"Matt, get out of the District. You are dealing with an evil boss who really doesn't care about anybody except himself."

"How will I get a good recommendation.?"

"You have memos from Central office that indicate your good work. The newspaper clippings of the fire and then your subsequent work is all out there for other Superintendents and Boards to read. Develop a folder that highlights all you have done. Use the Code of Conduct, hell use the PTA and their happiness with you. Even if you don't have a beautiful letter from the Superintendent, you can show what you are made of as you ran the school."

"Will this get me an interview?"

"Certainly and when it comes time to answer the real question you can talk about the three principals who were there before you. That is a pattern that the Superintendent has and it is known history."

"Thank you Professor Lebo."

"You are certainly welcome."

It was time to discuss the grievance the Music Teacher filed.

Sitting in his office were Jerry Jackson, Jennifer Stanton, the Union President, Sam England, Teacher Representative, and Linda Berlin, the Music Teacher.

Matt started. "Let the record show that I Matt Collins have received the initial complaint and I am responding on the third day of notification."

Matt then named the participants, their titles and the reason for the grievance.

"Mr. Collins, we know that since the fire there has been a sacrifice made by many of the teachers. The LRC Teacher complains of noise, yet she can deal with it. Teachers of the destroyed rooms complain, but they are dealing with it. It seems Mrs. Berlin cannot deal with her working conditions." Jennifer Stanton smiled at Matt as she finished her statement.

"Mrs. Berlin, specifically what is the problem?"

The grey haired teacher with twenty years in the District stood up. "Mr. Collins I have never filed a grievance in my life. I can't teach Music when I have a piano on the side of the auditorium and the kids are in auditorium seats thirty feet away from me. Its not right. I really want to teach them."

Matt thought for a moment. "Mrs. Berlin, if I had the piano moved to the stage and some desks and chairs placed on the stage near the piano, would that help."

Mr. Jackson spoke up. "Mrs. Berlin, I would call our Chief Custodian to find the proper furniture and we can order a furniture company to lift the piano onto the stage. This could be done by next Monday."

"You heard what my Assistant has said. What do you think?"

"I think this could work out."

Jerry Jackson stood up. "I will make this particular job my mission. Our job is to educate our students. I want the students to have a good musical experience."

Jennifer Stanton looked at Mrs. Berlin. "Yes or no for this plan?'

"Why of course, yes."

After the teachers left Matt asked Jerry to stay. "Jerry, thank you for the support. I think you were the person who made the deal. Nice catch!"

Jerry beamed from ear to ear. "I'm learning all the time. As they say in the program first things first."

Matt made sure to write a letter of commendation to Jerry. He thought about Jerry, and perhaps with a little more sober thought he would make a good principal.

The week ended without too many problems. In fact Jerry had the piano lifted to the stage and the furniture placed by Thursday afternoon. He was becoming a valuable aide.

On Friday morning Beth called Matt in his office. "I just got a lovely phone call from Celia Jackson. She and Jerry have invited us over for Sunday dinner. I told her my schedule was free, but I would have to check with you."

"Sounds good to me. Please get all the details."

* * *

On Sunday Matt and Beth drove just outside of Risenburg into a small community of some eighty homes. There were simple Cape Cod models, California ranch models, Split Level models, and large Estate models. The Jackson's house was one the small Cape Cod models  It was painted white and had red shutters.

Matt and Beth had brought cut flowers as a gift. "Here Celia, put them in water." Beth handed them to her.

Jerry shook Matt's hand. "Welcome to our home. It's small, but it's ours."

Celia took them on a tour. Downstairs there was a great room that was large enough for a living room area and a dining room. Near the dining area was a work kitchen with a small bistro table. The other side of the house had a master bedroom, about thirteen by thirteen with a walk in closet and nice size bath. Upstairs there were two small ten by ten bedrooms with a smaller bathroom.

"The house is seventeen hundred square feet with a two car garage." Jerry was glowing and seemed very proud.

"I love the way you decorated the house."

"Thank you Beth. It's quite contemporary, yet Jerry and I enjoy it. Since Jerry's been in the program he's helped me paint the rooms and if you notice we have a new wooden floor that Jerry laid by himself."

"Wow, nice work partner!" Matt was truly impressed.

Celia had a pitcher in her hand. "I can offer you lemonade or a soft drink. We decided to toss all alcoholic beverages away."

Beth responded quickly. "Lemonade for both of us would be fine."

Jerry lifted his glass. "To Matt and Beth as they prepare for their wedding. We hope it's a good one and that you are happy for the rest of your life."

They clinked glasses and drank their lemonade. Jerry was very helpful as Celia brought out the first course of shrimp cocktail. The meal followed with a delicious rump roast, roast potatoes, green beans and coleslaw. Dessert was homemade deep dish apple pie.

Beth wiped her mouth. "Where did you learn to cook? Your food is superb."

Celia smiled. "I graduated with a culinary degree from community college and worked as a chef for a few years."

"That's where I found my talented wife."

Jerry went on to tell about the courtship and Celia talked about the marriage. They seemed to be so happy. "I owe my new life to you Matt. If you didn't push me I would have been lost."

"You were the only one who could make the decision for yourself. You have a wonderful wife who supports you and I think you are ready to go out and start taking interviews. I think you can and will be a principal."

Beth whispered into Matt's ear. "Do you want to tell him?"

"Jerry. I'll be leaving at the end of the year. The Superintendent and I don't meet eye to eye. This may be an opportunity for you, if you play it right. My contract ends August first, but I'm owed twenty two days of vacation time so the reality is that I'm out of the school July first."

"God Matt, I really don't want you to go. You are the best."

"I'm the best because people around me want to work with me not for me. Jerry with me. If you get that going, then you will always be a winner!"

Beth took Jerry's arm. "Please hold back on telling anybody. Matt has to do this first."

Celia took Jerry's other arm. "You have to be a good soldier and hold your tongue. I'm sure you're going to get your turn."

Jerry was amazed that things were moving so fast. "I'm sure I can hold back. Matt, I owe you and I certainly respect your wishes."

"Thanks Jerry."

On the way back to Beth's apartment the couple stayed quiet for a little while.

Matt let out a long breath. "Let's hope that we can close school in seven weeks and do it peacefully. It's been one hell of a year!"

Beth replied. "Amen."

* * *

The next week went by quickly. There was great excitement about the Seventh and Eighth Grade Baseball Team. They had just won the League Championship and were heading to the Regional Playoffs.

Jerry walked into Matt's office wearing a school baseball hat. "I'd like to go to the game when the kids play for the regional's. The bus has already been scheduled. Is that okay with you?"

"No problem. Enjoy the game. The kids are doing great."

"Thanks to Rob Stuart. That kid has a great arm. The high school coach is relishing the thought of getting many wins from him next year. The kid is full of himself, but he really is good."

"Isn't that Maureen Stuart's kid? My PTA President's kid."

"Yep. Your PTA President has a budding super star to deal with."

" It would be nice to win the Regional Championship."

CHAPTER 49

Beth and Matt were pleased that they were able to exchange their airline tickets. It seemed that an extra day was tacked on to the school schedule for Memorial Day. They would have a four day weekend instead of three.

The rationale for this was the District's calendar planning. They had planned for ten extra snow days and only a few snow days had been used. This extra day was called a pay back day or adjustment day. It really did not matter what it was called since the staff and the kids were happy to have a four day holiday at the end of May.

Matt stayed with Beth over the weekend. "I hope your mom is feeling better. Is she?"

"I called her yesterday to tell her of the calendar change and she seemed guarded. My dad is quiet about her suffering and it's like pulling teeth to have him talk to me."

"I think he's trying to protect you from feeling stressed."

"This is the weekend to finalize everything for the wedding." Beth went to the cupboard and took out a folder. "Here, read this and see what you think?"

Matt opened the folder and let out a cool whistle. He read: budget, invitations, rings, RSVP, wedding party, guest list, photographer, florist, corsages for mothers, caterer, menu, table arrangements, wedding cake, band and music selections, limousines, hotel rooms, guest seating, marriage license, tuxedos, wedding dress, bridesmaid dresses, shoes and accessories, spa, hair, makeup, nails, gifts for bridesmaids and groomsmen, gift list and thank you cards, get addresses.

Every item had notations including names, dates, addresses, spaces, phone numbers, budgeted amounts, actual amounts, and backup vendors or service people.

"You amaze me. How did you do this while working?"

"I haven't watched much TV or anything else. My mom and I have talked about every item. Do you see anything missing?"

"Have you arranged the wedding ceremony"

"I'm Episcopalian and you're Catholic. I talked it over with your parents and mine and we decided to be married by a Catholic priest. We must make an appointment to see the parish priest. "

Matt kissed her on her cheek. "Thank you, it does matter to me."

"I know I left the honeymoon arrangements to you. Have you finalized the plan?"

"Yes. I know that we both work out, and we both like the outdoors, and we both like scenery and we both like fresh food so"

"Stop teasing me."

"Beth, we're going to the Harbourside Hotel, Spa & Marina in Bar Harbor Maine. It overlooks Frenchman's Bay from downtown. It's really a place that is a relaxed seaside haven. The hotel is right on the water and right in town. We can walk to the little shops and restaurants in downtown and have lobster for breakfast, lunch and dinner. If we want to we can go on a whale watching cruise or rent our own sailboat."

"That sounds wonderful!"

"It gets better. Acadia National Park is nearby. We can hike, bike, climb, and take all sorts of trails. There is even a tour of the area if we wish to do that. I've booked the airline tickets and car rental for July first through the seventh. Happy Fourth of July! And happy honeymoon.!"

"Where will we stay from the twenty seventh to the thirtieth?"

"I've booked us into the hotel where our wedding will take place. I figured your folks and mine could have some quality time together. I know how close you are to your mom and dad."

Beth started to cry. "Oh sweetheart, thank you for thinking of my feelings. Do my folks know about the schedule?"

"No. I figured I'd tell them over our weekend. My parents are staying over for another two days as guests of your parents."

She kissed him sweetly. "One more week and we can be in Florida."

"Let's go to dinner. I feel a lasagna coming to me."

Beth laughed and picked up her handbag. She grabbed Matt. "I want to be called Mrs. Collins so badly. I love you so much!"

The Italian food at "The Pizza Place" was excellent. The owners were long term residents of Risenburg and seemed to know everybody in the community. The owner greeted Matt with a big smile and brought over a carafe of white wine immediately. Matt thought. *I'm going to miss a great deal about Risenburg when I leave.*

\* \* \*

On Monday morning Matt met with Otto, Jerry and Maggie to go through final requests for summer projects to improve the school. The recent fire damaging four classrooms would have the highest priority. Rooms were to be repaired, painted and refurbished. Safety of the school was paramount and a request for an engineering report concerning the school's total electrical system was added. The outside of the school was to be repaired and painted as well. "Otto, thanks for your hard work on these repair lists. I'm sure the Board will go along with most of them."

"You're welcome."

"Jerry, when you get back from your summer vacation I would suggest you focus on all of the top priority items. Sometimes it takes a push from the building level to get things done. No Superintendent or Board would want to receive a memo from a school administrator stating that the school was not safe for the students."

Jerry smiled in a knowingly manner. "Right. First things first!"

Maggie closed her note pad and looked at Matt. "I'll make a PERT chart for all the projects so Jerry can check the progress."

"Great." Matt thought, *Well, at least some of my innovations will remain in the school when I leave.*

On Tuesday, late in the afternoon, Matt got a call from Mrs. O'Dwyer the School Nurse. "Mr. Collins I have a problem. Would you be so kind as to come to my office as soon as you can."

Matt hustled over to the Nurse's Office which was down the hallway some thirty yards away. Upon entering he saw a blond girl on the couch curled up in a fetal position. He walked over to Mrs. O'Dwyer. "What's wrong with her?"

"The girl is Betty Simpson. She's in eighth grade and will be fifteen next month. She was held back in grade school because of illness."

"Why is she all curled up?"

"She told me that her stepfather is sexually molesting her. He comes into her room at night and has sexual intercourse with her. Her stepfather told her that if she told anybody he would leave her mother and blame her."

"Where is her mother?"

"That's the problem. Her mother works as an exotic dancer in the 'Sweet Candy Club' outside of town."

Matt quickly responded. "Okay, we have to have Betty tell the police her story."

"It's not as simple as that. Her sister is eleven and Betty is worried that she will become abused. She broke down in my office and then just collapsed."

Matt picked up the phone and buzzed Maggie. "Call Ms. Andrews and tell her to drop everything and get to the Nurse's Office immediately. That's an order, not a request!"

Five minutes later Beth came into the office. She looked at the girl on the couch. "What is the story?"

Mrs. O'Dwyer filled her in as quickly as she could.

"We have to get Betty to speak to the police. Would you mind if both of you left the room and perhaps I can get Betty to talk to me. She is one of my eighth graders."

About a half hour later Matt and the Nurse were called back into the room. Betty was sitting on the couch with Beth right next to her holding her hand.

"How are you doing Betty?" Matt's voice quivered.

Betty looked directly at Matt. "Mr. Collins, I'm ready to call the police."

The sequence of events moved quickly. Matt explained the situation to the Chief of Police. Chief Miller responded by sending a female detective to the school. Less than an hour later the detective took Betty's story.

Matt was in his office when Maggie buzzed. "Detective Jayne Winston to see you."

Jayne Winston quickly opened the door to Matt's office. "Principal Collins, thanks for getting the child to speak to me. We are going to arrest Mr. Henry on rape charges. You have to call Child Protective Services and report this. That's the law. Since the mother doesn't know of this we are going to send a social worker over to her house to counsel her. Expect Mrs. Henry to come raging into school. Calm her down and tell her you have contacted Child Protective Services as well. She'll be pissed, but we have to protect Betty and her sister. Any questions?"

"No questions. You do your job and I'll do mine. I don't want to meet Mr. Henry because I'll be charged with aggravated assault. Thanks."

After calling Child Protective Services Matt called Beth. "Great job, Beth. I knew you were a good counselor. Now I know you're a great counselor. I called CPS and they have recorded my complaint. A social worker will counsel Mrs. Henry and Betty's stepfather is going to jail charged with rape."

"I hope Mrs. Henry files a protective order against her husband in case he makes bail. I'll call the principal of her sister's elementary school and fill him in. Matt, I'll watch Betty very carefully. I promise."

"Good. No kid should have that weight on her back."

The rest of the week went smoothly. The staff was preparing for the Annual Field Day to be held on Friday. All the teacher specialists and Team Leaders cooperated to plan for a full day of events. The staff and the kids looked forward to this tradition and Matt delegated it to Jerry who loved doing it.

On Wednesday Jerry came into Matt's office with a folder. "Here is the list of events and games planned for our Field Day. I need your approval."

"Jerry, did you look it over and did the staff say it was okay?"

"Why of course."

"Then I approve of it without looking through it. I trust you. You are a good schoolman!"

Jerry's eyes watered. "Thank you sir."

He wheeled and left the office beaming. Obviously he was thrilled with Matt's trust in him.

Matt opened the folder and was pleased to see the games were well organized and structured. There were the standard games as:

relays, tag games, tug of war, dodge ball, ten pin knockdown, limbo dance, hula hoop endurance, and softball throw. He read about some new and funny games utilizing balloons, traffic cones, and a huge obstacle course throughout the total field. The day would end with a student versus faculty softball game.

Matt read about community members taking part in the games as well. The PTA supplied ribbons and awards and the local restaurant owners supplied soft drinks, ice, water, hot dogs, hamburgers, chips and pizza. Obviously this event was one of the major events in Risenburg.

There was general excitement from the students during the week. They realized that Field Day and the Memorial Day weekend symbolized that school was nearly over. Many of their parents were already talking about summer vacations. There was a pleasant atmosphere of happiness in the school.

Matt realized that the Memorial Day weekend symbolized that his stay at Risenburg was nearly over. He would submit his letter of resignation the third week of June, resigning as of August first. That was more than the thirty day notice which was the norm. Matt was owed twenty two days of pay for his vacation days. The wedding was on Sunday, June thirtieth. . He thought. *That vacation pay will pay for our honeymoon.*

Beth called Matt. "We're having Maggie, Jason and Nancy over for dinner tonight. Will you please make sure that we have enough wine."

"No problem. I'm looking forward to the dinner."

\* \* \*

Beth prepared a huge lasagna for dinner. Every one ate with gusto and some drank with zest as well. It was a fun evening with all participants talking about previous vacations and foreign countries visited.

Beth sipped he wine. "I've never been to Europe, but hope to go soon."

Nancy downed her wine and responded. "Beth, if Matt doesn't want to go with you call me. I'll bet we would have a ball."

"I'd like to go to Ireland and trace my family's history." Matt declared, "It's the Irish in me!"

There was great laughter. Maggie lifted her glass of lemonade. "Here's to Beth and Matt going to Ireland soon."

Jason Carter lifted his glass of water. "Here's to your wedding. We got the invitations yesterday"

Nancy interrupted. "I got mine yesterday as well!"

"You have been great friends and we hope you will be able to make it."

"Sure, Florida in June. I'll buy new swim trunks. Maggie and I will be there."

Nancy Briggs was silent. Beth looked at her. "Do you think you can make it?"

"Oh I'll make it. The problem is that I'm dating two men and I don't know who I would want to take to your wedding. This is serious business."

Beth and Maggie both nodded. "Why is it serious?" Matt queried.

"When you take a date to a wedding, especially out of town, it tells the other person how you feel about him. It's serious."

"Thank you Beth, I could not have explained it any better."

Jason Carter finished his last piece of apple pie. "Have you invited any other people from Risenburg?"

"We invited Celia and Jerry Jackson. No one else."

"Well Matt. We promise to give your guests good behavior." Jason cackled.

After their guests left and the couple finished putting everything away Beth came up to Matt and kissed him gently. "Other than Jerry, does any other person know about you resigning?"

"No. I'll tell Maggie and Jason a week before school ends."

"What about Nancy?"

"Same timeline. If they want to cancel it will be alright with me."

"I think they will remain friends even when we leave the District."

Matt nodded. "Perhaps. I hope so."

CHAPTER 50

Late Thursday afternoon Jerry walked into Matt's office. "Don't forget to wear a gym outfit for tomorrow. The staff will be coming in dressed that way as well."

"Thanks for the heads up. I hope it will be a good day for the kids tomorrow."

Jerry smiled at Matt. "We're responsible for the effort not the outcome."

Matt realized the change that Jerry had shown over the last months. The A.A. Program was obviously making a difference in his attitude, personality and outlook on life. Matt really liked what he saw.

* * *

On Friday, Matt wearing his dark navy gym suit, spoke into the microphone to all of the school assembled on the field and bleachers. "Ladies and Gentlemen. Will every one please rise for the presentation of colors by the Risenburg Police Department Honor Guard. The singing of the National Anthem will be performed by our own Music Teacher, Mrs. Linda Berlin."

After the colors were posted Matt approached the microphone again. "Let the games begin. Remember to play fair!"

Matt walked around the field and felt really happy. The kids were having a great time and all was going well. The School Nurse had set up an emergency table in case of small scratches or bruises. Matt prayed that nothing would happen. He viewed the energy of the parents plus community volunteers and felt a bit sad that he would be leaving. Risenburg was a good town with good, hard working people representing the best values of the area.

He decided to go back to his office to relieve Maggie so she could go to the field and enjoy the happenings. "Maggie, I'll hold the fort. Go ahead out and join Jason who is volunteering at the tug of war. I'll see you in an hour."

Matt stayed in the front office and settled into Maggie's chair. He answered a few calls. The pizza delivery man came into the office. "Can I drive my truck onto the field?"

"No, but you can go along the right side of the building until you get to the bleachers. Then have some parent volunteers help you unload the pizzas. They'll show you where to go."

Beth finished her stint as a referee at the sixth grade dodge ball contest and needed to freshen up. She went into the school to the faculty lounge and came out five minutes later. As she passed by a custodial closet she heard voices in the closet and opened the door. Beth saw two students. A girl performing oral sex on a boy whose pants were down to his ankles. Beth yelled, "Stop this. Stop this now!"

Beth marched the boy and girl to the Principal's office. She said nothing to them until they were sitting on the bench outside the office. "I know both of you. Nora Costello, shame on you for your actions. Rob Stuart you should know better, shame on you as well. This situation is now in Mr. Collin's hands. I'm your Eighth Grade Guidance Counselor and I guess I haven't done a good job counseling you. I'm embarrassed as well."

The cute blond girl started to cry. "Please Ms. Andrews, let us go. My father is President of the Board of Education. My parents will be shocked."

The lanky young man nodded. "My mom is President of the PTA. She won't be able to show her face around here. Please, let us go and we'll never fool around again."

Just then Matt walked out of his office. He looked at Beth and the kids and instinctively knew that this situation was a bad one. "Ms. Andrews, why are the students here?"

"May I speak to you in your office?"

"Certainly. Both of you kids stay on the bench and don't talk and don't get up. That's an order!"

They went into the office and Beth spoke rapidly. "Matt, I caught them in a custodial closet. Nora Costello was performing oral sex on Rob Stuart. I brought them down to you."

Matt called Jerry's cell phone. "Jerry, please have Mrs. Stuart and Mr. Costello come to my office as soon as possible. They both volunteered for our Field Day."

"Okay. It may take a few minutes to find them."

Fifteen minutes later both parents arrived. They saw their kids sitting on the bench. Mr. Costello walked over to his daughter. "What are you up to?'

Nora started to cry and shake. She could not talk and would not look at her father.

Beth Andrews took Mr. Costello's arm and led him into Matt's office. Sitting at the small table was Matt and Mrs. Stuart. "We have a serious breach of our Code of Conduct. Ms. Andrews will you tell Mr. Costello and Mrs. Stuart what happened."

I was coming out of the ladies lounge when I heard noise in the custodial closet. I opened the door and found Nora performing oral sex on Rob. I took them to the office."

Mrs. Stuart shouted "Oh my God."

"Are you sure you saw this Ms. Andrews?" Dominic Costello queried.

"Of course I saw this. That's why you're here. We have a big problem."

"Mrs. Stuart and Mr. Costello, please take your children home. They are suspended for three days. Today, and after the holiday next Wednesday and Thursday. They will be allowed back to school on Friday. Are there any questions?"

Both parents left and took their children home. Matt looked out his office window and saw Nora Costello crying and Rob Stuart walking with his head down. "I guess the real punishment will be when they get home. I cannot condone sexual behavior in the school although I know the kid's hormones are intense. This is a tough call."

Beth shook her head in disbelief. "I never thought I would be involved in something like this. They didn't teach us to handle this type of situation in graduate school. Matt, you didn't even talk to the kids."

"What could I say other than you broke the Code of Conduct. I think the parents have to have the courage to confront this and work with their kids. I just cannot excuse this behavior in our school!"

"I'm going back to the field."

Matt called Jerry on his cell. "Have Maggie come back to the office. There is one chore I have to do and then I want to go outside again. I need a breath of fresh air."

Maggie came back to the office. "Please bring your pad. This letter will be sent to the parents of Nora Costello and Rob Stuart. It will be identical except for the names."

"Matt, are you okay? You seem upset."

"Oh yes, I'm really upset, but I have to do my job. Dear Mr. and Mrs. fill in the names. Your son/daughter, name of child, is suspended for three days. Starting today, date through next Wednesday and Thursday. The reason for this suspension is a serious breach of our school's Code of Conduct. The display of overt and improper physical contact with another student is not allowed. Please counsel your child in terms of proper behavior. Sincerely,

"What happened?"

"Both kids went to third base, in the custodial closet. Beth found them."

"Wow. This will upset the parents. Wait until the Superintendent gets this letter."

The phone rang. It was the Superintendent. "Mr. Collins. I just heard from Mr. Costello and Mrs. Stuart. They think your punishment is too harsh."

"I don't."

"Why don't you modify it for one less day?"

"No, I won't do it."

"Well, I'm directing you to do it."

"Put it in writing and deliver it to me. I'm leaving this afternoon for Florida."

"Come to my office immediately."

"Listen you bag of wind. You're covering your ass. I'll let my School Administrators Association attorney review your memos to me. We'll see who is manipulating the situation. I'm sure as hell willing to go all the way. This is chicken shit and you know it! Now I know why you can't hold onto any decent school principal!"

"Now Matt, don't get upset. Perhaps a meeting with all concerned in my office on Wednesday would be acceptable."

"I'll be there with Ms. Andrews who saw the whole thing."

"Alright. Nine in the morning."

"We will be there."

Maggie heard the whole conversation. "Matt, why don't you take the rest of the day off? We only have another hour or so."

"Hell Maggie, I've been in real combat. Wait until Dr. Hull meets with me next Wednesday! I'm going back to the field. Make sure to have the letters ready."

Maggie thought. *We just lost an outstanding principal.*

* * *

Beth and Matt talked on the plane as they were heading to Orlando. Matt was insistent that all the people involved would try to get him to withdraw the suspension letters and expunge the record. "Beth, these are people who have no value system when it comes to covering their asses. The Superintendent is a bureaucrat who will placate the Board President and the PTA President. He doesn't care about the discipline in the school, nor the kids, nor the community. He is quite self-centered about it. When I fight him he tries to weasel out by using some other strategy. The son of a bitch was willing to trade off an Assistant Superintendent position for me to take it easy on reporting the discrepancy in test scores. When I say weasel I mean he has all the characteristics of that animal."

"Come on Matt. You're just angry at him."

"No. Listen to me. A weasel is related to a skunk. They have quick minds and hide in a certain Machiavellian manner."

"Oh Matt. Come on."

"Listen Beth. The weasel is really a small animal so they are motivated to use devious tactics for survival. Sometimes a weasel will use as a weapon its charm. They still are carnivorous so they have to survive. That's Dr. Hull."

"Where did you learn all of this?"

"Survival training in the United States Army. Enough said!"

"Let's change the subject. There is a jeweler in Orlando who has been recommended by my mother. He fixed her ring and earrings and is quite reputable and fair. My mom said he has quite a nice selection of wedding rings."

"Wedding rings?"

"Don't you want to wear a wedding ring?"

"I never thought of it.'

Beth looked concerned. She reached over and took Matt's hand. "Is this thing in the school fogging your brain?"

"Yeah, I think you're right. Sure, I'd like to wear a wedding band as long as it matches yours."

Beth kissed his cheek. "That's the plan."

"Don't forget about the priest. We have to see him to discuss our marriage."

"What could he possibly say that we haven't discussed?"

"How about will you raise your children Catholic?"

"Oh. Matt. We really haven't discussed children in our marriage."

"It's a good time to discuss it now. We still have an hour or so left in the flight."

"I want children, but not right now. I want you to finish your doctorate. I want to finish mine as well. Perhaps in a few years, maybe four or five we could start a family."

"I'll be thirty three next month. That means when I'm thirty seven or so we start a family. When our child finishes college I'll be fifty eight. The next one and I'll be sixty. It looks like we will both have to work in order to raise a family."

"I'm twenty eight. So I'm five years behind you in every thing you said. If I'm able to get my doctorate in psychotherapy and counseling I'll have my own practice. That means I can set my own hours. Who knows, maybe you would want to teach at a university. Would you?"

"I really don't know. I'd rather become a Superintendent of Schools and perhaps be an adjunct professor for awhile."

"Well. Do we have a plan?"

"How about a boy and a girl?"

"I can't promise you their sexes, but I can promise you they'll have the best parents in the world."

The rest of the flight was peaceful. Matt slept and Beth watched over him, concerned about the stress he was experiencing.

## CHAPTER 51

The good news was that both Matt and Beth took carry on luggage. The bad news was that it took close to an hour to get their rental car. There was an accident blocking the main entrance to their car rental. They finally got their car and in thirty minutes they were hugging and kissing Beth's mother. Her father, usually a dignified man decided to hug Matt. "Welcome son. It is indeed a pleasure to call you son."

Matt was touched. There was a warmth and sincerity to this man who carried himself in a distinguished manner. "Thank you. I'm so pleased to be here."

"Mom, it's getting late and I'm tired. How about talking about the wedding at breakfast tomorrow?"

"That's fine with us." She kissed Beth and whispered in her ear. "I'm not doing too well."

When they were preparing for bed Beth started to cry. "My mom is not doing that well. She just told me."

"It's treatable hon."

"I know, but it certainly is taking a lot out of her."

"Would you want to talk to her oncologist? We're here until Tuesday evening."

Beth wiped her eyes and looked at her fiancé. She thought. *Thank God I have him. He supports me in so many ways.* "Yes. I'd like that very much."

"So be it!"

Matt was awakened by his cell phone ringing. He looked at the lighted digital clock in the bedroom. It was twelve thirty in the morning. "Matt, it's Steve. I'm sorry for calling so late, but I'll be in Orlando tomorrow for business. Is there a way we can meet?"

"Where are you staying?"

"The Ritz Carlton, Orlando."

"We'll pick you up. What's a good time?"

"How about six. I've got meetings all morning and afternoon."

"Done. Beth and I will see you."

"Oh, Linda is with me. She's anxious to see both of you. How about dinner?"

"Sounds good to me!"

Matt fell asleep within five minutes of the phone call. He smiled thinking that he would see his big brother soon.

In the morning when Matt woke up he did not see Beth. He opened the door of the bedroom and heard laughter. It was Beth and her mother. They were making breakfast and enjoying each other.

Orange juice was on the table when Matt got to the kitchen. Beth kissed him gently. "Sit down and my mom and I will show you what a good breakfast is all about."

Mr. Andrews was drinking coffee. "I've got some chores to do this morning, so I'll see you later."

"We have to see my brother for dinner tonight. He's in Orlando for business. I hope you don't mind?"

Mrs. Andrews quickly responded. "No problem at all Matt."

They served blueberry pancakes, sausage and bacon and the most delicious maple syrup. The pancakes were especially fluffy and tasty.

"The pancakes are wonderful. Where did you get this syrup? It's the best I've ever tasted."

"That was a gift from friends who spent their vacation in Maine. I'm almost out of it. I only serve it to special people." Mrs. Andrews came over to him and hugged him.

Matt's eyes watered. He thought. *If daughters are the reflection of their mother's than I will have a spectacular loving wife in the future. What a beautiful role model!*

"Beth and I will be going to Maine for our honeymoon. I'll buy you a jug of this syrup if I can find it."

The coffee was served with a home made pastry. Matt patted his stomach. "I think I'll skip lunch."

Both women laughed.

Matt looked up the number of the church where they would be married. He called immediately. "Father Hurley, this is Matt Collins. You are marrying Beth Andrews and me on June thirtieth. May we come in to speak to you.?"

"Come in at one today. I'll be available for an hour"

* * *

Father Hurley was about forty years old. He was tall and lean with hair that was wonderfully red. His face had freckles and his smile was warm and loving. There was an athleticism about him that Matt spotted.

Matt and Beth sat in his office. It reflected his personality. There were pictures of sailboats and speed boats and yachts. The furniture was modern and comfortable. The office was bright and cheerful. "Here is a list of items that you will have to work on for your wedding. Since you will be out of town you may call me at anytime. Beth, it's really about the type of ceremony you want."

"Thank you Father. I'll look it over and get back to you."

"I know you are short of time so I'm going to go through a list of questions with you. I need honest answers. Will you do that for me?"

The couple nodded as they held hands.

"Alright, please answer and if you don't know that's okay as well. Would you like to talk a little about your family situation? Would you say you have had a happy childhood?"

Beth answered first. "I had a very happy childhood. My mom is sick with a treatable cancer and I worry about her."

"I will pray for her recovery."

Matt laughed. "We were the Cleavers, that TV family that had a small house, white picket fence, two children and a loving mom and dad. I grew up in Levittown, New York. My folks are happily retired."

Father Hurley continued. "Obviously your relationship with your parents has been excellent. At any time was there any violence, alcohol abuse or drugs in the family?"

Beth quickly answered. "Not that I know of."

Matt shook his head in the negative. "No."

"Please think about this question before answering. Has suffering been part of your experience in life to date?"

Beth looked at Matt and decided to answer first. "I'm concerned about my mother. I sometimes worry that she will not be able to take care of her home and my dad. It worries me."

"Thank you for sharing this with me. A strong faith in God and a good doctor is all we can ask for."

"Thank you Father."

"Matt, any suffering in terms of your experience?

"Father, I was a Ranger in the service. I served in Afghanistan and Iraq. Yeah, I saw suffering and killing and maiming and everything else that war brings on. It takes time to get over it."

"Do you think you need special help to get over it?"

"I really don't know Father. So far it's been okay."

"Could you tell me a little about yourselves – your strengths and weaknesses? What do you find joy in? What makes you sad? What are your goals in life? What is most important to you?"

Beth responded. "I'm close to a doctorate in psychotherapy. I'm a guidance counselor and sometimes I feel so much for my clients that my professional judgment is clouded. I'm working on that."

Father Hurley stood up and opened a small refrigerator. "Do you want some water or soda? I'm having some."

"Water would be fine for Matt and me."

"Beth. You sound a lot like me. There are some of my parishioners who I deal with they really get into you."

"Oh I know. It's tough to be objective and rationale and still have a loving heart."

Father Hurley sipped his water slowly. "If you can, talk a little about past relationships and how they might differ from this one?"

"I had a boyfriend for two years and it ended up with both of us realizing that we were just using each other. I love Matt and it is completely different. We are partners in almost everything we do. Father, we really talk a lot."

The Priest started to laugh and was joined by Matt. Beth picked up on it and joined in the laughter. "Matt, how about your past relationships?"

"I had one relationship on Long Island and it ended up with my girlfriend trying to hold me back from moving up in my career. It was not a pleasant breakup. Beth and I are more compatible. We root for each other and are aware of each other's goals."

"Both of you have made this interview very easy. I'm going to skip my question about strengths and weaknesses. However, how do you view marriage?"

"I see myself in a marriage as a partner, supporter, nurturer, and eventually a mother. I'm twenty eight years old and I certainly know that there will be hills and valleys in our marriage. I'm confident that we can work it out."

Matt nodded his head. "Father Hurley, I'm thirty two years old, nearly thirty three. This is the most serious decision of my life. I view this marriage as a culminating event in my life. My duty is to protect the family, to be a true partner with Beth and to be a support for her. What I mean is that I will support Beth's career wishes and be there for her always."

"Will you be faithful to each other?"

Both Matt and Beth looked at each other and nodded.

"Where do you want to be in ten or twenty years.?"

"Father, if you are thinking about divorce, it's not in my vocabulary."

"I didn't mean that Beth. I meant your future goals?"

"I plan to have my own psychotherapy practice and integrate it with my family life. After that it's a matter of good health."

"Father Hurley, you really are covering more than we know right now. I plan to get my doctorate and be a high school principal or Superintendent perhaps teach at a university. It would be great to have kids as well."

"Talking about kids, how do you see parenting?"

"I believe in giving kids boundaries. As they begin to grow up the boundaries can get wider until they become young adults. Father, you know I'm a guidance counselor and that still doesn't change any of my thoughts. I believe this guideline within my career as well."

"Matt, how do you view parenting?"

Matt smiled. "Ditto!"

Every one started to laugh again. Father Hurley looked at the couple. "I am enjoying this interview. I see two mature people who have wonderful intellects and a great sense of humor."

"Father, I'm Irish. What did you expect?"

Laughter started all over again. "I'm going to skip my question about "natural family planning' and living together since both of you seem to be quite mature. Instead I'd like to discuss your faith. You are getting married in the Church – did you want to say anything about your faith? Who has been a witness of faith to you?"

"I'm Episcopalian and believe in the Nicene Creed. It is my belief that anything else in terms of the church trappings doesn't matter too much. I think I am a caring person and live my faith. My models are my parents. My father is so caring about my mother and her illness"

Beth began to cry and Matt rushed over to her. "Father, I think that's enough. Beth's mom is sick. She told you about that."

Father Hurley walked over to the couple and touched their shoulders. "Let us all pray together for Mrs. Andrews' recovery. Lord, we ask you to bless Mrs. Andrews and restore her to good health that she may take her place in her loving family in Jesus' name Amen."

Matt returned to his chair. "Thank you Father."

"It is my belief that both of you realize that marriage is a vocation – a calling – do you sense God's hand in your relationship as you look back on it? Can you sense how God has brought you together?"

Matt looked at Beth lovingly. He got out of his chair and walked over to her again. "We are together and it is truly a miracle to me. I can't wait to get married and be husband to my wife!"

Beth looked up at Matt and squeezed his hand. "Ditto!"

Every one started to laugh again. " Do you have any questions?"

"Yeah Father, where can we get a drink around here?"

Father Hurley took off his clerical collar and went to a wooden cabinet. He took out a bottle of scotch and placed three glasses on a tray. The cheerful priest poured a small amount of scotch into each glass. "I'm not on duty. My name is Peter. Here's to your marriage!"

The couple left with a feeling of joy and happiness. They were looking forward to the ceremony and realized that Father Hurley would do a marvelous job.

* * *

Matt called Steve to confirm their appointment. They were to meet at six thirty at "Norman's" a restaurant located in the Ritz Carlton.

After dropping off their car they entered the lush lobby of the hotel. Beth looked around the lobby. "Wow, this is certainly first class.

The choice of colors and arrangement of furniture are beautiful."

"We probably could stay here for a day or so. That is if we ate Raman dinners for a month or so."

Beth giggled.

The Bell Captain directed them to Norman's restaurant. The huge windows and outdoor terrace had spectacular views of the lake, golf course and gardens. Every aspect of the restaurant was first class. The women were dressed in smart and dressy dresses and the men in suits or sport jackets.

"I'm glad you looked up the restaurant on Google. I would have looked foolish wearing a tank top and shorts."

"I'm happy that your father was able to lend me his sport jacket. I would have felt underdressed here."

The maître d' greeted them.

"The Collins table please."

Steve spotted Matt and Beth first. He stood up and waved to his brother. When Matt came closer Steve hugged him. "Welcome little brother."

"Love you bro!"

Linda and Beth were already talking when the men entangled themselves from Steve's bear hug.

"How is the new Mrs. Collins doing?" Matt gently queried.

"The new Mrs. Kersey-Collins is doing just fine!"

"And how is the new to become Mrs. Collins doing?"

Beth started to giggle since she knew what Linda was up to. "Okay! The future Mrs. Beth Andrews-Collins is doing great."

More laughter from one and all. "Matt, watch out for these women. They charm us with their looks and beauty and then bang, before you know it what they want they get."

"Well Steve, isn't that the way we planned it?"

"Good catch bro. Perhaps the ladies are too intelligent to believe you."

"We know they are."

The meal was impressive. The menu was a blend of Asian and Latin food integrated with traditional European cuisine. Both couples agreed to share some Tapas. They ordered shrimp ceviche and fried green tomatoes. The men had for their second course conch chowder with a light sherry poured into it. Beth and Linda ordered a spectacular house salad with blue cheese, almonds and dried fruit as major components.

Steve ordered champagne and a round of toasts ensued. "May your marriage be as happy as Linda's and mine."

Linda spoke up. "May you train your man as quickly as possible."

That had the table in an hilarious uproar again. Beth could hardly keep her food in her mouth. "Oh Linda, please send me the manual."

More laughter and joy. Some other diners began to look at them and Matt put his fingers to his lips. "Shhh!"

The main course was delivered with flair. Both women ordered the pan cooked fillet of Florida yellow tail snapper. It was served beautifully with pan cooked asparagus spears and garlic mashed potatoes. Steve opted for the pork Havana with a mole sauce, smoky plantains and golden grits with a sweet corn salsa.

Matt ordered Mongolian marinated and barbecued veal chops with Thai fried rice, Japanese eggplant and Asian greens.

The couples agreed to share dessert, not because of cost but because of consumption. They were full. Key lime pie and a four layered chocolate decadence cake was served with vanilla ice cream on top. They managed to eat about half of the desserts.

Steve signed the bill. "Let's go to the lounge. It's quiet there and Linda and I want to talk to both of you."

They settled in a corner booth away from people. Linda opened her purse. Matt and Beth, this is an early wedding gift. We felt that it would be okay to give it to you now."

Beth looked at Matt who nodded. She opened the envelope and took out a gorgeous wedding card. Inside was a bank check for ten thousand dollars. Beth looked amazed and gave the check to Matt.

"Oh my God! Steve it's"

Steve interrupted. "I talked to Mom and Dad. They told me that for the most part both of you are paying for the wedding."

"Yes"

Linda interrupted Matt. "And we know that both of you are on a tight budget. Steve and I are overjoyed that we can assist you with your budget."

Beth moved to Linda and hugged her tightly. She whimpered a bit.

Matt looked at Steve and tears rolled down his eyes. "Thanks big brother. You have my back again."

"You always had mine Matt. This is a true pleasure for Linda and me."

The drive home to Beth's house was quiet. They seemed stunned that their money problem was solved so quickly. "I have to call my folks tomorrow."

"Knowing Steve and Linda I think your folks already know. Call them and share our joy."

"I told you we had a tight family."

CHAPTER 52

The rest of the long weekend was controlled by Beth and her mother in terms of the wedding. The check list that Beth had made came into focus. Small details as color of tablecloths and vegan menus were discussed. Beth and her mother worked very hard on all the details. Matt was amazed that almost every little detail was discussed and then finalized. It reminded him of some military missions where every detail was covered, down to the type of ammunition and weapons to take.

One of the problems that Beth had was contacting the band that would play for the reception. They were out of town and could not be contacted. "I have a list of our favorite songs and I don't know who to give them to. The band doesn't have a web page or e-mail address. The Manager of the hotel says that they are versatile and cooperative."

"Why don't you give that issue to me. I'll hunt them down."

Matt visited the Manager of the hotel. "We're having trouble contacting the band and we are leaving on Tuesday afternoon. Would you be so kind to let me know the phone numbers of the last three clients who have used the band. Perhaps they have a contact number."

The first two calls did not work out at all. The couples had no contact numbers. He was lucky enough to get a phone number on his last inquiry. The area code was from Georgia. Matt called the leader of the band. They exchanged e-mail addresses and cell phone numbers. The leader promised to review the play list and make sure to cooperate completely. Matt was really pleased that he could help, even if it was one item.

Matt came home and found no one home. The Andrews' car wasn't in the garage. His phone rang. "Matt, it's Beth. Mom passed out. We're in the emergency room of the hospital. The doctor thinks that she just needs hydration and rest. Oh Matt, we knocked her out. She is so weak."

"What can I do?"

"Go to the store and buy a barbecued chicken, some potato salad and coleslaw. I didn't prepare dinner and I know you and Dad will want dinner."

"Is there anything I can do?"

"No, just that."

Matt left immediately and picked up all the items that Beth requested. He set the table and hoped everything would work out. It was Monday and tomorrow, late afternoon they were going back to Risenburg.

Three hours later Beth and her folks came home. Mrs. Andrews looked pale. "Sit down Mrs. Andrews." Matt quickly pulled the chair out for her.

"Matt. It's about time you call me Mom."

"Yes ma'am. I mean yes Mom."

"That's better. Don't worry. I just have to drink more. I was dehydrated."

Matt looked at Beth. She had rings around her eyes. Obviously she was crying. He went over to her and took her into his arms. He whispered, "Rest, just rest in my arms."

Beth molded herself into Matt and held him tightly. She thought. *I know I can rely on him for anything. No wonder he and his brother are so close.*

Mr. Andrews put his hand on Matt's shoulder. "Thank you for being a rock. My daughter is in fine hands. Thank you Son."

After dinner Beth's folks excused themselves and went into their bedroom.

Matt cleaned up and Beth sat at the table and watched him. "It's almost ten. I am so tired I think I'll turn in."

"I'll join you later. I want to clean up a little better and watch the evening news. Sleep tight."

Beth came over to Matt and kissed him sweetly on his lips. "I love you so much."

During Tuesday's breakfast Matt told Mr. Andrews everything about the District's problems. He discussed the testing scores for the three previous years as well as the Superintendent's behavior. Then he told Mr. Andrews about the incident that Beth discovered. "You mean to say that the Superintendent did not back you up one hundred percent?"

"No sir. I suspect he wants to expunge the record and keep his political allies happy."

"Well you did the right thing by standing firm. Get every thing in writing. Your boss sounds as if he's a dishonest politician, not a school executive."

"I consider him a man without any scruples and without any positive values. He has no sense of right from wrong. Only what's good for him."

The former New York State Senator responded. "He sounds immoral to me."

Matt responded. "I think he is amoral. He doesn't get it and will never get it. I'm leaving the District at the end of the school year. Beth has told me she wants out as well."

* * *

The flight back to Syracuse was uneventful. Matt and Beth drove to a restaurant between Syracuse and Risenburg for dinner. Beth finished her salad and looked at Matt. "Tell me about tomorrow morning. We have to be in Dr. Hull's office at nine."

"I suggest we just tell him and whoever is there the truth. You saw what you saw and I did what I did."

"I'm worried about the kids. This can hurt them for a lifetime. It's traumatic."

"The consequences of letting them off the hook can also influence them for a lifetime. Beth, they have to live in a world with boundaries and standards."

"I'm concerned. There has to be some middle ground."

"Not for me."

Beth looked at Matt. His fists were clenched on his knife and fork.

They were so tight that she saw the outline of his knuckles against his skin. He was in a fighting mood. She decided to let the subject of the kids rest.

Matt dropped Beth at her apartment and went back to his place. He looked at the time. It was close to eleven in the evening. Matt called Jerry. "I'll be in Dr. Hull's office with Ms. Andrews at nine. Keep the lid on the school. I have no idea when I'll be back."

"Okay Boss. Don't forget, be part of the solution, not the problem."

Matt called Nancy Briggs. "Nancy, sorry for the late call, I have a problem and need your professional legal advice."

They talked for forty five minutes. Matt had some ammunition in his arsenal. He thought about Jerry's statement as he fell asleep.

* * *

Dr. Frederick Hull, Ed. D. was sixty years old. He graduated from the University of Wyoming. Born and raised in Laramie, Wyoming his early childhood was spent on a dairy farm. During the recession his father sold the farm and the family moved into town. His father ended up working as a waiter at a good restaurant and made a reasonable living.

Dr. Hull was an average student with average grades throughout his high school and undergraduate years. He ran track during his freshman year, but was never good enough to make the varsity. After four years he graduated with a liberal arts degree and did not know what to do.

Hilda Schaefer and Frederick Hull met on campus during their senior year. Hilda's major was elementary education. She got a job in Denver, Colorado and Frederick decided to go with her. When she told him how much she was making for ten months a year he wasn't impressed. However when he accompanied her to the personnel department he noticed a job bulletin for a high school principal. That salary was sixty percent higher than Hilda's salary. Frederick became interested.

He enrolled for a graduate degree at the University of Denver and eighteen months later he got his Masters in Math Education. During that time he worked as a substitute teacher in many of the Denver public schools.

He immediately got a job in the Denver school system and three years later Frederick Hull got his tenure. One year later he became Chairman of the Math Department and three more years later he became an Assistant Principal. Another three years and he became the High School Principal. He was a traditionalist who focused only on test scores and made sure that his school was one of the best.

Dr. Hull got his doctorate from the University of Denver and moved up to the position of Assistant Superintendent at the age of thirty eight. He spent eight years in that position.

His wife's father became very ill and Hilda had to go to Syracuse to take care of him. There was no one else to do this. After half a year of separation Frederick decided to check out the school districts near Syracuse, New York. He found an opening in Risenburg and applied for the position of Superintendent. The District was suffering from low scores in all their schools. Dr. Hull's record of improving scores in Denver was reviewed and he was hired at the age of forty seven.

Now at the age of sixty, with thirteen years of service behind him, he was confronted with another young principal. A man who had superior values, but did not know anything about school politics. Frederick Hull would make sure to get rid of him. The shrewd Superintendent had all of his people supporting him. He had set it up during the long weekend. There was no doubt that the Board President and the President of the PTA, having their children involved in this traumatic incident, would support the strategy of the Superintendent.

During the long Memorial Day weekend Dominic Costello and his wife Marie went over the story with their daughter Nora. She was frightened, confused and did not cooperate during the first few sessions. The girl cried constantly and refused to eat. Finally, her mother Marie, bribed her with a diamond tennis bracelet. Nora perked up and became a very good actress. She learned her lines very well.

Maureen Stuart and her husband Jack had no problem with their son Rob. He knew that if his suspension held he would not be able to pitch in the Regional playoffs. For this teenager it was the most important thing in his life. He was completely motivated to do anything.

Through careful coaching he became well versed with his script.

Rob rehearsed his lines like a real trouper. He was told that the Superintendent was on his side and there would be no problem. All he thought about was pitching in the playoffs.

CHAPTER 53

Beth Andrews arrived at eight forty five in the morning to the Superintendent's office. She was asked to sit outside and wait. Five minutes later the Costello family and the Stuart family arrived. The secretary told them to go right in. Beth thought. *I have a feeling this isn't going to go too well.*

Matt Collins arrived a minute before nine and the secretary waived him in as well as Beth. What Matt saw was a skirmish line of parents in front of their children. They were there to protect their kids. The Superintendent remained behind his desk.

"All right. Let us understand that we are concerned about Nora and Rob and we as adults must do the right thing. I am going to tape this meeting so there will be no distortions about what we say. Do we all agree?"

Matt realized it was a rhetorical question and did not even nod. Beth did not nod as well. They saw Dr. Hull press the tape recorder button.

"Let us start with the children. Nora Costello tell me in your words what happened?

The fourteen year old girl was dressed in a white blouse and a skirt below her knees. She stood up and started her recitation.. "Rob and I are boyfriend and girlfriend. We decided to talk about what we were going to do over the weekend. We went into the school and found the closet open. After we talked I kissed Rob on the cheek and that's when Ms. Andrews came in and took us to the Principal's office."

The Superintendent smiled. "Thank you Nora. Rob will you tell us your version of the story.

Rob Stuart was a lanky fourteen year old. He was dressed in a white short sleeve sport shirt and a pair of newly pressed blue dress pants. "Nora and I have been going steady since the beginning of eighth grade. I wanted to tell her about what plans we had for the weekend. We went into the school and saw the closet door opened. We went in and after talking Nora kissed me on the cheek. That's when Ms. Stuart saw Nora kissing me. She marched us down to the office."

"Thank you Rob. Ms. Andrews will you tell us your story."

"I'd prefer that the children leave the room."

Dr. Hull looked at the parents. They nodded in agreement. "Nora and Rob, please sit outside. We will call you in later."

The kids left and Beth looked at both parents. "It is with a sad and troubled heart that I have to tell you that the version of what your children said is a fabrication."

Jack Stuart yelled. "Are you telling me that my kid is a liar?"

Superintendent Hull responded. "Now, now Mr. Stuart, calm down and let Ms. Andrews tell her story."

"I was coming out of the ladies lounge when I heard noise in the custodian's closet. I opened the door and saw Nora on her knees performing oral sex on Rob. I told them to stop and brought them down to the Principal's office."

Mrs. Costello screamed. "How dare you accuse my sweet daughter of doing such a dirty thing. How dare you!"

"Now, now Mrs. Costello please calm down. Anything more to add Ms. Andrews?"

"No. Not right now."

"Mr. Collins what did you do? "

"I realized that both parents were on the field helping at the school's field day so I asked them to come into my office. Ms. Andrews told the parents about the incident and I summarily gave the kids three days of suspension. I never talked to the kids and the parents cooperated by taking their children home."

"Why did you give the children a three day suspension?" Dr. Hull's voice was shrill.

"According to New York State Education law I have the right as a school principal to suspend a student up to five days. If it is longer than that a hearing has to take place. Right now I would consider this a hearing. I decided what I thought was a minimal punishment because of morals and breaking the Code of Conduct. If you remember all the parents and students signed."

Dominic Costello responded to Matt immediately. "Do you think a kiss on a cheek is immoral?"

"Mr. Costello I consider oral sex by fourteen year olds, in a closet, in a school immoral."

"You don't believe the kids?"

"No sir. I believe what Ms. Andrews told me to be the truth."

Mrs. Costello stood up and in a piercing voice yelled. "That's a lie. You shacking up with Ms. Andrews is immoral! What do you think of that Mr. Principal?"

Matt stood up and addressed the group. "If you do not have enough faith in your teachers, counselors and administrators to run your schools than the system is broken and perhaps our civility goes out the window. Dr. Hull, if you please, bring back the kids again and ask them to tell their stories again.."

Nora was called in first. "Nora please tell your story again. Mr. Collins has requested it and we certainly want to cooperate."

Nora walked to her mother and grasped her hand. "Rob and I are boyfriend and girlfriend. We decided to talk about what we were going to do over the weekend. We went into the school and found the closet open. After we talked I kissed Rob on the cheek and that's when Ms. Andrews came in and took us to the Principal's office."

Rob came into the office. "Rob please tell your story again. Mr. Collins has requested it and we are sure you want to cooperate."

"Nora and I have been going steady since the beginning of eighth grade. I wanted to tell her about what plans we had for the weekend. We went into the school and saw the closet door opened. We went in and after talking Nora kissed me on the cheek. That's when Ms. Stuart saw Nora kissing me. She marched us down to the office."

"Thank you Rob. Mr. Collins what do you suggest next?"

"If you play back the students first stories and then their second stories you will see that they are exactly the same. Word for word. That means they have been rehearsed over and over again."

The Superintendent shut off the tape recorder.

"Please keep the tape recorder on because any judge or jury would see that they are lying. If there is collusion between you, Dr. Hull and the parents then you could loose your certificate to be a Superintendent. Do you understand where I'm going. I have already talked to an attorney. She has told me, that in discovery, phone records could be obtained. If there would be an inordinate amount of calling between the parties well, you know were I'm going. Don't you!"

Dr. Hull turned on the tape recorder. "Mr. Collins what are you suggesting?"

Dominic Costello got up from his seat. He walked over to Nora and took her arm. "You listen to me girl. You tell the truth now and I mean the truth so help you God. Tell them."

Nora wiped her tears away. "I did it. I did it just the way Ms. Andrews said. I love Rob and I heard that he was interested in another girl so I figured I would make him happy. Mom told me to lie, Dad didn't know anything." She started to sob and her mother grabbed her and hugged her.

Jack Stuart turned to his son. "Forget about what mom and I said to you. Tell us all what happened.

"Just the way Ms. Andrews said. We were doing it. So help me God it was the first time. I'm sorry Ms. Andrews for lying to you. You are the best counselor I ever had. I'm really sorry." He bowed his head and his father put his arm around him and took him to his seat.

The Superintendent muttered, "Alright I guess this conference is over. I'll keep the tape."

Beth stood up. "This conference is not over. Mr. Collins I'm speaking as both students guidance counselor and I'm requesting you remove the third day of your suspension. These children have suffered enough from our adult actions. The psychological trauma may affect them later on in life unless we make sure to tell them that we all make mistakes." Beth looked at the kids. "Nora, Rob, we adults make mistakes. Your parents make mistakes, your teachers make mistakes, your principal makes mistakes. This was one mistake that you made. Make sure to learn from it and move on with your lives. Mr. Collins please consider my request."

Matt was stunned by Beth's humanity. He loved her even more as he heard her talking to the kids. "Nora and Rob you are to report to school tomorrow. And Rob good luck pitching tomorrow!"

Fourteen year old Nora got up. "Ms. Collins what should we tell our friends?"

"Tell them you were caught making out. End of story!"

The parents and kids left. Matt looked at the Dr. Hull. "I'll be resigning from the District as of August first. I'm owed twenty two days of vacation time and I intend to get paid. Further I would recommend that Jerry Jackson become your Principal. He is ready and very able to do the job."

Beth Andrews took Matt's arm. "I'll be resigning as of July first. I don't want to work in this District anymore."

Dr. Hull nodded. "I understand."

As they left, an excited Eric Bolt rushed in. "Dr. Hull, bad news. The Inspector General from the Testing Bureau will be visiting us. It seems that our testing doesn't match their statistical analysis."

"How did this happen?"

"Some State Senator recommended this to the Governor who called the Board of Regents. That's all the Inspector General told me."

Beth and Matt left the building. In the parking lot Beth started to laugh. "I guess my father still has plenty of pull. Did you see the face on Dr. Hull? It looked like he was going to die!"

Matt kissed her and hugged her. You are a fine woman and a good woman. I am so proud of you that you spoke up for the kids. I love you!"

"Ditto!"

*End*

## EPILOGUE

After the Inspector General left Risenburg he wrote a report recommending monitoring of the George W. Bush Middle School for three years. He could not find any one person guilty, but blamed the Superintendent for shoddy supervision.

The Risenburg Board of Education bought out the last year of Dr. Hull's contract and started a nationwide search for a new leader.

Jerry Jackson was appointed to the position of Principal of the middle school in late August. He immediately started writing his first weekly newsletter to the teachers. He thought. *A great AA. slogan, look for similarities rather than differences. Thanks Matt.*

A month after her resignation from the Risenburg School District, Mrs. Beth Andrews Collins started her two year contract as a Teaching Assistant at NYU. Her free tuition and fifteen hundred dollar a month contract fit nicely into the couple's plan

A year later Dr. Matt Collins accepted a position as Principal of a moderate size high school in eastern Suffolk County, New York.

The only problem was that they would not see too much of each other during the week. They agreed it was worth the struggle.

Beth had an enchanting point of view. "I feel as if I'm still on a honeymoon. Each time I see Matt I'm ready to jump on him and make love to him."

Matt, in his Irish humor quipped, "One thing that the distance between us gives is that we don't have to pay a marriage counselor."

They both were right!

www.ingramcontent.com/pod-product-compliance
Lightning Source LLC
Chambersburg PA
CBHW061424040426
42450CB00007B/885